Concepts of Environmental Management for Sustainable Development

Concepts of Environmental Management for Sustainable Development

Madhab Chandra Dash
Formerly
Chairman, Odisha Pollution Control Board
&
Vice Chancellor
Sambalpur University

TECHSAR™
NEW DELHI

Published and Printed by

Techsar LLP
4435-36/7, Ansari Road, Daryaganj
New Delhi–110 002 (India)
E-mail: tech_info@techsarworld.com
Website: www.techsarworld.com

ISBN: 978-93-82332-27-5

Reprint 2026

Dedicated to the memory of my parents
Late Mrs. Mukta Dash & Late Harekrushna Dash
Who nurtured, educated, & loved me immensely

AND

My Parents-in-law
Late Mrs. Pravamayee Hatial and Late Dr. Manmathnath Hatial
Who gave me their daughter, Sovita in marriage and
loved me ungrudgingly and immensely

Preface

In the last century unprecedented deterioration in the state of environment occurred mainly due to huge human population growth, demand on resources, and loss of habitats, unscientific land use, industrialization and urbanization. This led to discharge of high volumes of effluents and municipal sewage which polluted the rivers and water bodies. Huge quantity of industrial emissions to the atmosphere caused environmental pollution and health hazards. This also led to the loss of biodiversity and environmental deterioration. The extent of deterioration could be judged due to the pollution of soil, water and air, global warming, ozone depletion in stratosphere, acid rain, eutrophication, loss and degradation of habitat, loss of vegetal cover and loss of biodiversity, excessive concentration of harmful chemicals and magnification through food chain, growing risk of environmental accidents, and threat to life support systems.

Concern over the state of the environment started building up in the second half of the last century. The undeniable reality is that human activities influence intensely the biological, chemical and geological processes on the earth. Humans have been around for 0.0001 per cent of planet's estimated 4.5 billion year history but they have put enormous pressure on planet's resources and natural environment. At present about 40% of planet's ice free land has been cleared for agriculture and farming. However, the impact of human activities started exploding the environment after the industrial revolution, in Europe. They developed technologies to produce value added products leading to have comfortable lifestyle and did not visualize the deterioration in the natural environment.

United Nations Organization (UNO) became concerned and it was reflected at the UNO-conference on the Human Environment held in Stockholm in June, 1972, and later in the Earth Summit at Rio de Janeiro, Brazil, 1992. Review of progress was done in Johannesburg, 2002 and review in June, 2012 at Rio de Janeiro, Brazil. Government of India actively participated in1972 conference and follow-up conferences. The Indian Parliament enacted laws to protect India's environment. Regulatory agencies have been set up to implement the laws and take steps to protect the environment in India.

Courses on, environmental science and on environmental management have been developed and incorporated in the syllabi of undergraduate and postgraduate classes in environmental science, environmental engineering and management studies. There are not many text and reference books which integrate the environmental science and environmental management into a single source for students. This up-to-date and comprehensive textbook integrates the concepts of environmental science with environmental management dealing with different management tools for achieving sustainable development. The text should be suitable for environmental science, environmental engineering and management, (MBA and BBA) students both at undergraduate and postgraduate levels.

This book deals with the concepts in ecology and environmental sciences, concepts of environmental management including corporate environmental indicators, legal, technological and managerial tools and concepts of sustainable development including indicators, priorities and practices. Besides, the detailed treatment of environmental laws, EIA and EMP, life cycle analysis, pollution control technology, EMS certification, environmental auditing, and accounting, industrial safety practices, disaster management, corporate social responsibility, etc. Waste treatment, municipal, hazardous, biomedical waste management, Hazchem Code, risk assessment and analysis etc., case studies, secured landfill, energy management and climate change have also been included.

For writing this book I have received assistance, computer support, data support, motivation, etc., from many people. Some university professors have gone through the contents or parts of the text. I wish to thank all of them profusely. They are - Er. Susanta Guru of Aditya Birla Group of Industries, Sambalpur, provided photographs of aluminium industry, mining activities; Dr. Appanna Mishra of Vedanta Aluminum Industry, Jharsuguda; Dr. Siba Prasad Panda of Hindalco Industries, Mr. Tushar Kanti Mishra of Bhusan Integrated Steel Industry, Dr. Dilip Kumar Behera, Dr. A.K. Swar, Er. Nihar Ranjan Sahu, Er. Simachal Dash, Sri Anupam Behera and Dr. S.S. Pati of State Pollution Control Board, Odisha, for data support, Prof. Padmavati Gahan, Prof. Sanjat Kumar Sahu of Sambalpur University, Prof. Jyotirmaya Mohapatra of Siskhya and Anusandhan University, Bhubaneswar, for reading the contents and parts of the text, Prof. P.C. Mishra, Prof. Niranjan Behera, Dr. Satyendra Prasad Mishra, and Dr. Sanjay Kumar Swain of Sambalpur University for discussion and data support. My wife, Sovita and other family members provided logistics support, and motivation to complete this project.

Madhab Chandra Dash

Contents

CHAPTER 1

Background: Environment and Ecology

1.0 INTRODUCTION

In the last century unprecedented deterioration of environment occurred mainly due to loss of habitats, unscientific land use, uncontrolled industrialization and urbanization. This led to the discharge of high volumes of effluents and municipal sewage into water bodies and polluted the rivers and water bodies. Huge quantity of industrial emissions into the atmosphere cause environmental pollution and health hazards. The extent of deterioration of the environment could be judged by global warming, ozone depletion in stratosphere, acid rain, eutrophication, loss of habitat, vegetal cover and biodiversity, excessive concentration of harmful chemicals and their magnification through food chain, growing risk of environmental accidents, and threat to life support systems. Concern over the state of the environment started building up as early as the 1960s due to the decline in environmental quality and deterioration in living conditions. United Nations Organization (UNO) became concerned and it was reflected at the UNO-conference on the Human Environment held in Stockholm from 5th June to 12th June, 1972, and later in the Earth Summit at Rio de Janeiro, Brazil, 1992. Review of the progress was done in Johannesburg, 2002 and recently in June, 2012 at Rio de Janeiro, Brazil. Government of India actively participated in the 1972 conference and follow-up conferences. The Indian Parliament enacted many environmental laws to prevent and control pollution, conserve biodiversity and wildlife, etc.

1.1 WHAT IS ENVIRONMENT?

Environment includes water, air and land and the interrelationship which exists between water, air, land and human beings and other living creatures, plants, microorganisms and property. [Section 2(b) of Environment (Protection) Act, 1986, Government of India]. As per the above cited definition, environment is the surroundings or conditions in which a human being, an animal, a plant or a microorganism lives, operates and their interrelationships. The environment includes the soil (pedosphere), the air (atmosphere), the water (hydrosphere) and the biodiversity and their interrelationship.

1.2 PEDOSPHERE

Life on planet earth has become possible due to favourable interactions between the soil (pedosphere), the water (hydrosphere), and the air (atmosphere) in a zone, we call **biosphere**. Therefore, biosphere includes these three spheres, and the biodiversity. Earth was formed some 4 to 5 billion years back. The earth has three layers: (a) the **crust**, which is in the solid state and has thickness varying from 16 to 50 km.The crust contains soil of thickness ranging from a few inches to a few feet. Soil is the abode of numerous organisms like bacteria, actinomycetes, fungi, protozoa and invertebrate fauna such as earthworms, collembola, mites, millipedes, centipedes, mollusks etc.; (b) the **mantle**, which is about 2900 km thick and made of hard rock containing mainly iron and magnesium, which respectively form 84% and 67% of earth's volume and weight; (c) the **core**, which is mainly made of iron and nickel with a temperature of about 8,000°C.

Soil has been formed by the interaction of complex physical, chemical, and biological processes of weathering of the parent rock. The mineral base of soil is the weathering of parent material. The decomposition of organic material, mainly of plant origin, is due to microorganisms and invertebrate animals. The climate, vegetation, parent rock and organisms play an important role in soil formation and formation of soil profile (Figure 1).

In a normal mineral soil, the profile has three horizons, usually termed A, B, and C layers. These soil horizons are differentiated by texture, physical structure, colour, porosity, root growth, nature of organic material and distribution of biodiversity.

The A horizon includes the top soil containing organic matter. The activity of microorganisms and soil fauna is greatest in this zone of soil. After the breakdown of organic matter into smaller particles and undergoing decomposition, it forms humus, which gets mixed up with mineral particles. In some soils, such as coniferous forest soil, the organic matter occurs in various stages of decomposition and forms a distinct zone called the O zone. The B zone is called subsoil

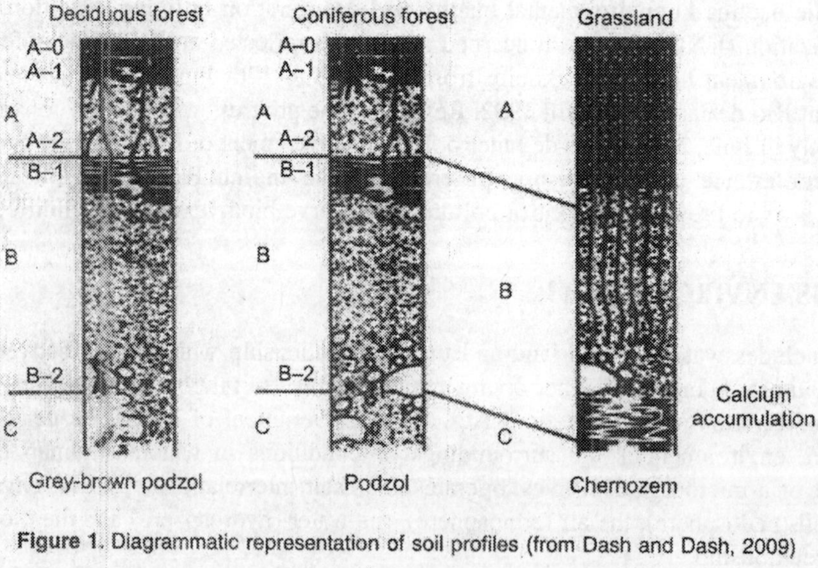

Figure 1. Diagrammatic representation of soil profiles (from Dash and Dash, 2009)

and is more brightly coloured than the A zone. The brightness is usually due to the presence of iron oxides. This zone may contain clay. In poorly drained soils, water logging may occur. This may cause alternate reduction, mobilization and reoxidation of iron compounds. Under such condition, the B horizon may appear grey in colour. The unchanged parent material is called the C horizon.

Soil texture depends upon the particle size of the constituent parts. Table 1 gives a classification of soils based on percentage of particle size.

Table 1. Soil Texture and Particle Size (mm) (from Dash and Dash, 2009)

Texture	Sand (2 to 0.05)	Silt (0.05 to 0.002)	Clay (<0.002)
Sandy	> 80%	Negligible	< 20%
Silty	Negligible	> 50%	< 40%
Clayey	Negligible	< 40%	> 40%
Loamy	< 80%	< 50%	< 40%

Forests have grown in areas in the world where precipitation (rainfall, snowfall) has exceeded evaporation. Grasslands have developed in areas where evaporation has exceeded precipitation. Heavy rainfall removes soluble constituents from top soil, particularly calcium to deeper soil through leaching. Due to leaching calcium may be deposited in deeper layers and becomes available to plants with deep roots. In cold temperate regions, coniferous forests grow on soil containing a distinct organic matter zone, called O layer. The soil is called Podzol. In these soils the B horizon may look brownish-red or black in colour. Podzols are acid soils, also called **MOR** soils. In deciduous forests, the A horizon consists of a mixture of organic matter and mineral soil which looks dark brown or black and this horizon may mix with the B horizon. The mixture of organic material and mineral soil is called **Mull** soil. Often soils develop with characteristics between mor and mull soils and these soils are called **Moder** soil.

The activity of microorganisms and soil fauna is intensive in the top soil. Their activity enhances the decomposition process manifold and helps release nutrients for plant growth.

Figure 2 shows the major biological systems operating soil and influencing soil processes. The litter system, the plant root area (rhizosphere), the earthworm passage (drilosphere) and the termite mounds (termitosphere) control soil processes and these activities show the important role of soil fauna and soil microorganisms. Life on the earth has become possible due to very favourable interactions between soil (pedosphere), water (hydrosphere), and air (atmosphere) in a zone, we call biosphere. Therefore, biosphere includes these three spheres, and the biodiversity. Scientific studies tell us that the earth was formed about 4.6 billion years ago).

1.3 ATMOSPHERE

The atmosphere, which surrounds the earth, can be divided into five distinct layers: (i) troposphere; (ii) stratosphere; (iii) mesosphere; (iv) ionosphere; and (v) exosphere, which is the uppermost layer extending to space. **Troposphere** extends from the surface of the earth up to a height of about 8 to 10 km in polar latitude, 10 to 12 km in moderate latitude and 16 to 18 km at the

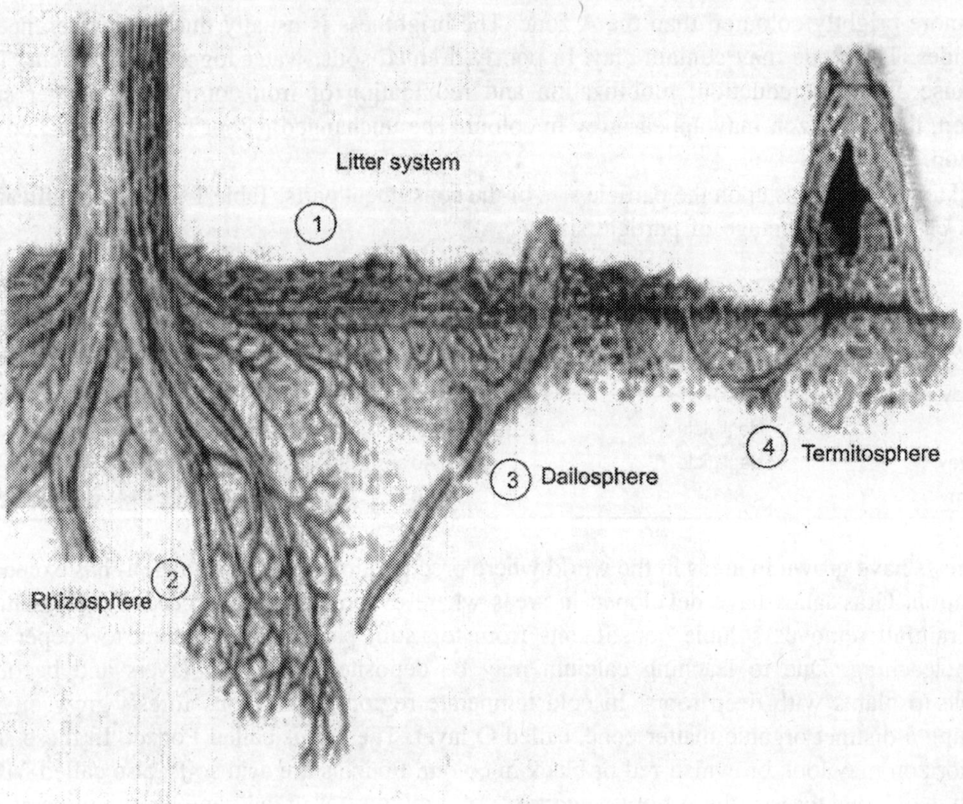

Figure 2. Major biological systems of regulations in soil (after Lavelle, 1984)

equator. In the troposphere the percentage concentration of different gases such as nitrogen, oxygen, carbon dioxide, etc., does vary with an increase in height. However, the water vapour content and the temperature decrease sharply with increase in height. Figure 3 shows graphically the stratification of the atmosphere.

The vertical gradient of temperature in the troposphere varies from 5 to 7 degrees per km; 5 km in the lower troposphere and 7 km in the upper troposphere. The transition of troposphere and the stratosphere is called tropopause which has more or less constant temperature. The upper troposphere is almost transparent as suspended particulate matter is not there. Therefore, the sun rays do not heat up the upper troposphere significantly. Most of the solar energy is absorbed by the earth's surface and heat radiates from the surface and lower troposphere to the middle and then to the upper troposphere. The particulate matter is concentrated mainly in lower troposphere. The non-uniform heating of the ground surface of the earth produces ascending and descending air currents, which cause turbulence and mixing of air masses vertically. Troposphere accounts for 80% of air mass. The temperature decreases with increase in attitude at the rate 0.6°C per 100 m rise. This is called lapse rate.

The average pressure at the earth's surface is 1,014 millibars (1 millibar = 1/1000 bar & 1 bar = 1.019 kg per cm^2, close to 1 Atmosphere, and 1.332 millibar = 1 mm of mercury). The

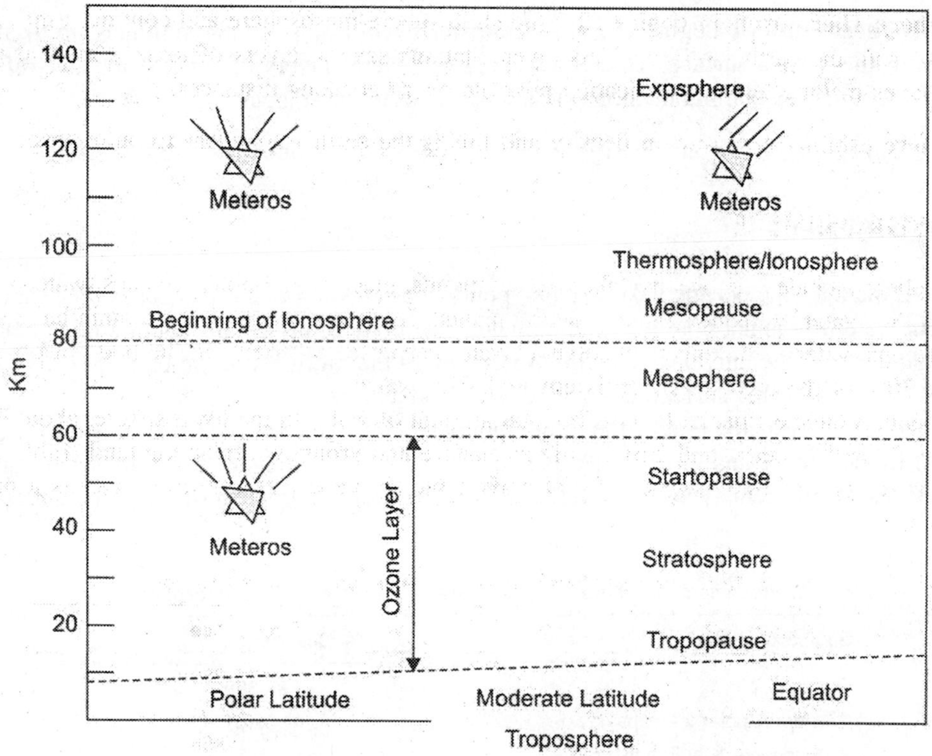

Figure 3. Stratification of atmosphere

pressure gradient is as follows: At an altitude of 5 km, the air pressure is half that at the surface of the earth, at 11 km the pressure is 225 millibars and at 17 km it is only 90 millibars. Since solar radiation causes water on the earth's surface to evaporate, the part of the troposphere over an ocean or big lake carries more moisture than over a land surface. The mass of water vapour decreases rapidly with increase in altitude.

Stratosphere is free from clouds and aeroplanes usually fly in the lower part of the stratosphere. The stratosphere extends up to 60 km from the earth's surface and its thickness varies from 50 to 55 km. This layer consists of ozone, which absorbs the ultraviolet radiation from the sun. Currently, there is serious threat of depletion of ozone by the pollutants produced by human activities. Thinning of this layer has occurred in the stratosphere of many regions, especially over the Antarctic region of the earth. This layer is full of ozone gas and there is continuous conversion of ozone to oxygen to ozone.

Mesosphere begins from the stratosphere and extends up to 80 km (20 km thick). This layer shows further fall in temperature due to decrease in the absorption of solar radiation. The ozone concentration goes on decreasing with increase in height.

Ionosphere/Thermosphere begins after the stratosphere-mesosphere and continues up to about 150 km from the earth's surface. This layer contains several layers of ionized air and reflects radio waves making telecommunication possible over very long distances.

Exosphere exhibits very low air density and this is the earth's boundary to outer space.

1.4 HYDROSPHERE

Hydrosphere includes the oceans, lakes, rivers, ponds, glaciers and polar ice caps, water vapours, etc. Without water life is not possible on the planet. The body of organisms contain large amount of water and water is the universal solvent. Water carries the nutrients in the body of organisms. Almost 70% of the earth's surface is covered with water.

Scientists have estimated that of the total amount of water in the hydrosphere, about 97.39% is available in the oceans and 2.61% only as surface and groundwater on the land. Table 2 gives the proportions of different types of water available. In view of this, fresh water is a precious resource.

Table 2. Proportions of Different Types of Water Available in the Hydrosphere

Source of Water	% Occurrence
Ocean	97.389
Glaciers & polar ice caps	02.01
Groundwater & soil moisture	0.58
Rivers & lakes	0.02
Atmospheric water as vapour	0.001
Total fresh water	2.611

The available fresh water in India is from rainfall and snowfall, which amounts to 4000 billion cubic metres per year. Out of this, about 1869 billion cubic metres is available as surface water and replenished groundwater that can be replenished . It has been estimated that out of this about 432 billion cubic metres from groundwater and about 690 billion cubic metres from surface water can be put for beneficial use. (Patnaik, 2006).

The National Water Council of India adopted the National Water Policy in 2002 and decided that water is a precious national resource to be planned, developed, conserved and managed as such and on an integrated and environmentally sound basis, keeping in view the socio-economic aspects and need of the country. Effort is to be made to develop, conserve, utilize and manage this national resource in a sustainable manner keeping the national perspectives in mind. The water allocation priorities have been decided as: (a) Drinking water, and for sanitation (b) Hydro power generation, (c) Maintaining ecological (environmental) demand, (d) Agriculture, (e) Industries, (f) Navigation and other uses. The per capita availability of fresh water in India was 1820 cubic meter in 2001 and it has been estimated that about 1200 cubic metres of fresh water per capita will be available in 2051 keeping the population growth in mind.

The total amount of water on the earth is more than 1404 million cubic km and most of it is salt water.

Water Cycle

The sun warms the planet. Water evaporates from oceans, water bodies and land, and stays as water vapour in the atmosphere. Water vapour in the atmosphere condenses to form clouds, which move over the land masses. If the air becomes cool enough, the water in the cloud falls back upon the earth as rain, snow, hail, or sleet. Much of the precipitation is absorbed by the vegetation and soil and the excess goes to low lying areas and ultimately moves to water bodies and oceans. In tropical forests, as much as 75% of the annual precipitation returns to the atmosphere by the vegetation that plays an important role in the water cycle. Some of the precipitation passes through the soil into deeper layers and gets stored as groundwater. Some water is stored on land in the lakes, ponds and some flows into the rivers and ultimately gets drained into oceans. Much of the precipitation falls on the oceans as the oceans cover almost 70% of the planet's area.

Streams and rivers wear down the rocks and transport huge quantity of small rocks, soil, mud, sand, etc., downstream and ultimately into the ocean. This process causes erosion of mountains and lands. Mountains store snow and ice on their peaks in winter and during summer, much of this snow melts and floods the rivers. Rainwater hitting the peak and slopes of the mountains brings huge quantity of soil, mud, rocks and sand. Mountain ridges and valleys become watersheds. Mountains with thick forest cover keep the area cool. The trees pump huge amount of groundwater into the atmosphere in the process of transpiration. Mountain ranges play on important role in water cycle and influence agriculture through the distribution of precipitation. Water cycle (Figure 4) involves evaporation, cloud formation, condensation, and fall of water as rain, snow, etc. The wind pattern and gravitational pull are responsible for brining water back to the earth. The sun provides the energy for the entire process.

Glaciers play a defining role in controlling climate and water cycle. In cold climate, especially in the arctic zone and high mountains and plateaus, some of the snow that falls each winter melts in spring and summer. A good quantity of snow remains without melting and every year snow accumulates and forms vast snow fields.

Year after year the snow cover becomes thicker and the lower layers become ice due to pressure. If the thickness of the snow field becomes about 60 metres, a huge slab of ice and snow begins to move down the hill. Such a thick slab of ice and snow is called a glacier. Two types of glaciers, i.e., mountain glaciers/valley glaciers/alpine glaciers and continental glaciers are known. Mountain glaciers cover only a few square km. The glacier destroys mountain slopes if it moves downward. A glacier maintains its integrity if the snow and ice accumulation per year equals or exceeds the evaporation and melting.

The continental glaciers are also called ice caps or ice sheets. The two major ice sheets are the Antarctica ice sheet, with an area of about 1,25,00,000 sq km and the ice cap of Greenland, which is about 18,00,000 sq km in area. There are many smaller ice caps in different continents. These glaciers and ice caps influence the climate and water cycles of the earth.

Figure 4 presents the water cycle diagrammatically. In the water cycle, part of the water always remains as vapour, part as liquid form and part as ice and snow. The cycle is largely regulated by the physical processes and the biodiversity, especially the vegetation plays an important role in maintaining the cycle.

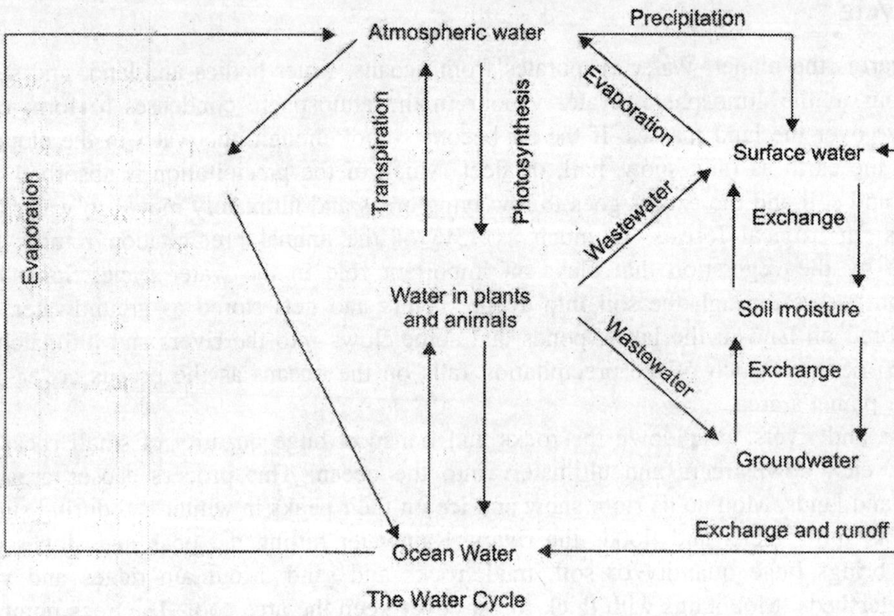

Figure 4. The water cycle (from Dash and Mishra, 2001)

Demand for use of fresh water is increasing as the population has grown manifold. Besides, the style of living affects the water consumption. The large cities and the urban systems, industries, agriculture, etc., consume vast quantity of fresh water. Due to human activities, water bodies have become polluted. None of the rivers in India is free from pollution. In view of these activities, fresh water has become a precious commodity.

Groundwater

Depending upon the amount of precipitation, soil type and surface topography, the zone of aeration in soil varies from few centimetres to many metres deep. Lower soil layers are filled with water and known as the zone of saturation, the source of water in most dug wells. The top of this zone is called water table. Geologic layers that contain water are called aquifers. It may take a few hours to years for water to move in aquifers depending upon the geology. If impermeable layers lie above the aquifer, pressure builds up within the water bearing layer, a well puncturing the aquifer flows freely at the surface and is called an artesian well or spring. Areas where surface water filters into an aquifer are called recharge zones. Pollutants can enter into aquifers through the recharge zones. Plants usually gather water from the aeration zone and with deeper roots may gather water from saturation zones. All these sources are called groundwater.

Groundwater is used for agriculture and domestic use. Rural India depends upon well water for drinking and other domestic purposes. Overuse of groundwater dries up wells, natural springs and groundwater-fed wetlands. Hence, measuring annual recharge of groundwater provides a clue about the amount of groundwater can be drawn. Water withdrawal at a faster rate and more than the recharge potential may bring a collapse of aquifers. Another consequence of aquifer collapse involves salt water intrusion if the area is near the coastline of ocean or bay.

Wetlands

Rivers, lakes, ponds, and areas containing water are called wetlands. Broadly the wetlands are the bogs, swamps, wet meadows, rice fields, marshes, rivers, ponds, lakes, etc. Wetlands play an important role in the water cycle. The ten largest rivers of the world carry half of all surface runoff on the earth (Table 3). The largest lakes of the world contain 100 times as much water as all the rivers and streams combined. Hence, if wetlands are disturbed, their natural water-absorbing capacity is reduced and surface water runoff quickly causes floods and erodes the banks in the rainy season.

Table 3. World's Ten Largest Rivers and their Discharge

River	Amazon	Orinoco	Congo	Yangtze	Brahama-putra	Mississippi	Mekong	Parana	Yenisey	Lena
Country	Brazil & Peru	Venezuela & Colombia	Congo	Tibet, China	India & Bangladesh	U.S.A.	South East Asia	Paraguay & Argentina	Russia	Russia
Annual Discharge (cubic metre/ second	1,75,000	45,300	39,200	28,000	19,000	18,400	18,300	18,000	17,200	16,000

The World Health Organization considers 1,000 cubic metres (2,64,000 gallons) of fresh water per capita per year as the necessary amount to maintain a healthy quality life. Some 45 nations in Africa and Middle East do not get this much water. In many African countries access to clean water is a problem. In India people in rural areas have less access to clean and fresh water, particularly in summers. More than two-thirds of the world's households (women & their children) have to fetch fresh water from outside their homes particularly in Africa and Asia. Being a very time consuming process this affects the education of children. Fresh water management is now a reality.

Oceans are extensively used for transportation of fossil fuels and commodities. Thousands of industries have developed in coastal regions and most of them discharge their wastes into the sea, causing serious pollution. Oil transport occurs largely in sea and oil is lost during production, refining, transportation and use. Ship/tanker accidents are very common nowadays. Marine pollution has become a serious problem. Depending upon its biological and abiotic features, the oceanic environment is divided into three divisions: (i) the open sea or pelagic environment; (ii) the ocean depths called benthic environment; (iii) the coastal waters. Figure 5(b) represents the ocean environment diagrammatically (Dash and Dash, 2009). The biodiversity in the sea is classified into: (a) plankton; (b) nekton; and (c) benthos. Planktons are of three types.

Nanoplanktons, which are less than 0.06 mm in diameter and the examples are diatoms, silicoflagellates, unicellular algae, etc., bacteria and many protozoa; Microplanktons,which are less than 3 mm and more than 0.06 mm in diameter. The examples are small diatoms and dinoflagellates; Macroplanktons, which are larger than 3 mm in diameter. The examples are mysids, salps, jellyfish etc. On the basis of nutritional requirements, planktons are classified as

phytoplankton, which are autotrophic, (diatoms, algae etc.) and **zooplankton,** (mysids, salps, jellyfish, etc.) which are holozoic.

Nektons are larger crustaceans, mollusks, fish, turtles, sea birds, and mammals. Nektons are largely plankton feeders and form a part of human food.

Benthos are sea bottom dwellers and consist of sessile forms such as limpets, chitons, mussels, oysters, sponges, crabs, lobsters, flat fish, etc. Benthos also include burrowing forms, called **infauna,** and creeping forms called epifauna. Ocean depths are cold, dark and devoid of autotrophs.

Figure 5(a) and (b) represent photic and thermal stratification of fresh water bodies and stratification of oceanic environment respectively. The coastal water is called the littoral zone. The surface water (open water-limnetic zone) is called euphotic/photic zone as sunlight is available and photosynthesis by phytoplankton occurs. The profundal zone includes the benthic zone. The surface warm water zone is the epilimnion and deeper cold water zone is the hypolimnion. In between, thermocline zone, which is a thermo-neutral zone, occurs.

Ocean currents

Ocean tides cause regular movements of the water due to the pull of the moon and the sun. Another movement of ocean water is due to the ocean currents. These currents (Figure 6) are like rivers of water flowing in the ocean and taking water from one region to another. These ocean currents influence the temperature of adjacent land masses. The examples are Atlantic Drift or movement of warm ocean currents poleward, which keeps the winter temperature in the western part of Europe warmer than it should be as per their geographical positions. Westerly winds in these areas carry the heat towards the land mass. Another example is that cold ocean current flows in the ocean near the western coast of southern Africa in summer and this current brings down the land temperature in the tropical region. Another ocean current which exhibits oscillations of 4 to 7 years cycle occurs in eastern pacific and is called **El Nino,**which causes temperature rise in surface water in the Pacific Ocean near Peru. This cycle is followed by drop in water temperature in Eastern Pacific in Asia and this decrease is called **La Nina**. These climatic cycles involve both ocean currents and temperature and are related to major pattern of air movement and location of land masses.

Europe's climate is different from North America or Asia in the same latitude and it has now been correlated to the ocean currents and wind flow patterns in the atmosphere. The ocean currents act as a salt conveyor that extends through southern oceans to Pacific and influence the world's climate. The monsoon climate in Southeast Asia, particularly in the Indian subcontinent, is largely influenced by the ocean currents in the Indian Ocean, Bay of Bengal and the Arabian Sea and the wind patterns in this region.

1.5 WHAT IS ECOLOGY?

All forms of life owe their existence to the mother Earth and to the maintenance of ecological order (ecological balance) in nature. This balance is maintained by:

(i) Rich biodiversity, (plants, animals, microbes, and man); (ii) Interdependence among the different life forms; (iii) Sustained productivity and food chain relationships; (iv) Maintenance of

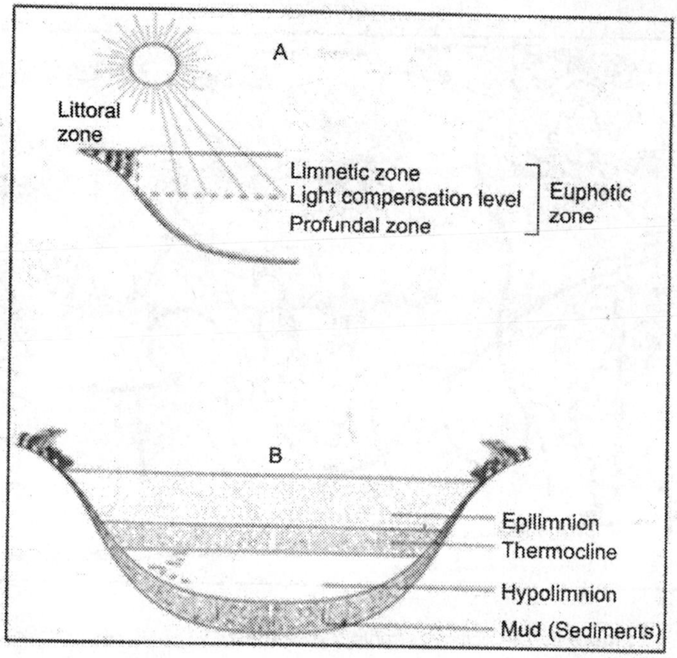

Figure 5a. Thermal stratification of fresh water bodies

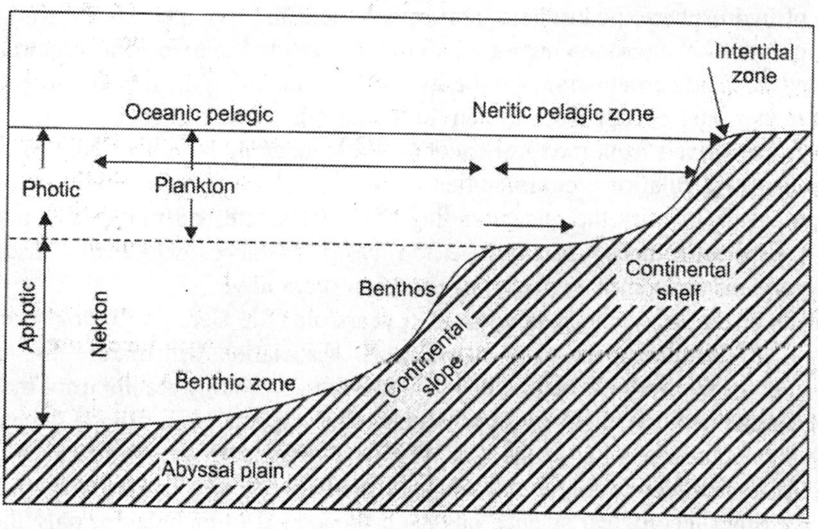

Figure 5b. The oceanic environment and its stratification. (Dash and Dash, 2009)

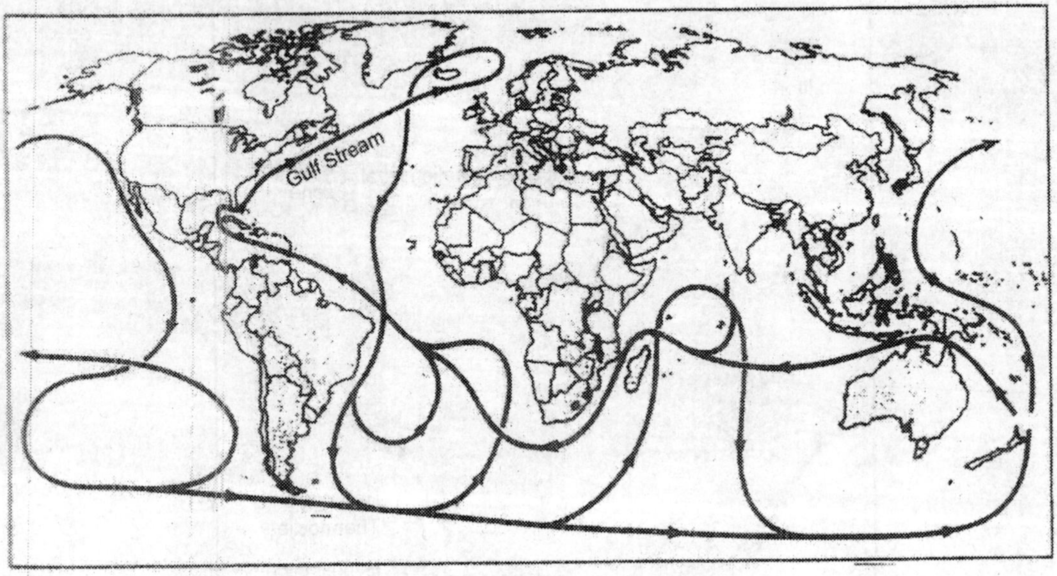

Figure 6. The ocean currents (Source: IGNOU publication)

natural processes of nutrient cycling energy flow, homeostatic mechanisms and evolutionary process; (v) Adapting potential of the living forms to the changing environment. The biosphere consisting part of hydrosphere, pedosphere, atmosphere, and the living forms have arisen in the evolutionary process. The microorganisms, plants and animals have specific requirements for existence, continuance and perpetuation. All the living forms including man get their requirements of gases, other matter, and energy from the environment where they live.

Ecology, a word derived from the Greek word **Oikos,** meaning house, is concerned with the biology of organisms, populations, communities and their functions in natural surroundings. In other words, ecology deals with the understanding of the structure and function of nature. This includes the living world including man and the non-living substances, which are constantly used by the living organisms from their surroundings to keep them alive.

As a scientific discipline, ecology is about 136 years old (the German Zoologist, coined the word ecology in 1876), although man is aware of its association with nature and non-living matter since the age of the Vedas. The practical importance of ecology results from the presence of man in the ecosystem. Man's evolution, its dependence, especially livelihood dependence on environment, his relationship with nature and the development of his position from one of struggle against natural forces to the recent adaptive methods used to control it are included in ecology. In recent times, ecological science has been broadened to include not only the biology and interactions of organisms, populations, and biotic communities but also many other aspects dealing with environmental degradation, pollution, resource utilization, restoration of degraded habitats, abatement of pollution, environmental management for sustainable development, etc. In view of this a new term called environmental science has been developed and has gained popularity. **Environmental science** can be defined as the systematic study of the structure and behaviour of the natural world, i.e., plants, animals, human beings, microorganisms and their interactions among themselves and with the dynamic environment through observations and experiments.

Pre-agricultural human society, agriculture, industrialization, the atomic age and the electronic age have brought the science of ecology to the forefront of human thinking.

The beauty of ecology lies in understanding the natural order, which keeps so many living organisms in a dynamic coexistence. This raises many fundamental questions in the human mind. What are the fundamental features of these natural systems? How the nutrients circulate and energy flows in natural systems? How efficient are the natural systems such as forests, grasslands, aquatic systems in comparison to man made systems such as agriculture, aquaculture, and industrial systems? Is there something called carrying capacity (Malthus-Darwinian concept) of an ecosystem? How can the ecosystem and its management knowledge be utilized to increase food, fodder and fuel production, to protect environment (landscape) from erosion, pollution, etc., and manage the resources? For sustainable utilization of natural resources, environmental management is important.

The functioning of natural systems is based on certain basic principles and understanding of these principles will help humans to solve many of their problems. The science of ecology has three aspects: (i) Theoretical; (ii) Practical; (iii) Socio-economic-cultural and aesthetics.

As per the modern concept, laws of ecology include not only unidirectional energy flow in the ecosystem, or nutrient cycling involving biodiversity, and abiotic components, or stability of the ecosystem related to rich diversity, etc., but also includes the following two concepts:

- First concept: "Nothing comes from nowhere, everything comes from somewhere".
- Second concept: "Nothing ever goes away, everything goes somewhere".

1.6 ECOSYSTEM CONCEPT

The living microbes, plants and animals of a habitat and their non-living environment function together as these are connected to each other through food chain, matter circulation, energy flow, etc., as one unit, which is called an ecological system or **ecosystem.** Man is a part of the ecosystem. This concept is holistic as all component parts of the ecosystem function together and has functionally obligatory relationship. A natural pond, lake, bay, ocean, forest, grassland etc., can be considered an ecosystem.

The component parts are: (i) **the abiotic** (non-living) substances found in the atmosphere, water, soil and factors like temperature, relative humidity, sunlight, rainfall, etc., associated with the environment. This component changes with time and affects the activities of living processes. (ii) Green plants called **producers (autotrophs)** or energy transducers, which convert solar energy into chemical energy stored in plant tissues and this energy becomes the source of energy for other living organisms including man in the ecosystem. (iii) **Consumers** like plant grazers (grasshoppers, cattle, etc.), flesh eating animals like frogs, snakes, some birds, and many mammals like tigers and omnivores like man form another component of this system. Plant grazers are called herbivores and animal flesh eaters are called carnivores, which may be classified under different categories like Carnivore-1, Carnivore-2 and so on. Consumers are heterotrophs. (iv) **Decomposers** form another component. They are detritus eating organisms like bacteria, fungi and some animals like earthworms. Decomposers are also heterotrophs.

Enumeration

The structure of an ecosystem refers to the diversity, distribution, numbers and biomass of living organisms in the ecosystem, the qualities and distribution of organic nutrients and the physicochemical conditions characterizing the system. Ecosystem function refers to the energy flow and its rate, nutrient cycle, biogeochemical cycle and the homeostatic mechanism that determine the structure and stability of the system. Courses in ecology in the senior classes of the high school and in the undergraduate curriculum must include the above aspects. Organism, populations (community) and ecosystem are three important and convenient levels, which can provide the most effective basis for the teaching of ecology.

The organism level of the integration deals with the relationship of the individual organism and its immediate biotic and abiotic environment. The structural and functional aspects of these systems correspond to the morphological, physiological, biochemical and behavioural adaptations of the organism and the characteristics of the environment, to which the organism is exposed and the interactions related to this exposure (Cox, 1970). The specialized fields of the functional morphology, ecophysiology and behavioural ecology direct much of their attention to relationships at organism level.

The population level of integration deals with the density, distribution and dispersion pattern, and sex and age structure of the populations, together with the descriptions of the biotic and abiotic characteristics of the environment. Function in such systems is characterized by natality and mortality, rates of transfer of nutrients and energy along trophic levels, and patterns of modifications of environmental conditions and the operation of mechanisms of population regulation. A community consists of population in a specified space.

Structure in the ecosystem level of integration includes diversity and relative abundance of species, number, distribution and the biomass of various trophic groups, the sizes, source and locations of energy and nutrient pools, and the conditions of the physical environment. Function in such system includes rates of energy and nutrient transfer and the operation of homeostatic mechanisms to maintain the structural stability of the system. None of these levels is more important than another with regard to teaching and research in ecology or understanding the structure of ecosystem.

The natural ecosystems of the world include Tundra, Desert, Lakes, Rivers, Ponds, Oceans, Forests (Tropical, Subtropical, Mangroves, Rainforests, Temperate, Alpine, etc.), and Grasslands in different latitudes and altitudes etc.

India is a mega biodiversity country having about 8% of world's biodiversity although land area is only 2.4% of the planet. On the basis of the presence of vascular plants and vertebrate animals, 18 mega biodiversity countries in the world have been identified. Figures 7-9 show natural ecosystems such as Canadian Prairie (grassland), Bhittarkanika Mangrove (Odisha, India), temperate region lake (Athabasca lake, Canada) respectively. These ecosystems have the same component parts such as producers, consumers, decomposers and abiotic components but the species of producers, consumers and decomposers may be different. These component parts perform similar functions in their respective ecosystems.

The natural systems are largely pollution free and less energy intensive systems.

Man made ecosystems are energy intensive, pollution generating but highly productive and fragile. Agro ecosystems, aquaculture systems, industrial systems, urban systems, etc., are man

Figure 7. Canadian Prairie—Drumheller, Alberta, Canada (Photograph taken in summer, 1970 by the author).

Figure 8. Mangrove ecosystem of Bhittarkanika sea coast in Odisha, India (Photograph by Dr. Chandra Sekhar Kar)

made systems and require huge amount of energy, resources and labour for their running. These systems, however provide jobs and are productive, although they generate pollutants that create health hazards. Figure 10 shows the conceptual framework of an ecosystem, i.e., natural or man made.

Figure 9(a). A temperate region lake—Athabaska Lake in Alberta, Canada. (Photograph taken by the author)

Figure 9(b). A tropical saltwater lake (Chilika Lagoon-Ramsar Site, Odisha, India) with painted storks and pelicans (photograph by Chilika Development Authority, Bhubaneswar)

Any disturbance in the system, whether natural or man made brings unpredictable changes in the system and may disrupt links and restoration involves money, time, etc. Disturbance in natural system may be unpredictable.

There is need for environmental management; the system may be natural or man made. Adoption of ecosystem concept and identifying component parts and functioning attributes has

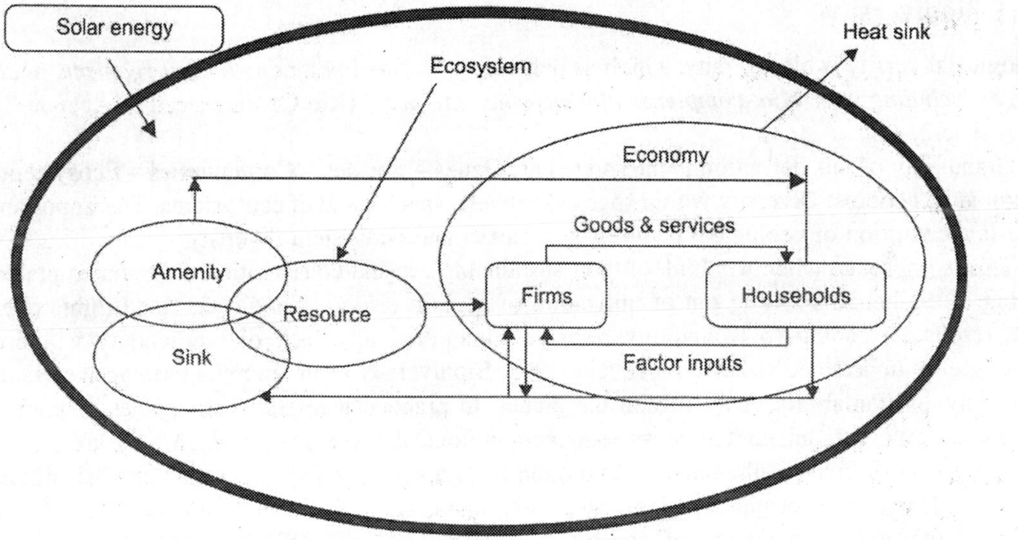

Figure 10. Ecosystem conceptual framework

helped man to manage the natural and man made ecosystems in an ecofriendly way and to its own advantage without creating much problem for other kinds of living organisms. Ecosystems can be modelled, and inputs, outputs, etc., can be quantified and predictions under defined conditions can be made. Modelling has become essential for ecosystem management. On the basis of energy flow in the ecosystem they can be classified into different categories like: (i) Unsubsidized, solar powered natural ecosystems, (ii) Nature subsidized natural solar powered ecosystem, (iii) Man subsidized but solar powered ecosystems, and (iv) Man made fossil fuel powered urban-industrial ecosystems.

Natural ecosystems have provided food, fodder, medicine, clothes, and ecosystem services to man since time immemorial but now they are under intensive pressure due to many anthropogenic activities.

1.7 ECOSYSTEM FUNCTIONS

Functional attributes of the ecosystem can be grouped as:

(i) Biodiversity, its role in ecosystem function and maintenance of stability
(ii) Food chain-food web relationships, ecological pyramids
(iii) Matter (nutrient) cycling: gaseous cycles, sedimentary cycles and their relation to pollutant movement in the ecosystems
(iv) Productivity (both plant (primary) and animal (secondary))
(v) Energy flow processes and energy flow modelling
(vi) Balance of Nature
(vii) Development and evolution of ecosystems including community evolution or coevolution.

1.7.1 Biodiversity

Biological diversity is biodiversity, which is defined as "variability among *living organisms in all sources including inter alia, complexes of which they are part*" (Rio Conference, The Agenda-21 and Article-2).

Granularity of this definition is interpreted as: Genes – Species – Communities – Ecosystems – Ecological patterns. Diversity within species, between species and of ecosystems. The important thing is recognition of ecological patterns, complexes and ecosystem diversity.

This is important when we think of their sustainable use and conservation. Fair and equitable sharing of the benefits arising out of utilization of genetic resources and access and rights over these resources leading to technology transfer. Functional approach of biodiversity is more meaningful to understand sustainable development. Biodiversity is an umbrella term and refers to the variety and variability of all life on the planet. In practice it refers to all species of plants, animals and microorganisms the ecosystems and ecological processes of which they are part.

Today's biodiversity is the result of evolution from a single celled organism some 3.5 billion years ago. This unitary origin explains why all organisms share the same basic chemistry: DNA is always the storage molecule of genetic information and the complex process of protein biosynthesis is virtually the same in all organisms. Separate species evolved when mutations between relatives no longer allowed for interbreeding, for instance after geographic or reproductive separation. Planet's biodiversity is organized into three levels, namely:

1. Ecosystems and ecological patterns, such as rainforests (Silent valley), lakes (Chilika Lake), coral reefs, Himalayan ecosystem, Western Ghats and Eastern Ghats.
2. Species level that comprise about 1.5-2 million species identified by scientists so far and may be another few million yet to be identified.
3. Genes that make up the heredity of each species is now considered the basic important tool for Genetic Engineering and creation of transgenic plants and transgenic animals and a tool for biotechnology research.

Ecosystem diversity refers to the diversity of a place at the level of ecosystems. This has three ecological perspectives:

(a) **Alpha Diversity:** Alpha diversity refers to the diversity of organisms sharing the same community/habitat within the biotic-community diversity.

(b) **Beta Diversity:** It refers to the diversity of organisms sharing two habitats (between community diversity).

(c) **Gamma Diversity:** Biodiversity of the habitat over the total landscape or geographical area is called gamma diversity. This has a broader perspective.

The rich biological diversity of India is largely due to the prevalence of wide range of soil, climatic conditions and habitats with food sources and it is reflected in the rich flora and fauna and diversified ecosystems. The total geographical area is about 328.73 million ha having a forest and tree cover of about 78.38 million ha. (~23.84%). India has about 47,000-50,000 plant species with 5,000 endemic species and about 89,000 animal species. India had earlier some 30,17,009 sq. km. of wild habitat and about 80% of it has vanished due to anthropogenic activities without replacement within half a century or so. Tables 4 and 5 give an estimate of the number of organisms identified so far in the world and in India.

Table 4. Number of Living Species of all Organisms (from Wilson, 1992)

Organisms	Number of species
Insects	751,000
Other animals	281,000
Higher plants	248,000
Fungi	6,900
Algae	26,900
Protozoa	30,800
Bacteria and similar form	4,800
Viruses	1,000

Table 5. List of Flora and Fauna in India

	Floristic Groups	No. of spy.	Aoristic Group	No. of spp.
•	Angiosperms	>15000	Mammals	> 372
•	Gymnosperms	> 64	Aves	> 1,200
•	Pteridophytes	>1022	Reptiles	> 399
•	Bryophytes	>2584	Amphibia	> 204
•	Lichens	>1200	Fish	> 1,693
•	Fungi	>23000	Insects	>60,000
•	Algae	> 2500	Molluscs	> 5,000

A biodiversity hotspot is a biogeography region with a significant reservoir of biodiversity that is threatened. An area is designated as a hotspot when it contains at least 0.5% of plant species as endemic. There are 34 such hotspots of biodiversity on a global level, out of which two are present in the Indian subcontinent.

These are: Indo-Burma (earlier The Eastern Himalayas) and the Western Ghats & Sri Lanka. These hotspots covering less than 2% of the world's land area are found to have about 50% of the terrestrial biodiversity. Internationally recognized Indian biodiversity hotspots are the Himalayan ecosystems and the Western Ghats. There are many internationally recognized aquatic, sites such as Chilika Lake, Bhittarkanika mangroves in Odisha, rich in aquatic biodiversity with bird fauna. Besides there are many nationally recognized biodiversity hotspots like biosphere reserves, sanctuaries, etc.

At the international level, eighteen countries are currently designated as mega-biodiversity countries as these countries possess very rich biodiversity. These countries are: (i) Australia (ii) Brazil (iii) Colombia (iv) Ecuador (v) India (vi) Indonesia (vii) Madagascar (viii) Malaysia (ix) Mexico,(x) Peoples Republic of China (xi) Peru (xii) Zaire and the newly added countries are: (xiii) Democratic Republic of Congo (xiv) Philippines (xv) Papua New Guinea (xvi) South Africa (xvii) United States of America (xviii) Venezuela (as shown in Figure 11 taken from WWF-Internet).

In these countries many ecosystems have been identified as biodiversity hot spots.

Areas defined on the basis of vascular plant diversity, endemic vertebrates and threat. 12 mega biodiversity countries (currently-18 mega biodiversity countries)
(now > 34 Hotspots – Conservation International)

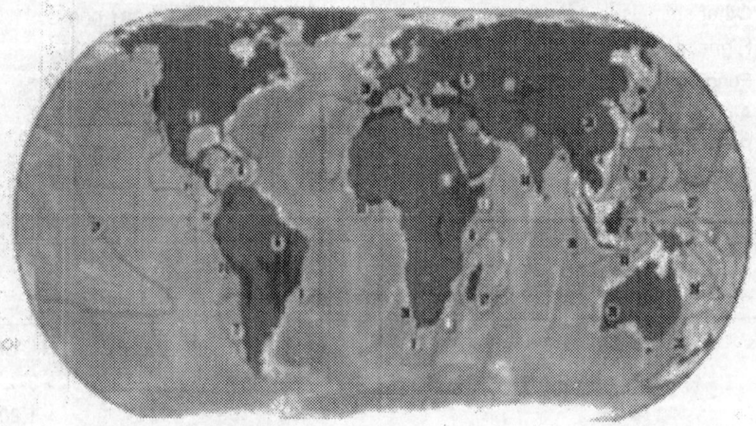

Figure 11. Biodiversity hotspots

The biodiversity hotspots are extensively distributed in the tropical regions. These regions are located in the vicinity of seas and oceans. Most of the hotspots are in tropical rainforests, Mediterranean-type vegetation, three are in temperate forests, one in tropical Brazil's dry forest (Cerrado), and one in semi-desert (Succulent Karoo). About 44% of all species of vascular plants and 35% of all species of the four vertebrate groups, namely, mammals, birds, reptiles and amphibians are confined to 34 hotspots. It has been found that about 62% of the total surface area of these hotspots is yet to be protected. This leads to huge loss of habitat and fragmentation of habitat in hotspot areas. In view of this majority of the endemic species of hotspot areas are considered as threatened species in the international red lists of species. The main types of biomes show the diversity of world's ecosystems. Most of these **biomes** are situated within the 30ºN and 30ºS of the Equator. These biomes are: (i) Tropical forest, (ii) Savanna, (iii) Desert, (iv) Polar and high mountain areas, (v) Chaparral, (vi) Temperate grasslands, (vii) Temperate Deciduous forests, (viii) Coniferous forest, (ix) Tundra (arctic and alpine). The major communities (biomes) are classified according to the predominant vegetation and by the unique adaptations the organisms exhibit to that particular environment.

Global pattern of biodiversity is conspicuous on the basis of latitudinal gradient in species richness. The pattern of the average species richness generally increases from high to low latitude, regardless of taxa (namely, plants, mammals, birds, reptiles, fish, insects), geographical position or time domain. Exceptions to this rule may occur, especially with regard to aquatic flora, and parasites and life histories. Since seasons, temperature, rainfall, duration of sunlight etc., vary latitudinally, it is not surprising to observe this biodiversity pattern.

Altitudinal gradient also influences biodiversity. Mountain ecosystems show drastic changes in vegetation and biodiversity and climate depending upon the height from the base of the mountain to its summit. It has been observed that in Norway and the Alps, the species richness of plants declines by 40 for every 100 m rise in elevation. The environmental factors like temperature, precipitation vary with increase in height. Besides, the mountain slopes reduce the land area with elevation. In general, in low elevation areas, species diversity is greater than at high elevation, where temperature is cooler and the growing season is shorter.

Generally speaking, favourable climate, parent rock material and geological stability, water courses and hydrology, land use and geographic isolation make mountain ecosystems in low and medium elevations rich in biodiversity.

Rainforests form the lifeline of ecosystem balancing. More than 50% of world's biodiversity is found in rainforests. The Amazon forest releases twenty billion tonnes of moisture every day, helping to water crops around the world. Healthy rainforests absorb about 10% of man's carbon emissions every year. Deforestation releases more CO_2 than all the transport. Saving the rainforests in the world, the Himalayas and the Western Ghats in India will be an essential first step. Deforestation is one of the largest contributors to climate change. Rainforests provide countless services to humanity, often unnoticed. (The Prince of Wales Rainforest Project, 1996). Man has a genius for survival, which often only manifests at the eleventh hour. Now is the time when we must act together to avoid the catastrophe of climate change and arrest biodiversity loss. In view of the discussion made above, it is concluded that *biodiversity forms foundations for* interdependence of organisms. Food chain relationships and multichannel food web, maintaining the balance of nature, maintaining sustained productivity and ecosystem stability, providing food, fodder, medicine, shelter, material, fuel, fibre and other utility material and foundation for agriculture, industry and civilization.

1.7.2 Rural Livelihood based Biodiversity

In developing countries the livelihood options and rural economy are largely bio-resource based, especially on agriculture and horticulture, (crops and fruits), forestry (firewood, minor forest products), home gardens (vegetables, fruits, flower), diary (milk, cowdung, ploughing), fishery (fish, prawn, turtles), goatery (meat, milk, skin), poultry (meat and egg), artisan work based on bamboo, wood, cane, grass and other resources. Traditional ecological knowledge and bio-resource management is important for rural systems. Biodiversity provides us food, shelter material, raw material for medicines, gases for survival, other ecosystem services like recycling of water and other materials. We need natural protectors around us, like the mangroves of Bhittarkanika (Odisha), and Sunderbans (West Bengal) as coast guards and the "green-friends" (jungles) like Similipal, Himalayas, Western Ghats, and Eastern Ghats, and rainforests to generate and supply life supporting oxygen or sequester the atmospheric carbon preventing global warming.

1.7.3 Agricultural Biodiversity

In addition to biodiversity in the wild, the biodiversity of organisms used for farming and other human activities is very important. In agriculture, 7000 species of plants are used by farmers in the world, but only 30 species provide 90 percent of our calorific intake. The top three crops are wheat, rice and maize (corn) with around 500 million tons annual production of each. Data from various sources indicates that India has contributed about 167 cultivated plant species (7%) to the world. Within these dominant crop species, there are many hundred thousands of varieties (landraces, cultivars) adapted to local climates, farming practices, and cultural predilections like taste, colour, structure, ability to store the products, etc. Much of this large crop diversity is important for providing the initial material for breeding.

1.7.4 Biotechnology and Biodiversity

World's population is about 7 billion at present and has been projected to grow to about 9 billion by 2050. Poverty is a major concern in the world. Assuming perfect distribution, it is projected that food production at the current level would feed 6.5-7 billion people. It is crucial that food production keeps pace with the increasing population.

To feed a huge population, the food production has to be doubled. This will be a tall order as water is scarce, additional agricultural land may not be available and constraints in the form of other factors including climate change. For the improvement of food security and alleviation of poverty, the proponents of genetically modified crops believe that the use of this technology would help reduce poverty and improve food security. The only answer at present is to adopt new farming systems and modern technology to increase food production. Availability of sufficient food and nutrition, and bio-energy and environmental protection are now universal concerns. In this context, use of biotechnology to increase crop productivity and improve crop quality from nutritional angle may be the only answer. The genetic modifications of cereals, pulses, fruits and vegetables are required not only to increase productivity, but also for better nutrition. Biotechnology is also a tool to increase biodiversity and to conserve biodiversity. The bio-safety aspects of genetically modified food are an emerging field for research and require immediate attention.

Scientists and farmers have been changing the genetic structure of plants and animals for thousands of years to increase food productivity and to get desired animals for human use for various purposes. Vertical gene transfer between cultivars and wild plants has always occurred within the limits of species, if the two types of plants were in close proximity and flowered at the same time. Hybrid production is an age old practice. When apple cultivators take an apple tree that produces juicy and sweet apples and crossbreed it with an apple tree that is resistant to frost or a particular disease, the cultivators produce a hybrid, which is a genetically modified apple tree to produce juicy and sweet apples even under the adverse condition of frost. This manipulation happens in nature and man acts as an agent, like crosspollination by bees or insects or the wind.

But modern biotechnology deals with altering genetic material, the DNA in an organism in a way that does not occur naturally. The genetically changed organism is called genetically modified organism or GMO. Genetic mediation permits desirable genes to be transferred to another plant to create a GMO-crop that can be productive, more nutritious, and have resistance to herbicides and pests. The following examples will explain the situation.

Example 1: In Europe strawberries were genetically modified to withstand severe cold conditions that prevail in Europe. Biotechnologists isolated an anti-freezing protein, found in the DNA of a fish called the winter flounder and inserted it into the DNA of strawberries. This altered DNA was then passed on to subsequent generations of strawberry plants. The purpose was to get the benefits of the introduced gene without taking away the good attributes of strawberries. Thus, the GM-strawberries should withstand the severe cold condition without tasting fishy. Ethical questions are involved. But a from scientific angle and from the angle of nutritious food production, this appears to be an excellent solution if the GMO-food does not create health problems.

The World Heath Organization estimates that the world's population will exceed nine billion by 2050. There will be severe scarcity of food unless we increase food production. In view of this biotechnology is the answer.

Example 2: In the United States of America, a GM-crop such as golden rice has been trialed by combining rice with beta-carotene. Beta-carotene intake prevents blindness in children by supplying vitamin-A.

Another example is the production of Bt-corn, Bt-maize or Bt-cotton, which involves the transfer into the crops of a gene of a bacterium (*Bacillus thurengenesis*) that naturally releases an insecticidal toxin which gives protection to crops from bollworms that eat cotton leaves and many other crop plants. GM crop technology can improve the yield of important staple crops by creating varieties of crops which are disease resistant and which can withstand extreme climatic conditions such as low rainfall and uneven soil fertility. In Mexico, for example through genetic engineering, it was possible to create GM maize that was able to grow in acidic soils. This has helped the poor Mexican farmers who were able to grow GM maize that produced 30% more yield and thus improved their economic condition by increasing profits.

Other notable examples are virus resistant GM potatoes in Colombia and Kenya, insertion of genes against aluminium toxicity in Mexican wheat. Research is being conducted to produce GM crops that could produce bio-pharmaceuticals. Examples of such crops are potatoes that have the cholera causing bacterial gene inserted to produce tiny amounts of cholera toxin that immunize against cholera or tomatoes engineered to carry plant-derived vaccines. The advantage of edible crops with vaccines is that they would be cheaper to grow locally. Biotechnology tools are now used to conserve biodiversity and also to create new biodiversity. However the biosafety of these GM Foods are to be carefully dealt with.

1.7.5 Soil Biodiversity

Soil organisms include microorganisms, such as bacteria, actinomycetes, fungi and algae, and soil animals, such as protozoa, helminths, nematodes, annelid worms (enchytraeids and earthworms), collembola, mites, insects and their larval forms, pupae, arachnids, other arthropoda, gastropods, etc. Some mammals and birds use the soil for various purposes. They play an important role in determining the physical and chemical properties of soil, soil fertility, and so on. Earthworms and termites play a significant role in soil formation. Earthworms may burrow two metres into the soil, make numerous transverse burrows and produce worm casts by eating the soil and soil organic matter. These casts are very rich in nitrogen and mineral substances, and increase soil fertility. The burrows facilitate aeration and increase water-holding capacity. Dash and Patra (1979) measured 77 tonnes of dry weight of earthworm cast production per hectare per year in an Indian grassland site. Edwards and Lofty (1972) have estimated that earthworm cast production ranges from 2 to 247 tonnes per hectare per year in different world sites. This is equivalent to bringing up layers of soils between 1 to 5 cm thick to the surface every year. In addition, a large amount of soil is deposited in burrows as casts. Thus the soil turnover provides a stone-free layer about 15 cm deep on the surface. Earthworm casts contain more water-soluble aggregates than the surrounding soils.

Microbes form a vibrant living community in the soil contributing to a number of nutrient transformations and ecosystem functioning. They are involved in organic matter decomposition, N2-fixation, solubilization and immobilization of several major and minor nutrients (Alexander, 1971). Microorganisms play important roles in soil structure maintenance, plant growth promotion through secretion of hormones and soil-borne disease control. The diversity and richness of soil microorganisms are huge and subject of interest to scientists over the years. But till today much is yet to be is known on the complex living biota in the soil and their biophysical, biochemical functions and interactions in the soil ecosystem. But during the last 50 years, many beneficial effects of microbes in temperate and tropical soils have been discovered. We have been making use of microbes for improving productivity in agriculture, industry and pharmaceuticals and they are used in biotechnology.

1.7.6 Depletion of Biodiversity

Biodiversity is vanishing. It has generally been agreed upon by scientists that the rate of species extinction is now 100-1000 times greater than before the evolution of the modern human society. Species disappeared naturally at the rate of about one species per million per year and newly evolved species replaced them at the same rate. Thus, equilibrium was maintained. But the equilibrium is now getting disturbed because of human interference. The principal cause of both extinction and slowing of evolution is the interference of man by degrading and destroying natural habitats.

The rainforests, storehouse of biodiversity, are losing about 10,000 square kilometres every year due to habitat clearance for other uses of man. The other rich ecosystems, namely, coral reefs, salt marshes and mangrove swamps are also cleared for uses of man and for other purposes. Some 967 tree species are classified as "living dead" as they face extinction problems. The other familiar members of this category are the Java-Sumatran Rhinoceros, Philippines Eagles, Hawaiian Crow, River Dolphins in China and India, the giant Pandas, mountain Gorillas and many bird species. Since tropical humid forests are particularly rich in biodiversity, their destruction is disproportionately damaging to biodiversity.

Habitat loss is the prime reason of depletion of biodiversity. Habitat loss comes not only from taking more land under the plough, but also from expanding urban centres, roads, and buildings for developmental projects. In addition, habitats are damaged by flooding, lack of water, climate changes, salination, etc., which may be both natural and man made.

The loss of biodiversity can be measured by a loss of individual species, groups of species or decrease in the number of individual organisms. In a given location the loss will often reflect degradation or destruction of a whole ecosystem. First reason is habitat loss (most of it through the expansion of cultivated land), second is the introduction of exotic species. Habitat loss comes not only from taking more land under the plough, but also from expanding cities and road building. In addition, habitats can be damaged by flooding, lack of water, climate changes, salivations, etc., all of which phenomena that may be both natural and man made. Since tropical humid forests are particularly rich in biodiversity, their destruction is disproportionately damaging to biodiversity. Burning and selective logging may damage greater area.

Biodiversity is not homogeneously distributed over the humid tropical forests; rather there are hotspots with a particularly high level of biodiversity. These hotspots are of particular interest for the implementation of conservation measures.

The second most important reason for loss of biodiversity is the invasion by exotic plants and animals. Knowingly, or unknowingly, imported plant species threaten the native ones by being highly competitive and often by lacking local predators, such as insects or birds. One of the most extreme examples is seen in the pampas of Argentina, flat grasslands with a moderate climate, from which nearly all the native grasses have disappeared and have been replaced by European plants. This invasion was brought about by European farmers who introduced animals and crops, in addition to accidentally spreading many different weeds.

This phenomenon was already noted in 1833 by Charles Darwin. Yet today, droves of gardeners transport seeds all over the globe and never think of the possible threat to the local biodiversity, as suggested by Amman in 1997. It has been estimated that one in ten imported plants may spread in a modest way and that one in a hundred may turn into a nuisance weed. Even in today's Europe, invasion by exotics may threaten ecosystems. In the Ticino region of Southern Switzerland *Robinia pseudo acacia*, a native of North America, is displacing chestnut and oak trees, whilst in the northern regions of the country *Solidago canadensis* is replacing native irises in swampy areas. Islands are particularly threatened by invaders, as is well documented for Hawaii, New Zealand and the Galapagos Islands. For North America, it has been estimated that the damage caused by exotics amounts to137 billion dollars a year. Although such calculations are fraught with uncertainties, there is no doubt that the costs of exotics are tremendous. Exotic biological control agents are often introduced to agricultural ecosystems on purpose, in order to control pests or weeds without resorting to chemical control agents. Whilst there are some success stories, Strong pointed out in 2000 that such systems may also go wrong. One example is the introduction of the seven-spot ladybird, which was intended to fight the Russian wheat aphid. The consequence, however, was the disappearance of the native ladybirds, for which the seven-spot import was a competitor and an actual predator. Another example is the decimation of the large American moths, which are killed by European *Compsilura* flies, introduced nearly a century ago to control the gypsy moth. Field experiments recently done by Jensen showed that caterpillars of the American moth *Cecropia* were killed by massive infestations of *Compsilura* maggots.

The endangered species according to the International Union of Conservation of Nature and Natural Resources (IUCN), are the species that are considered to be in imminent danger of extinction and whose survival is unlikely, if factors causing their decline continue to operate. Out of about 47,000 species of plants in India, 7000 are considered endemic. India contains 172 species of animals considered globally threatened by IUCN, or about 2.9% of the world's total number of threatened species. These include 53 species of mammals, 69 species of birds, 23 species of reptiles and 3 species of amphibians. As many as 3,000-4,000 higher plants are threatened in India.

Over population (currently 7 billion people) has led to over exploitation of natural resources, destruction of wetlands, fragmentation of habitats due to developmental projects such as mining, road construction, railways development etc., Moreover, introduction of harmful substances and toxic materials into the ecosystem, poaching of wildlife and trade in wildlife and climate change cause the depletion of biodiversity.

1.7.7 Biodiversity Conservation

Conservation is being done either by *in situ* (either in the natural or semi-natural habitat) or *ex situ* (in some purpose-built environment). The choice is contextual.

In situ conservation involves maintenance and protection of natural habitats. Conservation of species in its natural ecosystem is called '*in situ*' conservation. This strategy emphasizes protection of total ecosystem through a network of "protected area", which is an area of land and/or sea specially dedicated to the protection and maintenance of biological diversity and managed through legal and effective means. There are different categories of protected areas which are managed with different objectives. These include; biosphere reserves, national parks, wildlife sanctuaries etc. At present we have 11 major biosphere reserves, 80 national parks, 420 wildlife sanctuaries, in India covering 4% of the geographic area. The JIM CORBETT National Park was the first national park to be established in India.

Similipal in Odisha is a Biosphere Reserve. *Ex-situ* conservation involves botanical gardens; zoo and seed banks/germ-plasm bank.

Ex situ is defined as "the conservation of component of biological diversity (sample of genetic diversity, particularly of endangered species) outside their natural habitats".

Ex situ involves maintenance and breeding of endangered plant and animal species under partially or wholly controlled conditions, e.g., zoos, botanical gardens, aquaria, nurseries, DNA bank, seed bank, Gene bank etc.There are more than 1500 botanical gardens in the world containing more than 80,000 species. There are more than 800 zoos around the world with about 3000 species of mammals, birds, reptiles and amphibians. Both *in situ* and *ex situ* processes require precise knowledge of taxonomy.

Conservation requires a selection of the most appropriate areas, called the hotspots. Conservation also embraces various components of agro-biodiversity like crop varieties, land races, semi-domesticates and crop relatives. The role of indigenous communities in maintaining agro-biodiversity is stressed by the Global Biodiversity Assessment and the Leipzig Plan of Action, two recently concluded international agreements. United Nations convened the CBD (Convention of Biological Diversity) and succeeded in having it adopted in 1992. It entered into force in 1993. CBD requires that all Member States take measures to conserve both native and agricultural biodiversity.

As the human population expands, the need for food is expected to double in the next 30 years. Increasing crop productivity on the land already under cultivation would prevent or at least reduce habitat destruction. CBD recognizes that states have a sovereign right over biodiversity within their own territory. Living organisms or their products may, under the terms of the CBD, only be removed from a country under mutually agreed conditions. The CBD is a comprehensive approach to biodiversity conservation of both wild and domesticated species.

Scientific data shows that the biological diversity has increased slowly but steadily through the evolutionary process over geological time. However, mass global extinction of species has occurred due to natural processes of glaciation, volcanic eruptions, earthquakes, etc. At present on an average we are loosing one specie of mammal, one bird specie and many invertebrate species from the planet every year. This realization has helped to develop the concept of environmental management and planning so that in the scenario of accelerating economic development, the biodiversity and quality environment is maintained and a sustainable society is evolved.

Remedial measures: The remedial measures are summarized below. It is important to identify unique ecological patterns and conserve them to create biotic resource inventory. Periodic monitoring (biological, chemical and physical, remote sensing, etc.) is very important to know the status. Identifying endangered, rare, vulnerable, and threatened species and conserving them is another important aspect. Biotic salvage operations include restoring wilderness, habitat and niches, restoring food webs, understanding the home range and territorial requirement, doing captive breeding and understanding their fitness values and establishing biospheres, national parks, sanctuary, zoological gardens, gene banks, etc., creating awareness by environmental education (curricula, media, folk dance, jatra (opera) etc.).

Environmental laws are a good instrument to protect biodiversity. Law implementation is important. 'No development" without adequate environment al protection and addressing human issues should be allowed.

Action Plan: The Biodiversity Act

The Biological Diversity Act, 2002 received assent of the President of India in February, 2003. It is expected that this Act will be a valuable instrument for biodiversity conservation and to achieve sustainable development. Traditional knowledge is also used as an input into pharmaceuticals, ayurvedic medicines, agriculture, biological pesticides, cosmetics and toiletries, etc.The traditional knowledge is being widely disseminated and commercially exploited with only a small proportion of the benefits flowing back to the people/communities.

Questions arise about who own the traditional knowledge patents? It is expected that the Biological Diversity Act has considered this aspect also.

The India Seed Act and Patent Act should be reviewed keeping the Biodiversity Act in view and the interests of Indian farmers, industry and people' interest.

India has taken important steps like: (i) setting biotic resource inventory; (ii) identifying the endangered, vulnerable, rare and threatened species and ecosystems; (iii) identifying disease causing organisms, vectors, etc., and devising methods for their eradication or control in the context of environmental management; (iv) biotic salvage operations for ecosystems and threatened species populations; and (v) creating trained manpower for taking up ecosystem analysis especially from the biological damage control point of view and for sustained yield point of view. The problems, however, are extremely complex.

We are compassionate for biodiversity conservation for the sake of continuance of man on this planet. World Trade Human rights, traditional knowledge on alternate medicine and other aspects are linked to biodiversity.

1.8 FOOD CHAIN-FOOD WEB RELATIONSHIPS, ECOLOGICAL PYRAMIDS

Green plants (autotrophs) convert solar energy into chemical energy stored in plant food material. The transfer of this food energy from plants, through a series of organisms, forms a food chain. Grass may be eaten by a grasshopper, which may be eaten by a frog, which is eaten by a snake, which forms the food source for other large snakes, birds and so on. This is called a food chain. For example:

(i) A diatom > zooplankton > small fish > large fish > man

(ii) Grass > grasshopper > frog > snake > bird

These two examples indicate that the base of food chain forms a plant, which is eaten by a herbivore, which in turn in predated by a carnivore and so on. The arrangement is generalized as:

Plant > Herbivore > Carnivore 1 > Carnivore 2 ....

In nature the food chain relationship is not so simple as the plant is eaten by many herbivores, which are eaten by many carnivores depending upon their food habits. Hence, the relationship becomes web-like called a food web. For example, grasses can be grazed by grasshoppers, rabbits, cattle, and they in turn can be predated by frogs, toads, snakes, some carnivore birds, small sized carnivore mammals, large sized carnivore mammals etc. The small sized carnivores can be predated by large sized carnivores. Thus, a food web is formed rather than a simple food chain. The green plants occupy the first food level (trophic level), called producers; the plant eaters form the next trophic level, called herbivores, (primary consumer). The herbivores may be predated by animals called carnivore 1 (secondary consumers), which in turn can be predated by larger carnivore 2 (tertiary consumers).The larger carnivores can also predate herbivores. The dead plant and animal materials and their excreta can be eaten by another group of organisms; (microorganisms/some animals) usually found in soil and are called detritus feeders, and/or decomposers. All types of green plants (producers) form the first trophic level. All type of plant grazers (grasshopper, rabbit, cattle) form the second trophic level, called herbivore or primary consumer.

Carnivores depending upon their size and food habits can be carnivore 1, carnivore 2 and soon (secondary consumer, tertiary consumer). The decomposers form another trophic level. Except the green plant (autotrophs), all other organisms are called heterotrophs (herbivore, carnivore, etc). Charles Elton was the first ecologist to observe that the number of links in any food chain in nature rarely exceed five links because of energy constraints. In the process of energy transfer, there is loss of energy due to dissipation as heat and thus the energy transfer between trophic levels determines the number of links. Charles Elton concluded that 'One hill cannot sustain two tigers'. The tiger being a tertiary consumer, sits on the top of food chain. A hill, because of limitations of primary production (production by plants), may not sustain many primary or secondary consumers. Hence, a number of tigers will starve to death as they will not get enough food in a small hill ecosystem.

1.8.1 Significance of Food Chain

Food chains/webs show the feeding relationships and the interaction between organisms in the ecosystem. Besides, it shows the role of biodiversity in the energy flow and matter circulation in the ecosystem. Food chain studies can show the movement of toxic substances and biomagnifications in the ecosystem and can indicate the health of the ecosystem.

1.8.2 Ecological Pyramids

Charles Elton (1927) observed that the primary consumers at the base of the food chain are relatively abundant while the consumers at the end of the food chain are relatively few and there is a progressive decrease in between the two extremes. He found that if the number of consumers at different trophic levels are plotted, it may look like a pyramid. Ecologists call it Eltonian (after the name of Charles Elton) Pyramid. Later intensive studies showed that the ecological pyramids can be broadly of three types, i.e., (a) Pyramid of Numbers (number of organisms in different trophic levels are plotted in the graph), (b) Pyramid of Biomass (biomass of organisms in different trophic levels plotted), (c) Pyramid of Energy (the total quantity of energy utilized by the different trophic levels or in a unit area in a given period of time plotted). The energy pyramid remains upright always because of the energy transfer mechanism but the pyramid of numbers and pyramid of biomass may be upright or inverted depending upon the situation or ecosystem. (Figure 12)

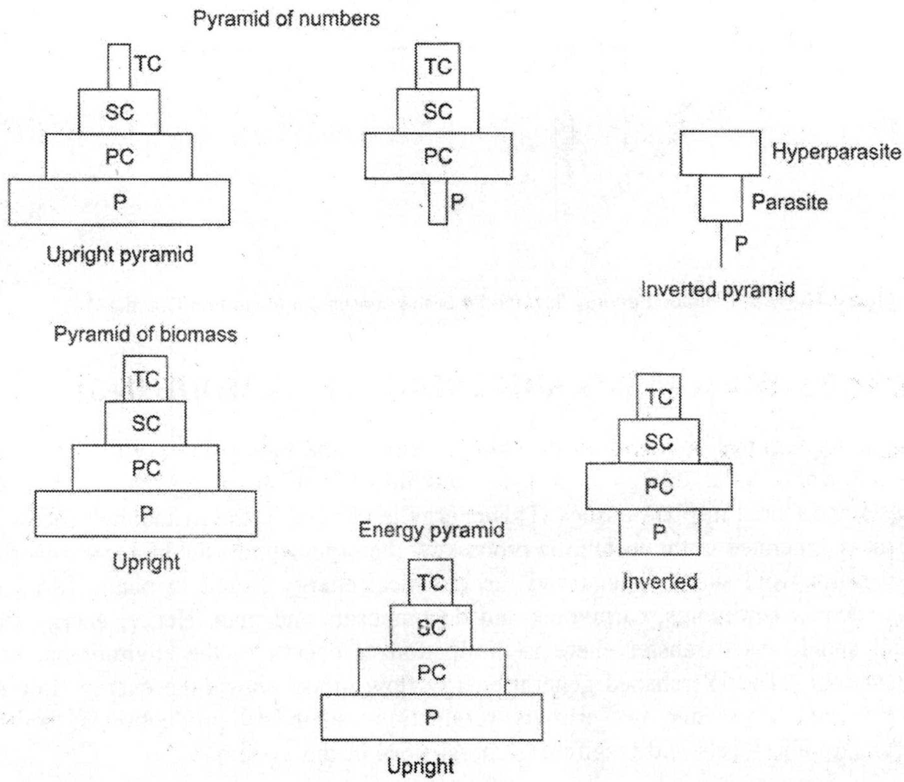

Ecological (Eltonian) pyramids: Pyramid of numbers can be both upright and inverted, pyramid of biomass can also be both upright and inverted but the pyramid of energy is always upright (see text for explanation) (P = producers. PC = primary consumers, SC = secondary consumers. TC = tertiary consumers). A parasitic food chain is also shown.

Figure 12. Ecological pyramids (from Dash and Dash, 2009)

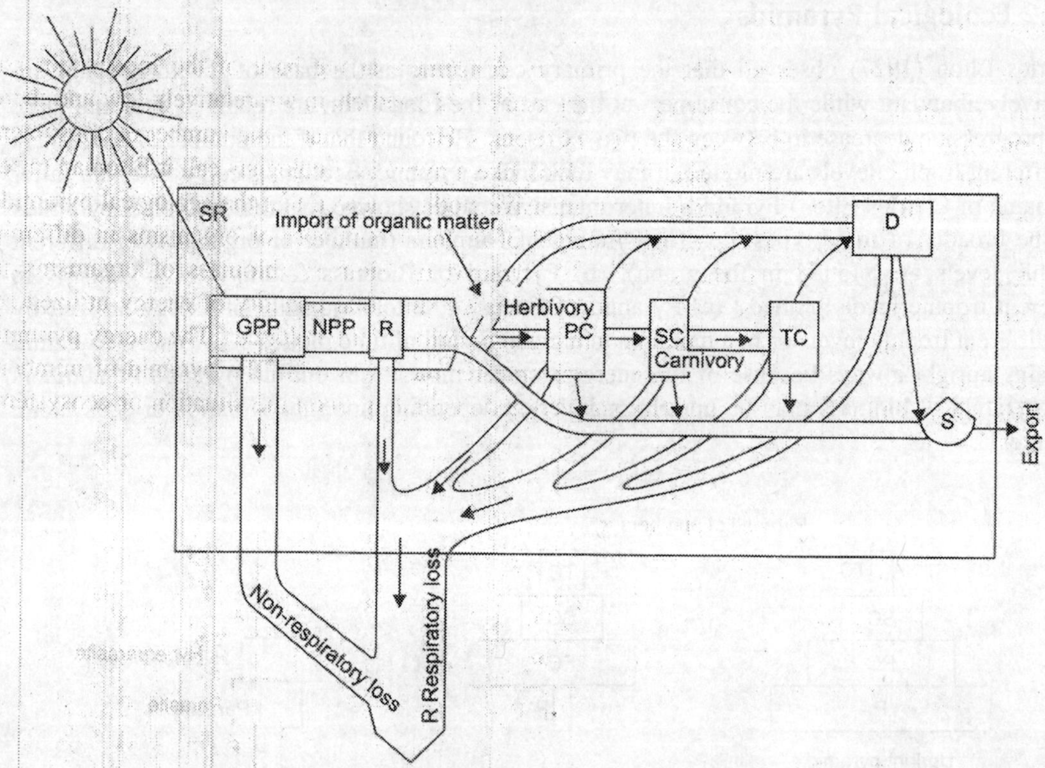

Figure 13. The 'Y'-shaped energy flow model of the ecosystem (based on Odum 1971)

1.9 ENERGY FLOW PROCESSES AND ENERGY FLOW MODELING

Biological activity requires energy. Sun provides energy to the biological world. Energy is the capacity to do work. Solar energy is transformed into chemical energy by the process of photosynthesis and stored in plant tissues. This energy is utilized in the metabolic process to do work and heat is generated in the metabolic process by the organism. In the biological world, the solar energy flows from sun to plants and the chemical energy stored in plants flows to all heterotrophs such as herbivores, carnivores and decomposers and man. Hence, energy flow is unidirectional and in each transfer, there is dissipation of energy to the environment as heat (Figures 13 and 14).The 'Y' shaped general energy flow model shows the energy flow in the ecosystem involving gross and net primary production, secondary production at herbivore, carnivore, etc., trophic levels and respiratory energy loss in the system.

Energy and Global Environment

Only the fifty-millionth of sun's energy output strikes the earth's outer atmosphere, at a constant rate called solar flux, which is defined as the amount of radian energy of all wavelengths that cross the unit area per unit time. The solar flux is about 8.37 joules (2 cal/cm^2 min).The solar flux at a place varies diurnally because of the earth's rotation on its axis. It also varies seasonally

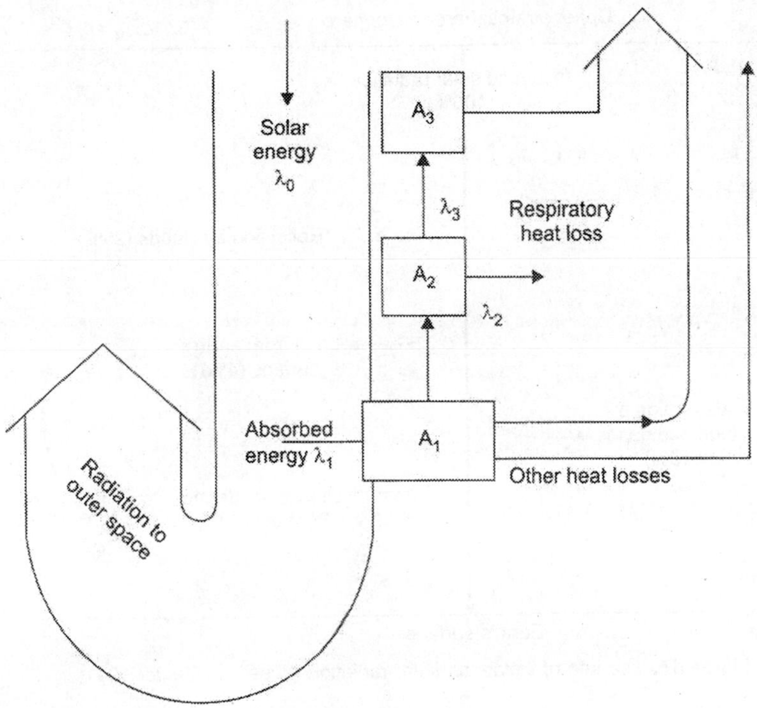

Figure 14. Lindeman's energy flow model showing different trophic levels (A1, A2, A3) and heat losses, etc. (Dash and Dash, 2009)

with the latitude because of the earth's rotation around the sun and due to the inclination of the earth's equatorial plane with respect to its orbital plane. About 42% of the solar flux is reflected back to space (33% from the clouds and 9% from the suspended particulate matter or dust) and about 10% of the solar flux is absorbed or diffusely scattered by the atmospheric gases like ozone, oxygen, water vapour etc. About 48% (0.96 cal/cm^2 min.) of the total solar flux strikes the earth's surface (Geiger, 1941). Of this 48%, part of the sunlight is reflected back from light surfaces or from clear and bright sand. The radian energy absorbed in the troposphere keeps the

Table 6. Total Spectrum of Solar Radiation Wave Length

Up to 0.0 01μ	0.001- 0.39μ	0.39 to 0.42μ	0.42 to 0.49μ	0.49 to 0.535μ	0.535 to 0.586μ	0.586 to 0.647μ	0.647 to 0.760μ	0.760 to 10.0μ GHG absorb ↕	>10.μ Radio waves
X-rays, r-rays, cosmic rays	Ultra-violet	Violet-Visible spectrum	Blue-Visible spectrum	→ Green Visible spectrum	→→ Yellow Visible spectrum	→ Orange Visible spectrum	Red-Visible spectrum	Infra-red	Radio waves

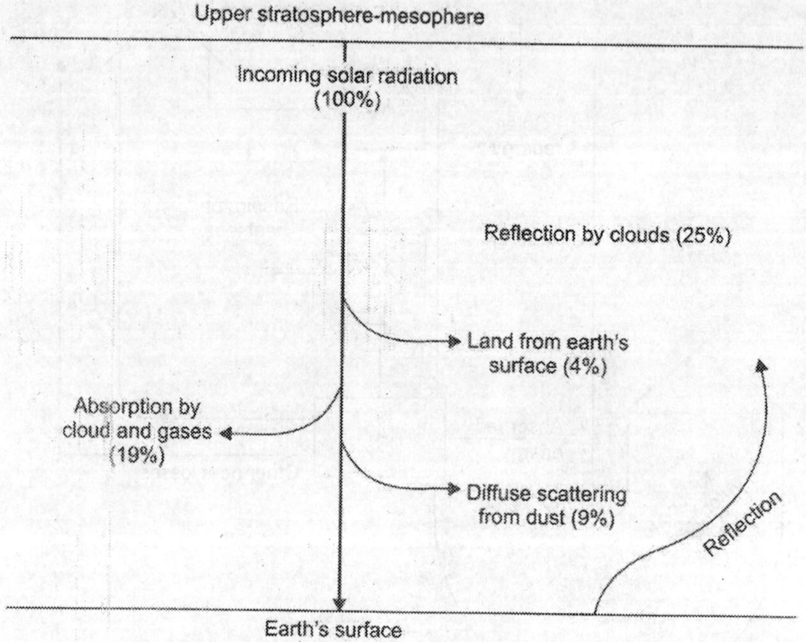

Figure 15. The fate of incidental solar radiation (based on Geiger 1941)

atmosphere warm and is radiated outward in the infrared portion of the spectrum (Table 6 and Figure 15) and some infrared radiation strikes the earth's surface.

Life is abundantly found in the small zone where the atmosphere, hydrosphere and pedosphere interact and this zone lies at the bottom of the atmosphere. The troposphere experiences an average temperature of about 14.43°C ranging from about – 40°C in high altitudes to about an average of 15°C at the surface. The stratosphere has negligible to nil water vapour and contains nearly thousand times more ozone than the troposphere. Seventy five percent of the total mass of the atmosphere consisting of gases and water vapour lie in the troposphere. The stratosphere absorbs the ultraviolet radiation, causing warmer temperature towards the top of the stratosphere. In contrast to the troposphere, there is little mixing of air in the stratosphere. In the troposphere air moves continuously, redistributing heat and moisture from one region of the globe to another. The composition and behaviour of the different layers of atmosphere, especially troposphere and stratosphere control the weather (temperature and humidity content) in a place and the climate of the area. Because of air movements and wind pattern, the air pollutants easily move from one place to another in the troposphere. The situation is different in the stratosphere as there is negligible mixing of air and therefore, pollutants remain suspended for a long time. Air density and pressure decrease with increase in distance from the earth's surface until a near vacuum is reched in space. Gases like carbon dioxide and water vapour absorb heat and play an important role in the energy balance of the earth.

The incoming solar radiation is stronger near the equator than at high latitudes. Gases like carbon dioxide, water vapour, methane, ozone and other gases absorb heat and this heat absorption warms the atmosphere to some extent and therefore, the earth's surface which reflects solar radiation usually has a high albedo. Earth's surfaces containing forests, water bodies, black soil

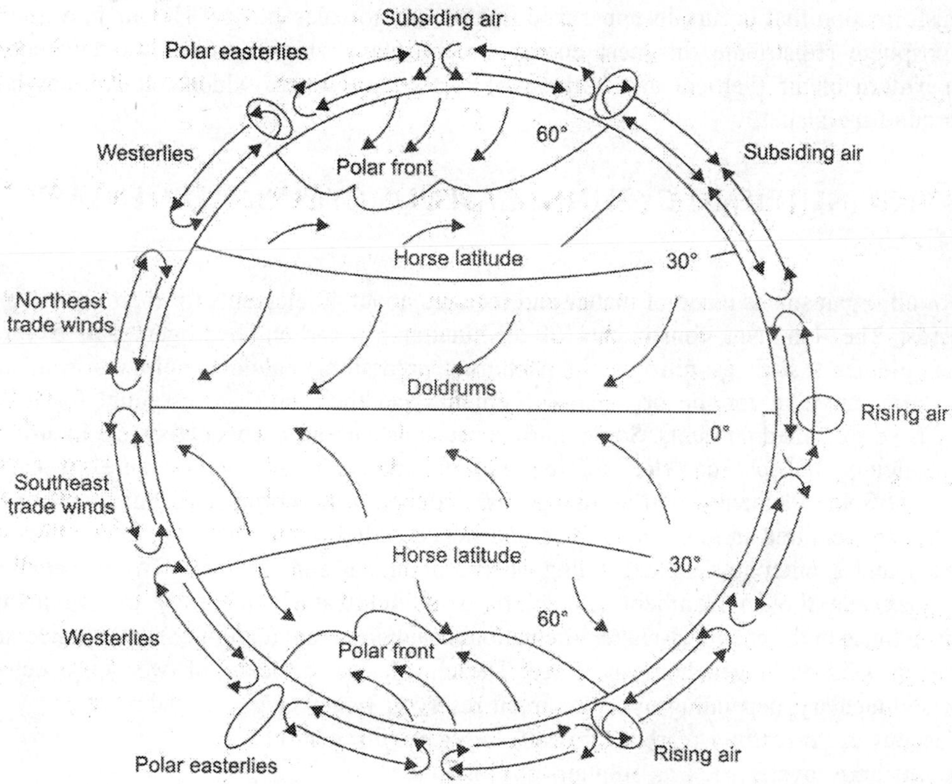

Figure 16. The general circulation pattern of air in the globe (from IGNOU publications)

etc., absorb solar radiation and then have low albedo and surfaces that are densely clouded, snow covered, etc., which reflect solar radiation have high albedo. Energy absorbed by forests and plants provides the energy for photosynthesis and in this process of energy transformation, the low quality diffused energy becomes high quality concentrated energy.

A brick-cement building absorbs solar radiation and remits the absorbed energy in the form of heat. Part of the solar energy comes in the form of intense high energy light in the form of infrared wavelength. The upper atmosphere absorbs longer infrared wavelengths and most of the short wavelength light (visible spectrum) reaches easily at the surface. From the earth's surface, the energy is reflected in longer wavelengths and some of it gets absorbed by the atmospheric gases, and keeps the lower troposphere warm, a phenomenon called **'greenhouse effect'** and these gases which absorb the heat are called **'greenhouse gases'**. Burning of fossil fuels like coal and petroleum products and deforestation also affect the energy balance of the earth. The planet earth is now experiencing global warming, which causes unpredictable environmental changes including climate flip-flop. Every gram of water on evaporation absorbs 580 calories of energy as the water transforms from liquid to vapour. Thus, water vapour contains a huge amount of stored energy called latent heat. When water vapour condenses usually in the upper troposphere, it changes from vapour to liquid form and in the process, 580 calories of heat energy are released from each gram. This simple calculation shows the huge amount of heat energy transformation that occurs in upper troposphere due to solar energy. The air movements in the troposphere redistribute this heat energy on the planet. Figure 16 shows the general circulation pattern of air (vertical and horizontal) in the atmosphere which redistributes heat moisture around the planet.

1.10 MATTER (NUTRIENT) CYCLING: GASEOUS CYCLES, SEDIMENTARY CYCLES

The body of all organisms is made of matter and requires about 40 elements for their growth and life processes. The dominant constituents of this matter are carbon, hydrogen, and oxygen. Many other elements such as nitrogen, phosphorus, potassium, calcium, sulphur, iron, and magnesium are important for the organisms. Elements and their salts are essential for living processes. These are called nutrients. Some nutrients such as carbon, nitrogen, oxygen, hydrogen, potassium, calcium, phosphorus, etc., are required in large amount and are therefore called macronutrients. Some elements such as manganese, copper, zinc, boron, molybdenum, cobalt, chlorine, etc., are required in small quantities and hence called micronutrients. Sodium can be both a macro and a micronutrient depending on the organism and situation. These matter on circulating between the environment (especially soil and water) and body of organisms. (biodiversity). Since in the chemical-matter circulation the environment (earth-geo) and biodiversity are involved, it is called biogeochemical cycles. These cycles are basically of two types such as gaseous or sedimentary, depending upon the main reservoir (whether gas or sediments).

(a) Gaseous cycle (carbon (carbon dioxide), ogygen, nitrogen, etc.

(b) Sedimentary cycles such as sulphur, phosphorus.

Besides the water cycle (water as vapour, water as liquid, water as solid-snow and ice, and ground water) operate in nature.

In the cycling of these matters (chemical), biodiversity and their activities play a very important role. Pollutants, being chemicals, also circulate in the ecosystem involving biodiversity and cause health problems. Major gaseous and sedimentary cycles and some pollutants, movement are represented in the graphs. (Figures 17, 18 & 19)

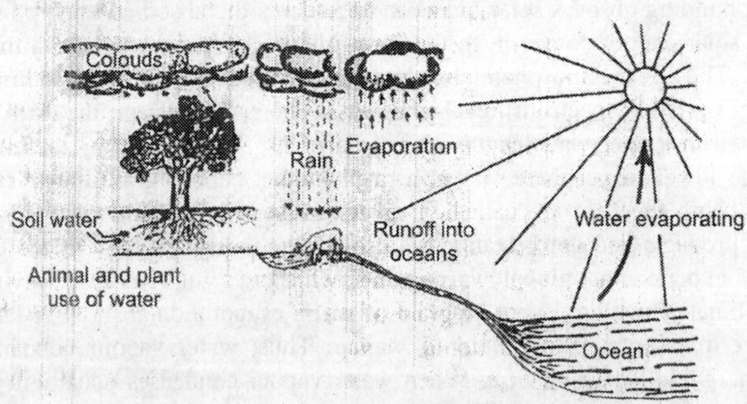

Figure 17. The water cycle (from Dash and Dash, 2009)

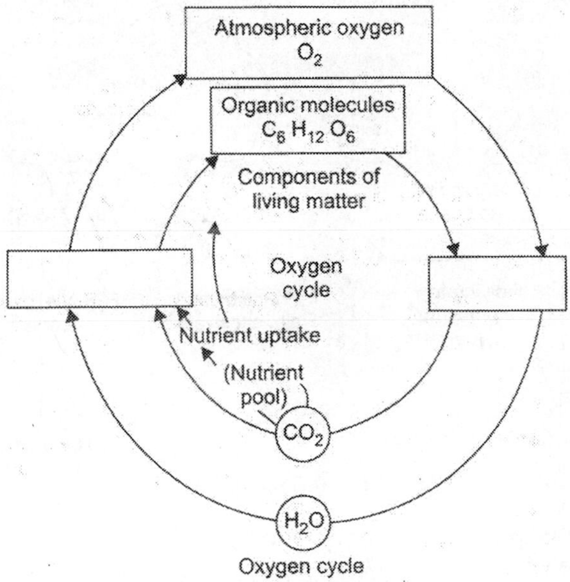

Figure 18(a). The oxygen cycle (from Dash and Dash, 2009, 2001)

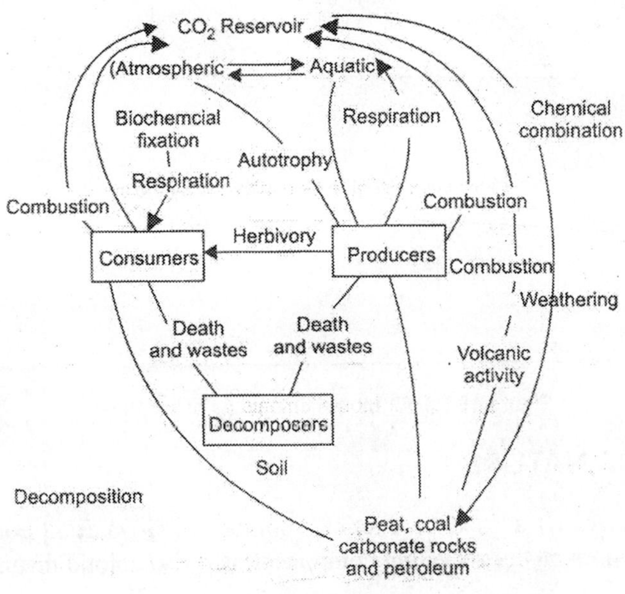

Figure 18(b). The carbon cycle (from Dash and Dash, 2009)

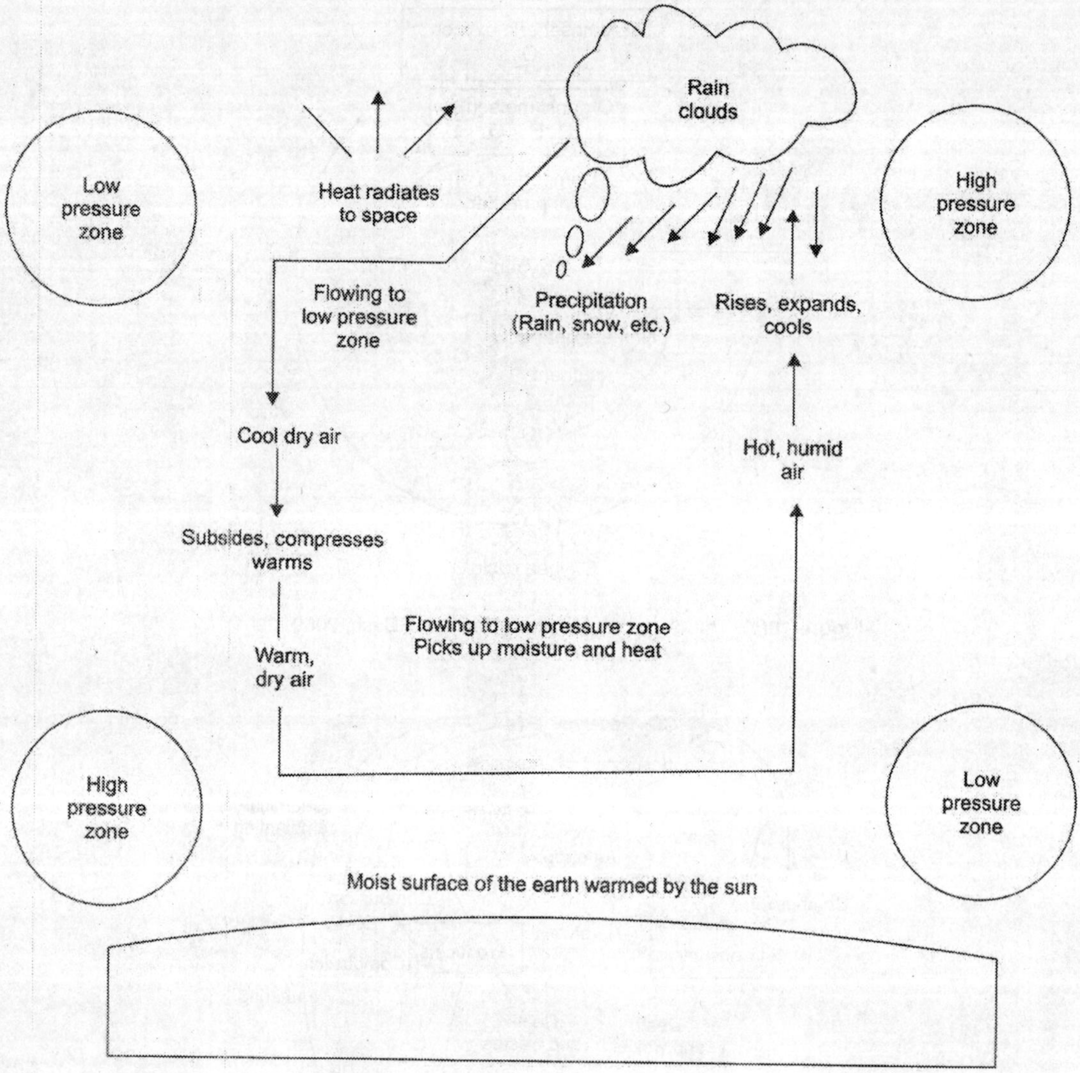

Figure 18 (c). Air movements in the atmosphere

1.11 BALANCE OF NATURE

All the ecosystems have: (i) a food production component, (ii) a food consumer component, (iii) a detritus-decomposer-matter recycling component, and (iv) abiotic matter and its movement component.

A balance exists between these components. The basis of maintenance of this balance are ecosystem processes like matter cycling, energy flow through food chain and many natural processes. Each individual depends upon other organisms for food and for other requirements for existence, continuance and perpetuation.

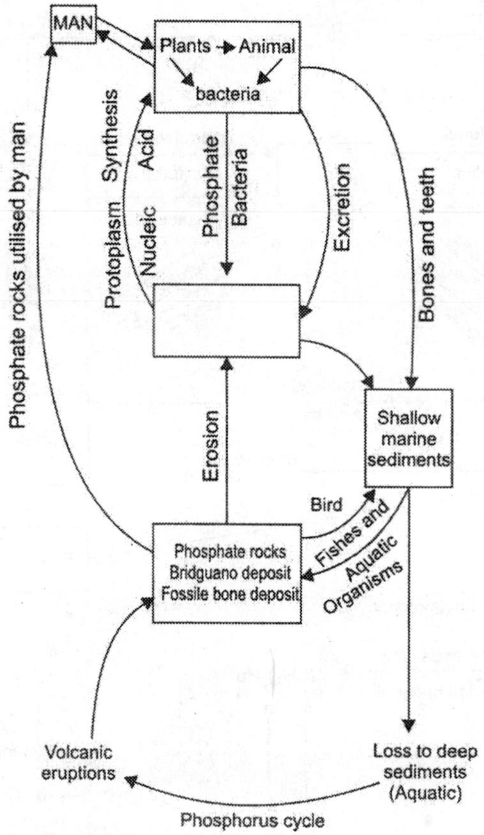

Figure 19. Sedimentary biogeochemical cycles (phosphorus cycle) (from Dash and Dash, 2009)

Since different forms of living organisms depend upon each other, there exists a balance in their numbers or biomass and if one is disturbed, the other's activity is affected.

For example, the number of deer (herbivores) in a forest and the number of tigers (carnivores) in the same forest must maintain a balance.

If the deer population is decreased it will affect adversely the tiger population. Alternatively, in the absence of tiger population the deer population may increase rapidly to such a level that it will deplete the vegetation component in a very short time and then start starving – dying or migrating to another place. In this example the grasses, the deer population and the tiger population depend upon each other for their existence, continuance and perpetuation. Another example can be that the material cycles like oxygen, carbon dioxide, sulphur, phosphorus, calcium, magnesium, etc., operate in nature due to the interaction of biodiversity and abiotic components. Plants utilize carbon dioxide in food production during day time and release oxygen. Animals and men utilize oxygen for metabolism and release carbon dioxide. A balance is maintained.

Because of anthropogenic activities like deforestation, use of automobiles on a very large scale, heavy industrialization, urbanization, etc., we are producing more carbon dioxide (green

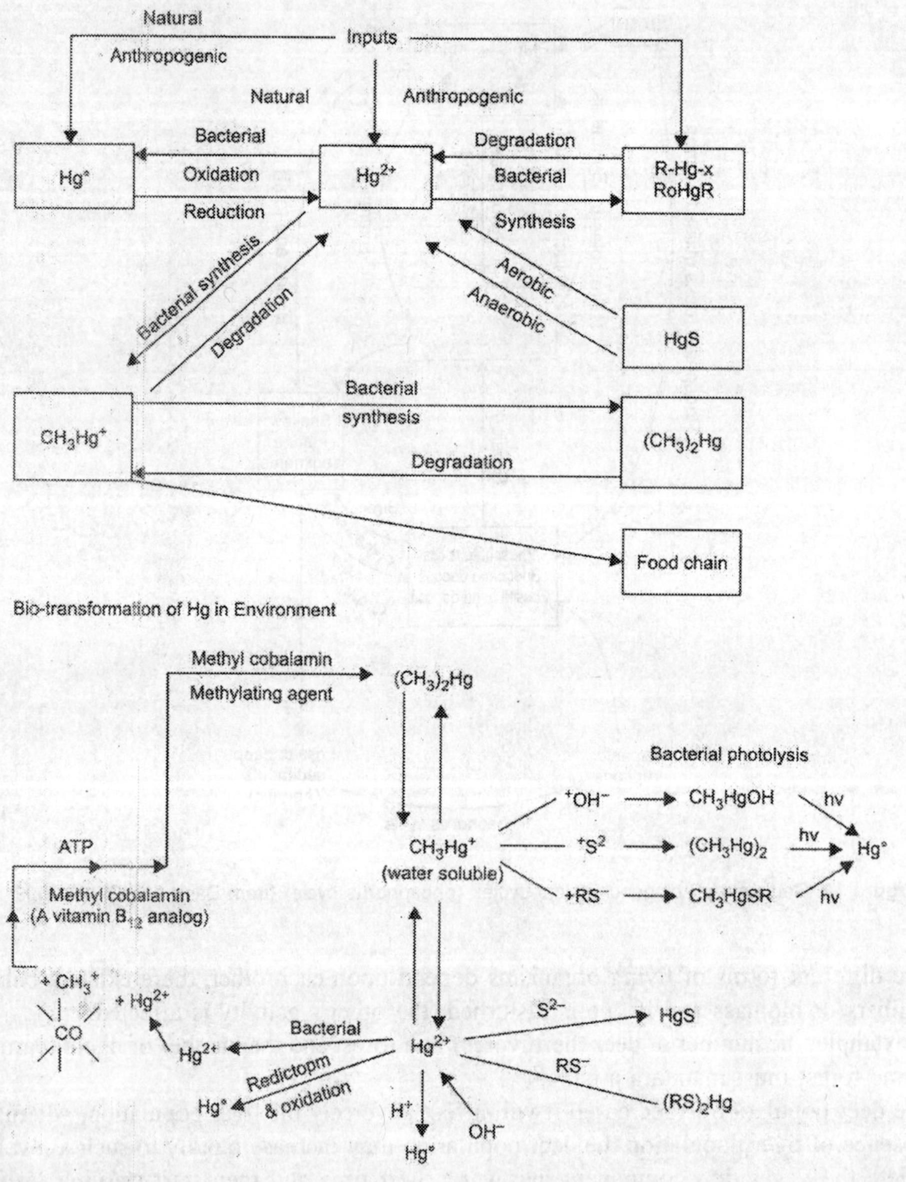

Figure 20. Movement of mercury (heavy metal) in the environment (from Dash and Dash, 2009)

house gas) than is being utilized by plants. More carbon dioxide in air absorbs more heat and makes the planet (troposphere) warmer. The balance of nature is not maintained.

Man's interference disrupts ecosystem processes as every ecosystem has a limit to its carrying capacity for normal functioning pressure on the life supporting system.

1.12 PRESSURE ON LIFE SUPPORTING SYSTEM

As per scientific evidence, hominids have existed for the last 3 to 4 million years and man has existed for the last 100,000 years. The chief source of living for man was hunting and gathering food and other requirements from the environment. The hunter-gatherer man was nomadic and hence family bonding and social commitment were largely nonexistent. Because of his living manner individual man-woman bonding was weak. The hunter-gatherer was not able to maintain a large family. But in course of cultural evolution, man could learn to domesticate animals and plants some 12,000 years back. Thus, the technological advancement started in a big way, family bonding became strong, and villages, towns, etc., developed and man started producing more food in a given area of land than by hunting and collecting food. People could spend more time at home. Man-woman bonding became more intense. The population started increasing.

In the course of cultural evolution, man could learn the use of many tools and with new discoveries and inventions man could make advances in the scientific and technological fields. The industrial revolution in Europe came in the 17th & 18th centuries. Goods and services became readily available. With the advancement in the transport system, the movement of human population became easier and due to the advances in medical science infant mortality decreased and the population started growing very fast.

In an age of explosive population growth, unbelievable scientific and technological advances, there is immense pressure on the life supporting system. Because of anthropogenic activity of industrialization, urbanization, use of fertilizers and pesticides to raise more food and for many other activities, man has cleared forests and produced substances, which were either not there in the environment or increased their concentration in the environment in alarming quantities. The area of deserts is increasing. These activities also create pollution, bringing numerous diseases, health and other problems and destroy ecological order. During the last 200 years man has created so many imbalances in nature that his own survival is in danger. The greed for more materialistic comfort and to meet the pressure of population explosion, there has been environmental degradation to such an extent that unless urgent steps are taken with modern technological inputs these adverse factors cannot be mitigated.

Pollution Stress

Some of the global pollution problems are: (i) Climate change, green house gases and their effect (ii) ozone hole, (iii) acid rain, (iv) photochemical smog, (v) eutrophication, (vi) land degradation, (vii) deforestation, etc., which cause damage to the environment and the ecological order. Besides some other issues are: (viii) The fly ash pollution, (ix) solid waste and municipal waste disposal, (x) hazardous waste including medical waste disposal, (xi) coastal zone degradation and pollution problems, (xii) pollution in river systems, (xiii) fluoride pollution, (xiv) heavy metal pollution, especially mercury, arsenic, etc., (xv) biodiversity loss due to mining activities, pollution in aquatic systems etc. (Figure 21)

1.13 NATURAL RESOURCES

1.13.1 Concept of Resource and Natural Resources

A resource is a means for satisfying human and social requirements in a given space and time. Resources are basically of two kinds: (a) renewable, and (b) non-renewable. Some resources, such as plants (crops, forests, etc.) and animals (milk and meat producing) are replaced from time to time because they have a life cycle, and a continuous harvest is possible. These resources are said to be renewable; examples of such resources are wildlife, aquatic life, pastures, and forests. Some resources do not have a life cycle but can be recycled. These resources, like water, are also classified as renewable. Resources which are not regenerated because they do not have a life cycle or are not recycled are termed non-renewable. Mineral deposits are formed slowly over millions of years and once used cannot be regenerated, e.g., fossil fuels, such as petrol and coal. Since the formation of soil takes thousands of years and is not renewable in the lifespan of many generations, it is thought of as a non-renewable resource. These resources provide food, fodder, fuel, medicine and clothes for man and hence sustain life on this planet. Natural resources are also classified as: (a) inexhaustible, and (b) exhaustible. Resources which

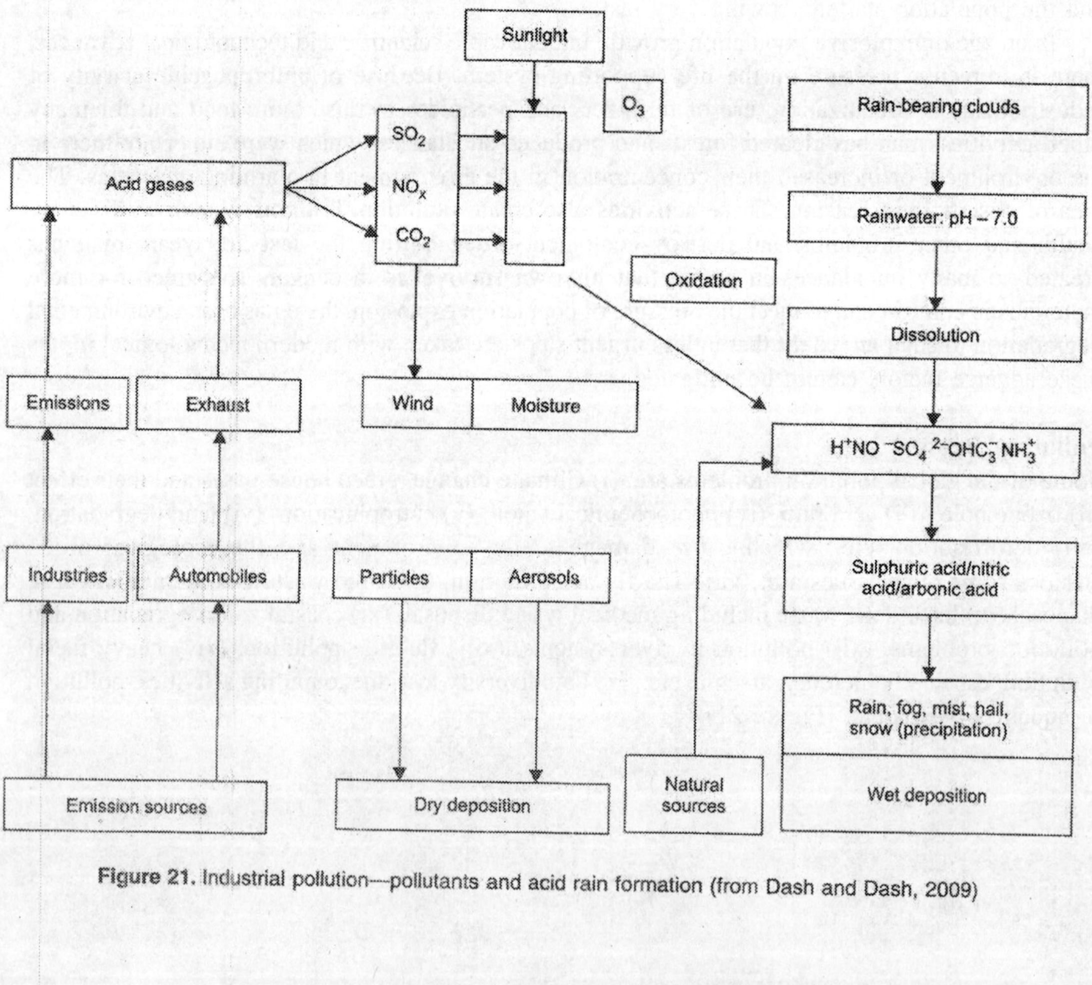

Figure 21. Industrial pollution—pollutants and acid rain formation (from Dash and Dash, 2009)

are usually not changed by man's activities, and are abundantly available and expected to be available for millions of years, are said to be inexhaustible. Solar energy, atomic energy, wind power, power from tides and so on are classified as inexhaustible. Renewable resources can also be classified as inexhaustible because they can be managed properly and renewed. Resources like coal, petrol, and so forth are classified as exhaustible because their deposits on this planet are finite. Renewable resources such as plants and animals become extinct if not managed properly. They are maintainable. But purely exhaustible resources like fossil fuels and some minerals are non-maintainable.

1.13.2 Non-renewable Resources of India

Mineral Resources: Mineral resources include all inorganic and organic substances derived from the earth. A number of minerals, such as coal, iron ore, chromites-chromium, copper, bauxite-aluminium, petrol, etc. are essential for our industries. Man has been using minerals since the dawn of civilization. Man used stone implements and stones for the construction of pyramids, and clay bricks to build houses. As civilization progressed, he learnt to use and manufacture iron implements. Iron and steel are used for the manufacturing of machinery, houses, automobiles, ships, rail tracks, and so on. Other metals like copper, lead, manganese and zinc are now used for various purposes. Minerals usually occur as ores, combined with many other substances. These ores are first processed to get rid of impurities and then the minerals are extracted. These industries depend upon the large scale use of petroleum, natural gas and coal as energy source.

India has a thriving mining industry with mineral sector contributing about 5-7% of gross domestic product. The number of minerals mined in India are about 89 and can be grouped into: (i) fuel minerals like coal, petroleum, natural gas, lignite; (ii) metallic minerals like iron ore, chromium ore, bauxite, etc., and (iii) non-metallic minerals like limestone, dolomite, phosphorite, clay, etc. India produces 89 minerals including four fuel minerals, 52 non-metallic minerals, 11 metallic minerals and 22 minor minerals. India stood as the world's largest producer of mica blocks and mica splitting and ranked second in the production of chromites, third in coal and lignite, and barites, fifth in iron ore, sixth in bauxite and manganese ore, eleventh in aluminium and twelfth in crude steel in the world (IBM, 1999).With its contribution of about 16 percent in exports and 20 percent in imports, the mineral sector is an important component of India's foreign trade.

Fuel minerals contribute 88% of the total value of mineral production (coal 42%, petroleum 33%, natural gas 10.5% and lignite 2.5%). The metallic minerals and the non-metallic minerals account for 6% each of the value of the minerals produced. India possesses about one-fourth of the world's iron-ore deposits located largely in Jharkhand and Odisha. It now produces more than 100 million tonnes of iron ore annually. It has been estimated that India has about 1,250 million tonnes of bauxite deposits, located in Jharkhand, Chhattisgarh, Odisha, Andhra Pradesh, and Gujarat. Alumina is extracted from bauxite and is used to produce aluminium. About 80 million tonnes of manganese deposits are also in India with Odisha as the leading producer state. Out of 193 million tonnes of chromite deposits, about 140 million tonnes are in Odisha. Copper deposits are scanty and are in Jharkhand, Bihar and Rajasthan. Gold deposits are meager. India also has good reserves of uranium and thorium in Jharkhand, Bihar and Rajasthan. These are important for the generation of atomic energy. India is rich in some 35 minerals. About 6% of the value of mineral production is due to metallic minerals.

It has been estimated that the coal reserves of India amount to about 86,000 million tonnes. At present more than 575 coal mines are present in India. Annual production is more than 400 million tonnes and consumption is more than 500 million tonnes. In 1998-99 some 300 million tonnes of coal was mined. The annual production of petroleum is more than 10 million tonnes and our reserves are located in the valleys of the Brahmaputra, the deltas of Cauvery, Krishna, Godavari and Mahanadi rivers, coastal areas of Kerala, Andhra, Odisha and offshore sites near Mumbai and so on.

The world's oil deposits are found mainly around the Persian Gulf. About 60% of the world's oil reserves are located in south-west Asia and the main countries that produce oil are Kuwait, Saudi Arabia, Iran, Iraq and the USA. The largest producer of oil is Russia and the largest consumer is the USA although it has only 7% of the world's total oil reserves. India mined some 170 million tonnes of non-fuel minerals in 1994-95.

1.13.3 Land Resources

Land is the most precious resource, since it is put to diverse use by man. India with a land area of 32,8800 km^2 which is about 2.4% of the world, supports 16% of the world's population. Land is now under great pressure due to the increase in population. There were about 238 million people in India in 1901 and now there are about 1200 million. The per capita land resource available now in India now is less than 0.30 hectare, in comparison to about 0.8 hectare in China and about 8.3 hectares in the erstwhile USSR. With the present rate of population growth the per capita land resource in India may be reduced to 0.25 or less hectare in the near future. About 44% of our land is used for agriculture, 23% is covered with forests, 4% is used for pasture and grazing fields, 8% for housing, agro forestry, industrial areas, roads etc., 14% is barren and about 8% is used for miscellaneous purposes (data source – Indira Gandhi National Open University Publication). However, 1988 forest policy of Indian Government envisages 33% of land under forest cover. The rapid increase of urbanization and migration of population from rural area to towns and cities has created many problems. It has led to the utilization of agricultural land for housing, construction of office buildings, industries, and so forth. Land use policies are, therefore, very important for any country, particularly India. The rational use of land resources is possible only by adopting an integrated land use policy, which involves prevention of land misuse and reclamation of degraded and under utilized land, wasteland, fallows, etc. Reclamation of abandoned mines and brick kilns may yield some much required land.

1.13.4 Soil Resources

Soil supports the life system and is formed through the combined action of parent rock material, climate, weathering process, vegetation and the decomposition process. Soil formation is an extremely slow process, taking thousands of years. Soil is, therefore, practically a non-renewable resource. It is important in that it stores water and plants, which provide us food, fodder, fuel, medicines and fibres grown on it. The type of soil varies from place to place – we have already discussed the different types of soils found in India. This resource is now threatened because of large scale deforestation and erosion of the top soil by wind action, floods and water flow.

1.13.5 Non-renewable Oceanic Resources

At a depth of 4,000-5,000 metres below sea level, mineral nodules are found. These are mainly sulphides of cobalt, nickel, copper, iron and manganese oxides. These resources are now being exploited. Besides, natural oil and gas deposits are also found below the oceanic floor and are now tapped by digging offshore wells. Some important minerals like monozite (used for the generation of atomic energy), gold and platinum deposits are found in the sea bed or sea sands.

1.13.6 Renewable Resources

Renewable resources are of conventional types, such as forests, crops, other plants, wildlife, and aquatic resources, and non-conventional, such as solar energy, wind energy, wave and tidal energy, biogas, atomic energy, and so on. These resources can also be grouped as water resources, energy resources, agriculture, rangelands, forest resources, wild life, aquaculture, etc.

1.13.7 Water Resources

We have already discussed the importance of water in the cycling of material. Water is needed for daily use by organisms, for irrigation, navigation, industrial use, electricity production and domestic use. Of the total water resource of the earth, 97.3% is salt water and the rest fresh water. This 2.7% amounts to about 1.4 billion km^3 of water.

Of this, about 77.2% is permanently frozen, 22.4% occurs as groundwater and soil moisture, 0.35% is found in lakes and wetlands, and 0.01% in rivers and streams (World Resources, Basic Books, New York, 1986). The total volume of groundwater found in underground reservoirs, called aquifers, is estimated to be 42.3×10^{10} m^3. At present about 25% of the groundwater is being used by man. Agriculture uses the maximum amount of water in the world. This amounts to about 73% and leads to a lot of pressure on groundwater. Excessive use of groundwater depletes aquifers, lowers the water table and may lead to stalinization, waterlogging and alkalinisation of soils. As the population goes on increasing, so do agricultural and industrial activities. Thus there is considerable demand for water resources (Figure 22). It has been estimated that the fresh water needs (drinking and food) of a person are about 3 litres per day. This does not include the water requirement for other purposes. As per the present population of the world, 6 billion m^3 of water is required per year. But the distribution of fresh water is not uniform in all countries and the pattern of use also varies. Therefore, there is a scarcity of fresh water in many parts of the world. The use of ground water at rates higher than those at which it is recharged should be avoided. Water pollution should be avoided and steps taken to store runoff water. One estimate shows that about 1.3 billion people in the world do not have access to clean drinking water.

India receives huge amount of rainfall, which amounts to about 105 to 117 cm annually. This is a huge water resource and the largest in the world. But almost 90% of this precipitation falls between mid-June and October. Fourteen major river systems, such as the Ganges, Narmada, Brahmaputra, Mahanadi, Cauvery, Krishna and Godavari, account for 85% of surface flow and

Figure 22. Water stress: collection from village well (from Er. Susanta Guru-seminar presentation)

share 83% of the drainage basin. They serve 80% of the total population. There are about 100 medium and minor rivers. The storage capacity is 3.65 million m^3. Of the total annual precipitation, India utilizes only 10%, which may increase to about 26% by 2025. The groundwater is also not well tapped except in a few states. We need to apply improved technology to increase water harvesting and storage capacity and groundwater recharge and utilization.

The Central Ground Water Board has estimated that the available groundwater in India is 210 billion m^3 and the annual utilization potential is about 42.3 million hectare, only one-fourth of which is used at present. However, the groundwater availability is not adequate in provinces like Tamil Nadu and Andhra Pradesh. Due to large scale deforestation and monsoon failure, there is a regular occurrence of drought in Kalahandi and some other districts of Odisha, Karnataka, Rajasthan and Maharashtra. The supply of drinking water in Indian villages is not adequate. There is no organized water supply in many villages and even in some small towns. Although there is a lot of precipitation in India, sufficient care needs to be taken to manage this water efficiently.

1.13.8 Energy Resources

Non-renewable energy resources like oil, gas and coal account for about 90% of the world's commercial energy requirement (petrol 45%, natural gas 20% and coal 25%). They are now in short supply and also generate a huge amount of environmental pollutants when burnt.

The conventional sources of energy are mainly:

(i) Biomass or dried organic matter (renewable). These are renewable sources of energy. Fuel wood consumption provides about 43% of the total energy consumed in all developing countries taken together but this amounts to about 14% of the total energy production of the world. Fuel wood demand in India was about 150 million tonnes in 1985 and this doubled in 2005. As natural forests are depleted, they will be able to provide 50-75 million metric tonnes and the rest of the demand will have to be met with fuel wood plantations, which require a lot of effort and sound management strategy.

(ii) Fossil fuels (non-renewable). Fossil fuels are non-renewable source of energy although these are still forming very slowly as compared to their consumption. Table 7 provides information on the production and reserve of fossil fuels.

Table 7. Production and Reserve of Fossil Fuels in the World (from various sources)

Fossil fuel	Reserve (estimated)	Production per year	Life span years
Coal	27,350 billion tonnes	>2730 million tonnes	1000
Oil	356.2 billion tonnes	>2888.0 million tonnes	120
Natural gas	600,000 billion m^3	>1250 billion m^3	450

1.13.9 Renewable Energy Resources

Cloud (1969) gave the concept of demographic quotient (Q), which is defined as

$$Q = \frac{\text{Total resources available}}{\text{Population density} \times \text{Per capita consumption}}$$

If the value of the quotient goes down, so does the quality of modern life. The demand for energy doubles every 10-14 years and in modern times energy consumption is taken as an indicator of a country's development. India, with about 16% of the world's population, consumes only about 2% of the world's energy production while the USA with 6.25% of the world's population, consumes 33% of the world's energy production (Table 8). The nature of energy consumption varies. In India, 80% of the population depends upon dung, wood and agricultural waste as the main energy source.

Due to the indiscriminate felling of trees, forests have been depleted and fuel wood has become scarce. Cattle dung, which could have been used for agriculture, is used as fuel. Hence, non-conventional renewable resources are essential for India.

Solar energy: It is the sole source of energy for the biological world. Plants utilize solar energy in photosynthesis for the production of food. Millions of years ago, forests were buried, and were converted into coal and oil under great pressure and temperature. This fossil fuel is in reality the sun's energy. In recent times, technologies have been developed to trap solar energy

Table 8. Per Capita Income and Energy use in the World (from SPAN)

GDP/ Capita↓ kW/ Capita→	<1	<2	<4	<5	<6	<7	<8	<9	<10	<12
< $5000	India	Brazil, China			Russia					
10000		Argentina	World Average				South Arabia			
20000				Spain						
25000					France					Canada
30000					UK					
40000					Japan					USA

for generating electricity, and for cooking. Solar energy is converted into electricity with the help of a photocell. Since India receives abundant solar energy, it is advantageous to develop photovoltaic devices to harness this energy. In India with an average of 250 clear sunny days in a year, such systems have proven viable and cost-effective. The efficiency of conversion of sunlight into electrical energy is up to 15-22% of at the present level of knowledge of photosensitive materials and technology. Advances in molecular biology and nanoscience may provide promise for a break-through. At present (2005) Japan, Germany and Spain generate 2422 MW, 1500 MW and about 50 MW energy respectively from solar source. India's target is 20,000 MW installed capacity by 2020.

Wind energy: Windmills convert wind energy into mechanical energy for raising water from wells and rivers to the ground surface. Alternatively, wind energy can be converted into electricity for supplying to a small town or village. Windmills are in use in many countries, notably Holland. At present wind energy accounts for more than 50% of the 8000 MW energy produced through renewable sources in India. This has great potential in India, as there is a long sea coast. In 2005 wind energy generation in Germany, Spain and the USA was 18428 MW, 10027 MW & 9149 MW respectively.

Wave and tidal energy: Waves and tides can be converted to electrical energy. In many hilly regions of India flour mills are run by water energy. Hydroelectric power is generated if a natural or artificial waterfall is created to turn a turbine (comparable to a pedal wheel) rotating fast. Areas where rivers flow into the sea experience waves and tides, and electricity can be generated thereby. India, having a large coast line and major river systems and mountain ranges through which these rivers flow, has immense potential for generating electricity from waves and tides.

Geothermal energy: In hot springs we find superheated steam. In India there are 46 hydrothermal areas where the water temperature exceeds 150°C. These hot springs can be utilized to generate electricity. The superheated steam can be used to run machines, turbines, and so on.

Biogas: Cattle dung is used to produce biogas. India has 185 million cattle, 61 million buffaloes, 45 million sheep, 97 million goats, 1 million horses, 1 million camels, and 1 million other livestock. These animals produce a huge quantity of dung, which can be utilized for biogas

Table 9: Energy Sources for Rural India (from Sharma, 1987)

Renewable	
Wood	68.5
Animal dung	08.3
Others	03.4
Non-renewable	
Oil products	16.9
Coal	02.3

production. Water hyacinth, *hydrilla*, duckweeds and algae can act as supplements for production of biogas. Besides cooking, biogas can be utilized to produce steam, which can be used to run machines and turbines for generating electricity. Leftover slurry can be utilized as manure. India has appreciable potential for biogas energy (see Environment and Resources-4, Foundation Course in Science and Technology, Indira Gandhi National Open University, New Delhi, 1989).

Some 1,500 to 2,000 million tonnes of wet animal dung is available per year in India and at a 66% collection rate, 25000 million/m^3 of biogas can be produced. The slurry can produce 200 million tonnes of organic manure per year, equivalent to 1.5 million tonne of nitrogen, 1.5 million tonnes of phosphate and 1.0 million tonne of potash as fertilizers. At present the amount of dung production is much more. There are about 0.7 million biogas plants in India now.

Biomass energy: Some conventional energy resources, such as biomass fuels (wood, etc.), are also renewable. The principal energy sources (Table 9) for rural India are as follows.

The present (2000s) firewood demand in India is more than 350 million tonnes Biomass such as firewood, agricultural residue, bagasse, crop stalks, coconut shells, waste from agro based industries, and animal dung can be used to produce power. Direct burning of these wastes is inefficient and leads to pollution. If these wastes are combusted in a gasifier at low oxygen and high temperature, they can be converted into a gaseous fuel called producer gas. This gas, though has a lower calorific value compared to natural gas or liquefied petroleum gas, can be burned with high efficiency and without emitting smoke. India generates more than 600 million tonnes of agricultural residue per year. These wastes can generate 79000 MW of power if all of this waste is gasified (SPAN, 2006). This energy will form more than 60 per cent of the total power available in India from all sources. It is feasible to set up a biomass based power plant of 10 to 20 MW in every village block, consisting of of 100 villages.

Atomic energy: Atomic reactors are utilized to harness energy from the atom in a controlled manner. Nuclear reactors produce heat, which is used to produce steam. One kilogram of natural uranium (written as U^{238}) generates energy equal to that generated by 35,000 kg of coal. In India the nuclear energy capacity was only less than 4% of the total installed power generating capacity. The plan is to produce about 10% of the total energy needs of the country from nuclear source by 2020. An hour of coal-generated 100-watt electric light creates a half-pound of atmospheric carbon, a bucket of ice makes a third of a pound, an hour's car ride 5 pounds. A Massachusetts Institute of Technology study forecasts that worldwide energy demand could triple by 2050. Finland has ordered a big Nuclear Power reactor specifically to meet the terms of the Kyoto Protocol on climate change.

China's new nuke plants will be 26 numbers by 2025 and this is part of a desperate effort at smog control. The United States should be shooting to match France, which gets 77% of its electricity from nukes. Belgium derives 58% of its electricity from nukes, Sweden 45%, South Korea 40%, Switzerland 37%, Japan 31%, Spain 27% and the U.K. 23%. France, where nukes generate more than three-quarters of the country's electricity, is privatizing a third of its state-owned nuclear energy group. The 103 reactors operating in the United States pump out electricity at more than 90 percent of capacity, up from 60% when three mile Island made headlines. So atomic power is less expensive than it used to be – but could it possibly be cost-effective? What is a rapidly carbonizing world to do? The high-minded answer, of course, is renewable and nuclear energy. (*Source*: SPAN: 2005 & 2006 & other sources).

Forests as Renewable Resource

Forests constitute 90% of the global biomass. These are natural ecosystems dominated by trees. About a third of the world's land surface is covered by forests, of which tropical forests constitute about 50%. Forest ecosystems are great resources, since they provide habitat for wildlife, fuel wood, fodder, fibre, fruit, herbal medicines, timber, and several raw materials, which are primarily used in wood-based industries, including paper and pulp industries. Forests regulate climatic conditions, such as rainfall, humidity and temperature regime of the area and protect the soil and landscape from wind and erosion. Thus, they have three broad functions: (a) *productive*, (b) *regulative*, and (c) *protective*. The productive function involves the transformation of solar energy into plant biomass and ultimately to animal and human biomass through the food chain.

Forest products like wood, fruit, resins, latex, fibre, and essential oils are produced directly or indirectly by photosynthesis. A climax forest may account for 400 tonnes of dry matter per hectare, equivalent to about 22 to 156 $\times$ 10^{10} cal per hectare. The large animal biomass may account for about 1,000 kg per hectare. The regulative function includes absorption, transformation of radiant energy into plant biomass, absorption, storage and release of carbon dioxide, oxygen, water, and mineral nutrients. These cycles in turn (particularly the water cycle and gaseous cycle) regulate the climate and the quality of environment. The protective function includes the protection of the soil and land surface from wind and rain action. Soil erosion leads to low fertility, since the rich soil is washed away. Nutrient cycling involves the uptake of nutrients by plants, storage in plants and other organisms and the subsequent return to the soil through urine, excreta and dead organic matter. A large amount of mineral substances are stored in the vegetation, particularly in tropical forests. It has been estimated that some 2 tonnes to 53 tonnes of minerals per hectare are accumulated in tropical forests. The long-term stability of the forest ecosystem depends upon the input and output of nutrients.

Importance of forests to human society: The diverse functions of forests can be stated to be that they provide timber, firewood, nuts, fruits, seeds, medicinal plants, etc., to man (productive function). Forests shape natural environment by influencing such factors as temperature, humidity and precipitation (regulative function). Forests shape natural environment by influencing such factors as temperature, humidity and precipitation (regulative function). Forests shape the soil environment by affecting its composition, structure, the chemical properties, water contents, etc., and play an important role in bio-geo-chemical cycles (regulative function). Forests check soil erosion by obstructing currents of water or air. Roots of plants bind soil particles together in larger lumps preventing erosion (protective function). Forests influence flood conditions by intercepting surface runoffs, infiltration, evaporation, etc., which is helpful in water retention by the soil and in recharging groundwater resources (protective function). Forests help in public health protection by reducing contaminants of the environment. Forest soils and vegetation acts as an effective sink for a number of pollutants (protective function and regulative function). Forests provide suitable habitats for a number of plant and animal species. They help in maintaining a broad genetic base from which future strains and varieties could be developed (resource and protective function). Nearly 23.8% of the total land area of India (328.8 million hectare) is occupied by forests, amounting to about 78.4 million hectares. It has been estimated that since independence, India has lost about 45 million hectares of good forests, of which only 6 million hectares have been replaced. The principal factors for deforestation are an increase in human population and livestock and consequent increased demand for timber, fuel wood, and grazing. Urbanization and industrialization are important factors causing the destruction of forests. Other important causes are the construction of roads and mining activities. The construction of hill roads, particularly in the Himalayan region, has destroyed many forestlands. One estimate shows that some 683,672 hectares of land was under mining activity in 1973. Mining activities are still continuing in many states in full swing – the bauxite, coal, iron, chromite mining in Odisha and neighbouring states is a case in point. Wood consumption worldwide amounts to more than 4 billion m^3. Of this around 46% and 54% are consumed by industry and as firewood respectively. The corresponding figures for developed countries are 84% and 16% while for developing countries the trend is reversed, most of the wood being consumed as firewood. In India, fuel wood production was 212.6 million m^3 in 1983, about 23% higher than the figure for 1973. (FAO year book of forest products, Rome, 1985). Paper industries consume a huge amount of bamboo, which is now in short supply in peninsular India. Paper mills now depend upon supply from Arunachal Pradesh (Sharma, 1987). The Himalayan mountain areas amount to 12,49,000 km^2, which forms about 38.4% of India's land resource. Deforestation is now a major problem in the Himalayan regions. It has caused soil erosion and other damage. Besides, a number of industries have come up in this region as raw materials are easily available. The growth of industries has also caused air and water pollution. No detailed survey on the rich wealth (fauna, flora, minerals, water resource, etc.) of Himalayan ecosystems has been made.

Social forestry involves plantations on government, private and village panchayat lands, roadsides, canal banks, along railway lines, land not suitable for agriculture and so on. The aim is to grow fast growing trees, which are commercially valuable. These trees are meant to raise firewood for people, pulpwood for the paper industry, fodder for cattle and act as windbreaks or shelterbelts. Social forestry also involves the participation of people on a large scale, so that natural forests are not destroyed. It helps create plant resource genetic banks, nurseries, recreation gardens, and so on. Although a few years ago monoculture (culture of one species of trees) was practised for social forestry. polyculture (growing more than one tree species in the same land) is now considered better. Polyculture is based on indigenous or exotic species of plants which can provide not only timber but also much required fodder and fix nitrogen to increase soil fertility. The following species of plants are now widely used for social forestry: (*Acacia, Lucaena* (Subabul), *Prosopis* (Jhand), *Sesbania* (Agastha), *Casuarina, Tectona* (Teak), *Dalbergia* (Shisham), *Moringa* (Shajan), and *Azadirachta indica* (Neem). *Eucalyptus* plantation was once considered a panacea for our economic ills. It is a quick growing tree which is used in the paper pulp industry. But it is not very suitable as firewood or timber, nor can it be used as fodder or for consumption of fruit. Besides, there is now a controversy regarding its water uptake and transpiration rate. Some studies tell us that its water requirement is very high and that the water table goes down if it is planted. Some other studies have expressed reservations on this finding, but the eucalyptus has lost the popularity it once had. Social forestry also aims to provide a good income to the farmer. Therefore plants which grow faster and reach a marketable size in 3-8 years should be chosen. A modified version of social forestry is called agro forestry. Woody perennials are grown on the same land management units as annual agricultural crops and farm animals. These are grown either simultaneously or sequentially and the purpose is to maximize output on a sustained basis. Community forestry is practised around villages and panchayats. The three terms, social forestry, agro forestry and community forestry have much in common and are considered more or less the same thing. The social forestry programme has made the people conscious of the importance of afforestation and is gaining in popularity.

Compensatory afforestation: The basic objective of the Forest (Conservation) Act, 1980 amended 1988 is to strike a balance between development and forest conservation. Compensatory afforestation is stipulated by the Indian Government, while approving proposals for dereservation or diversion of forest land for non-forest uses. Compensatory afforestation is insisted over equivalent area in forest land or double the area of non-forest land. The purpose is to compensate for the loss of forest cover due to its diversion so that the net area under forest cover remains the same. If non-forest land is not available or is available in lesser extent compared to the forest area being diverted, compensatory afforestation may be carried over degraded forests twice in extent to the forest area being diverted or to the difference between forests land being diverted and available non-forest land, as the case may be. The non-availability of non-forest land for compensatory afforestation is, however, accepted by the Central Government only on the certificate from the Chief Secretary to the State/Union-Territory Government to that effect. As an exception to the above, compensatory afforestation can be undertaken to double the degraded forest land without insisting on a certificate from the Chief Secretary in the case of: Extraction of minor minerals from the riverbeds. Proposals involving diversion of forest land up to 20 ha in hill districts and also the districts having more than 50% of geographical area under forests, laying of transmission lines up to 220 kV diversion of linear or 'strip' plantation declared as protected forest along the road/rail/canal sides for widening or expansion of road/rail/canal and for central projects.

Livestock as Renewable Resources

Livestock are important resources, as they provide milk, eggs, meat, skin (leather) and other products. The total livestock in India a mount to a huge population consisting of more than 185 million cattle, 118 million goats, 61 million buffaloes, 45 million sheep, 1 million horses and ponies, 1 million camels and about 1 million other livestock. Besides, there are 156 million tonnes poultry, fowls, ducks, turkeys, etc. They provide about more than 1 million tonnes of meat, 100 million tonnes of milk, 40 million kg of wool and 13 million eggs. The amount of dung produced is huge and is used for biogas production and as manure. Livestock are also used for rural transport and agriculture. To get a sustained yield, their proper breeding, healthcare, management diet are essential. Recent advances in biology have helped produce better livestock. The milch breed (milk producing) cattle are the Gir, Red Sindhi, Deoni and Sahiwal and the draught breed (work animals) cattle are the Nagari, Malvi, Kenkatha, Khillari, Hallikar, Amrit Mahall, Ponwar, and Siri.

The total milk production has increased from 17 million tonnes to 100 million tonnes in 2006-07. Some examples of dual-purpose (both for milk and work) cattle are the Rewati, Kankrej, Ongol and Danji. The humped zebu cattle originated in India and there is evidence that humpless cattle were domesticated in India during the Harappan period.

India has the best water buffaloes in the world. These buffaloes are the Murrah, Surti, Nili-Ravi, Jaffarabadi and Mehsana. The common breeds of Indian sheep are Kashmir, Chokla, Magra, Kali, Gaddi and Bhakarwal. Breeds of Merino and Suffolk sheep have been imported for production of better wool. Milk breeds of goat, such as Saanan, Alpore, Nubian and Toggenberg, have been introduced to develop better breeds to suit the Indian environment. The wool and textile breeds are Ashman and Chegu, Beetal, Jamunapari, Barbati, Deccan, Black Bengal and Malbari. The niche requirements of sheep and goats are different. Livestock contributes at least 40,000 million rupees a year to our national economy. Of this, poultry contributes about Rs.10,000 million. Almost all the world's fowls trace their origin to India's red jungle fowl (Gallus gallus). Ducks constitute about 10% of the total poultry in India. In India, we have the Assel, Kadaknath, and short-legged Nicobari breed fowls. The important broiler strains are B 77, JBL 80, IBB 83, ILI 80 and ILI 82.

Women largely form the work force in animal farms and hence this sector helps in women empowerment through financial security. Marginal and small land owners are the owners of 71% of cattle, 83% of buffaloes, 88% of small ruminants, 70% of pigs and 74% of poultry (government of India-publication, 2005). In view of this the village livelihood sustainability is dependent on animal resources. The live-stock contributes about 25% of the agro-sector of the country in terms of money. This is the important sector for scientific research to increase the milk, egg and meat production. There is good scope to enhance this production and other welfare measures are required. Genetic selection of animal breeds, feed and nutrition aspects, health and disease aspects and opening of veterinary dispensaries and hospitals in villages are the priority areas.

Aquaculture as a Renewable Resource

Fish are an excellent source of protein. They feed on plankton (phytoplankton and zooplankton), weeds and organic matter. Crabs, prawns, molluscs, etc., are also aquatic organisms and are a very good source of animal protein for human beings. Over half the population in developing countries gets at least 40% of its animal protein food from fish (FAO, Status of Food and Agriculture, 1984, Rome). The natural pearl industry depends upon oyster culture. Fishery includes capture fishery and culture fishery. Capture fishery is usually practised in oceans, large

Table 10: Important Constituents of Marine Catch from India (Data from CMFRI).

Name	% of total landing
Oil Sardine	11.91
Other Sardine	5.20
Sciaenid	7.92
Harpodon nehereus	6.76
Mackerel	4.93
Elasmobranchii	4.93
Catfish	4.24
Hilsa	3.86
Ribbon fish	3.36
Pomfret	2.78
Leiognathus	2.73
Anchoviella	2.70
Perch	2.52
Caranx	2.43
Prawn	13.52

Table 11: Fish Production in India

	Fish production (lakh tons)		
Year	Marine	Inland	Total
1950-51	5.34	2.18	7.52
1960-61	8.80	2.80	11.60
1970-71	10.86	6.70	17.56
1973-74	12.10	7.48	19.58
1980-81	15.55	8.87	24.42
1981-82	14.45	9.99	24.44
1982-83	14.27	9.40	23.67
1983-84	15.19	9.87	25.06
1984-85	16.98	11.03	28.01
1985-86	17.16	11.60	28.76
1986-87	17.13	12.29	29.42
1987-88	16.58	13.01	29.59
1988-89	18.17	13.35	31.52
1989-90	22.75	14.02	36.77
1990-91	23.00	15.36	38.36
1991-92	24.47	17.10	41.57
1992-93	25.76	17.89	43.65
1993-94	26.49	19.95	46.44
1994-95	26.92	20.97	47.89
1995-96	27.07	22.42	49.49
1996-97	29.67	23.81	53.48
1997-98	29.50	24.38	53.88
1998-99	26.96	26.02	52.98
1999-00	28.52	28.23	56.75
2000-01	28.11	28.45	56.56
2001-02	28.30	31.20	59.56
2002-03	29.90	32.10	62.00
2003-04	29.41	34.58	63.99
2004-05	30.10	35.00	65.10

Source: (i) CMFRI Up to 1970-71 (ii) State Govts./ UTs (iii) Ministry of SPI, Govt. of India

lakes and other aquatic ecosystems. Culture fishery is usually practised in inland water bodies and artificial ponds.

The global marine fish catch was about 76 million tonnes in 1984 and is on the increase. India's marine fish catch was about 1.2 million tonnes in 1984 and it has increased to 3.1 million tonnes in 2005. India has a very long coast line (about 5600 km) and a continental shelf of about 2, 59,000 km^2. Thus, there is a vast area available for tapping. Marine resources include the Bay of Bengal, Arabian Sea, and Indian Ocean, numerous gulfs, coral reefs and mangrove swamps. The estuaries of major rivers, backwaters, lagoons, and brackishwater lakes like Chilka, add to India's marine resources. They form an additional 2.6 million hectares. There is a good possibility of increasing fish catch along the Indian coast using sophisticated scientific techniques now available. In 1984, India produced about 3 million tonnes of fishery products, occupying the eighth position in the world. It has increased considerably (4.3 million tonnes in 2011) and it has been estimated that this production can be increased to about 12 million tonnes per year. The important constituents of India's marine catch are given in Tables 10. & 11.

However, fishing remains confined to a narrow coastal region of 16 km and the rich offshore and deep waters remain poorly exploited. India has about 1.6 million hectares of inland waters. It has many major river systems, such as the Ganges, Jamuna, Brahmaputra, Narmada, Mahanadi, Cauvery and Krishna. Besides, there are canals, ponds, lakes and irrigation channels where culture fishery can be practised. The main fresh water fish are carps (*Labeo rohita*, other *Labeo sp.*, *Catla catla, Cirrihina mrigala*, etc.). The exotic carps available are the Chinese carp (*Cyprinus carpio*), green carp (*Ctenophryngodon idella*), mirror carp (*Hypophth-almichthys molitrix*), catfish, and so on. Some Clupeids like *Hilsa* are also found in river systems like Hoogly, Subarnarekha, Mahanadi, and Chilika Lake. The total fresh water fish production is about 1.77 million tonnes (1996), (about 50% of the total catch). Now culture fishery has been started in pond cultures, artificial enclosures and net pens, providing fertilizers such as cow dung, domestic and agricultural waste and other animal excreta. Pond culture can be: (i) Monoculture, involving one species only; usually trouts, eels and cat fish, (ii) Polyculture, involving the culture of more than one aquatic species, common combinations are milk, fish with prawn, Chinese carp with Indian carp, and carps with *Tilapia*. Besides, intensive rearing pond culture with high stocking density and water quality control and rich artificial food, eels, trouts, and catfish are usually grown in such cultures. An extensive rearing pond where stocking density is low and food is natural is also practised. In semi-intensive rearing ponds, natural food supplemented with artificial food is given; usually fertilizers are used to increase food production. Carps, *tilapia*, trouts, salmon and some other fish are also cultured in net pens. Milkfish, mullets and some other fish are cultured in enclosures or bamboo fences. In India, fish culture is also done in irrigation canals, paddy fields and other small wetlands. Air breathing fish, such as *Channa* sp., *Clarias* sp., *Heteropneustes, Anabas* sp., and so on are cultured in swamps and cage culture systems. In 2011 the total production from fish culture was about 4 million tonnes. A study of the foodchain relationships of fish with a view to shortening the chain is important for aquaculture. Recently, technologies have been developed in Odisha, India to culture prawns (*Paeneus monodon* and *Paeneus indicus*) in confined salt water tanks.

The average aquaculture production is about 600 kg per hectare per year in India. This yield can be increased considerably using composite fish culture (using surface, column, and bottom feeding fish in the same pond and thus avoiding competition among them for food). The yield of air breathing fish in swamps is now 15 tonnes per hectare per year.

Fish, prawn, and turtle form part of the livelihood support in Indian villages. The total fish production (capture and culture) in India was about 8.29 million tons in 2010-2011, and out of this, fresh water aquaculture amounted to about 3.84 million tons, mariculture and coastal aquaculture 0.15 million tons and the capture fishery (both marine and fresh water) amounted to 4.30 million tons (Dilip Kumar, 2012). About 90% of fish production is consumed in the country. However, the average per capita fish consumption is only 5.48 kg compared to that of 12 kg internationally. However, about 30-40% people are vegetarian in India. In view of this, the per capita fish consumption is estimated to be around 9 kg among the non-vegetarian people. There is good scope to increase capture fishery considering 8,118 km of coastline and 0.506 million sq.km of continental shelf and 2.03 million sq.km of Exclusive Economic Zone (upto 22 m depth). The area under ponds, tanks, beels and fresh water lakes, etc. amounts to about 3.42 million hectare. There is need of renovating village ponds for water harvesting and fish culture on priority. Rice-fish integration systems, cage culture, etc. are innovative systems, which should be widely practiced. The cleaning of rivers and canals for fish culture will boost the village economy. Serious efforts are to be made using modern technology to increase the production to maintain at least 10-12 kg of per capita consumption even if the population grows to 1.6 billion by 2050.

CHAPTER 2

Concept of Sustainable Development

2.1 DEFINITION

Sustainable developement is the development which meets the needs of the present without compromising with the necessities of the future generations (Brundtland Commission, 1987).This concept, developed as the present model of unlimited growth in a limited environment, is not the right answer to the complex problem that every country faces. This is indeed a tall order to achieve. It also means redistribution of resources as it will reduce inequalities. Redistribution may include technology transfer, financial aid and compensation to prevent environmental degradation, resource conservation, etc.

2.1.1 Concept of Sustainability

In Europe, the concept of sustainability can be traced back to the 14th century. In the 14th century, "sustainable" forestry was practised, based on the principle of not cutting down more trees than the growth rate for replacement allowed. In 1795, the economist George Ludwig wrote that the forests are to be used in such a way that "future generations will have just as many advantages as the present generation does". In India the concept is very old and linked to Vedic times and sustainable forestry was practised in ancient India.

The Stockholm Conference in 1972 led to the establishment of UN Environment Programme (UNEP) and gave emphasis on protection of environment for the future. The concept of sustainable development was first introduced by the International Union for Conservation of Nature and Natural Resources (IUCN) in 1980. The World Commission on 'Environment and Development' (popularly known as Brundtland Commission) was established in 1983 and brought out its report 'Our Common Future' in 1987. Dr. Gro Harlem Brundtland, the then prime minister of Norway was the chairman of the commission. This report highlighted poverty, depletion of natural resources, deterioration of environmental quality and quality of life. The report of the commission highlighted that (i) today's needs should not be detrimental to the ability of the future generations to meet their needs; (ii) a direct link exists between economy and environment; (iii) the needs of the poor in all countries must be met; (iv) our environment is to be protected so that the economic conditions of world's poor be improved; and (v) in all our actions, we have to consider the impact of the present activity upon the future generations. In other words, ecological sustainability was considered very important. These actions led to the organization of the Earth Summit in Rio de Janeiro in Brazil in June, 1992. A definition of sustainable development was first given by the World Commission on Environment and Development in 1987 as a development process that "meets the needs of the present without compromising the ability of the future generations to meet their own needs".

The Brundtland Commission considered: (i) population control, (ii) food security, and (iii) energy security as critical components of sustainability. Since the Rio Summit in June 1992 and the adoption of Agenda 21(includes biodiversity-forest conservation, climate change, pollution control, etc.) by the global community, many nations have set sustainability as a key goal of their development. Rio conference gave widespread visibility to the important concept of sustainable development. This concept placed environmental management in a position to address the environmental impact of developmental projects so that the environment is protected for the present and future generations.

The UNO-conference in Johannesburg, South Africa in 2002 provided opportunity to review the actions taken and benefits made and review the different aspects of resource utilization and conservation. Biodiversity-forest conservation received top priority. Besides, the important issue of energy use and climate change and its effect on developmental projects, on human activities and future of mankind was very much focused.

According to the World Resources Institute, the four dimensions of sustainable development are social, economic, environmental and technological well-being (Figure 23). These dimensions provide a framework within which one can specify details for countries at a given stage of development.

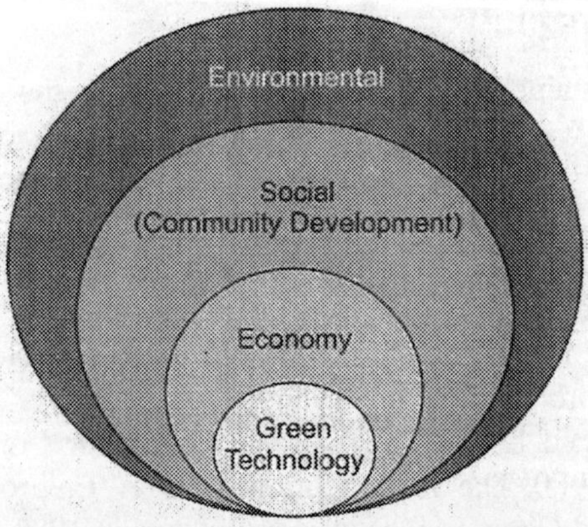

Figure 23. Conceptual model of the components of sustainable development

The 1992 Rio Conference brought forward the international concern for deteriorating environment at the global scale. The Conference focused on the "Green Agenda" comprising issues concerning global warming, ecosystems management, ozone depletion, etc. On a separate platform, professionals have highlighted the concern for local issues in urban areas referred as the "Brown Agenda". These are related to poor sanitation, solid waste collection, pollution of air, land and water, traffic congestion, accidents and noise which have more direct and immediate negative impact on human health and safety, especially for the poor, and on business productivity than does the "green" environmental agenda.

Therefore, these concerns are more akin to the urban agenda and form part of the future challenges for sustainable city (green city/ecocity) management. It draws greater importance since the future of human settlements is in cities if present rate of migration is taken into account.

Millennium Development Goals: In September 2000, world leaders came together at United Nations Headquarters in New York to adopt the *United Nations Millennium Declaration*, committing their respective nations to a new global partnership to reduce extreme poverty and setting out a series of time-bound targets - with a deadline of 2015 - that have become known as the Millennium Development Goals. Eight issues were included. These are (i)to end poverty and hunger; (ii) to provide Universal Education; (iii) to promote Gender Equality; (iv)to care for Child Health; and (v) Maternal health; (vi) to Combat HIV/AIDS; (vii)to promote Environmental Sustainability; and (viii) Global Partnership. These aspects of human development are also intrinsically linked to sustainable development.

2.1.2 Malthusian-Darwinian Carrying Capacity Concept

The concepts developed independently by the economist Malthus and the biologist Charles Darwin emphasized that there is a capacity of any area/region to sustain the population and its growth. The population size, food availability, and natural factors determine the carrying capacity of the area. In other words, the concept emphasizes critical limit for population growth as natural resources and space availability have a finite limit (Figure 23). It recognizes that the population density and natural factors put a limit on food availability. Further it emphasizes conservation of resources, and limiting the growth rate. The concept can be extended to interpret the recognition of equity within and between generations.

Figure 24(a) shows the carrying capacity concept. As there is a limit to space availability, and the population is growing fast and there is a limit to food production, the population crash was thought to be the ultimate outcome. However, in recent times technology development and intervention, medicare availability, intervention of management techniques, and family planning combined have prevented large scale population crash from happening. For example, India has a land area about 329 million ha (both productive and unproductive land).The population was about 330 million in 1947, grew to about one thousand million in 2000, at present is about 1210 million and may increase to 1800 or 2000 million by 2050.The per capita land area goes down as population increases, thus putting enormous pressure on lesser land area to produce more food.

2.1.3 Enumeration of the Concept of Sustainability

Each development process has its own distinct imperatives. Rio conference emphasizes that economic development favours market expansion, industrial expansion, externalization of costs and sustained private profit. Community development favours basic human needs like food, shelter, water, sanitation, recreation, education, economic and social equity, community self-reliance and security. Ecological development favours maintenance of natural order, wilderness,

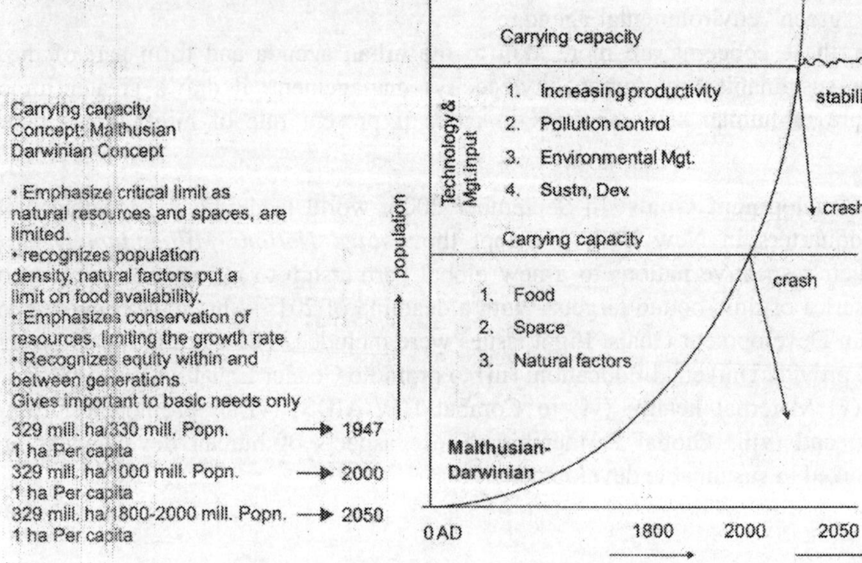

Figure 24(a). The carrying capacity concept graph

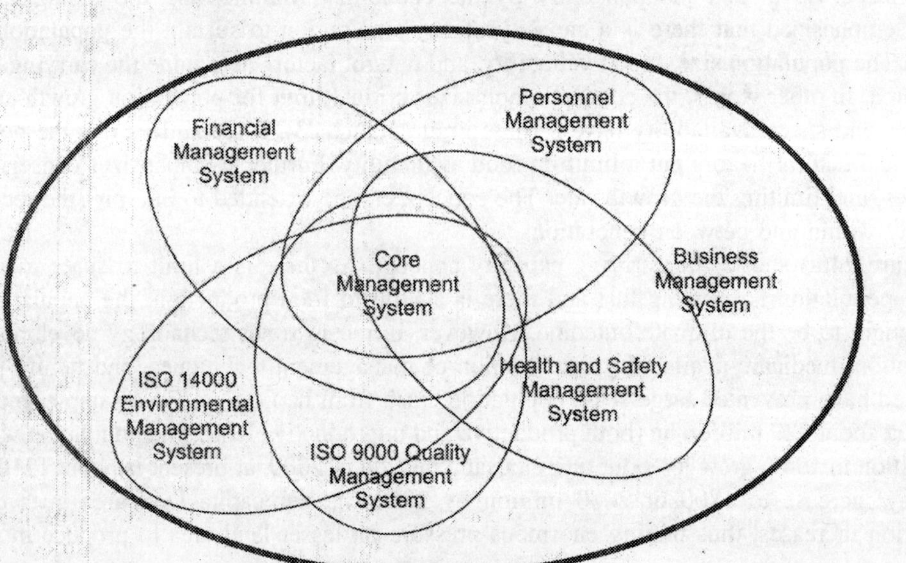

Figure 24(b). Relationship between management systems for sustainable development (from CII & ICC publications)

aesthetics, resource conservation, man and biodiversity as integral parts of nature. Imperatives of these developmental processes often contradict one another. For example, the externalization of costs in order to maintain rates of private profit can contradict ecological development.

Table 12. Example of Pressure-State-Response Framework (from Dash (ed), 2006)

Sustainability dimension	Goal	Driving force/ pressure indicator	State indicator	Response indicator
Economic	Poverty alleviation	Inadequate means of livelihood	Poverty index	Employment generation
Social	Acess to basic service	inadequate public infrastructure	Electricity consumption (per capita)	Off-grid electricity Services
Environmental	Reduction in health effect from indoor air pollution	Inadequate access to clean cooking fuel	Morbidity from particulate concentrations	Provision of fuel emissions and efficient chullhas
Technology	Reduction in carbon and pollutant emission	Climate change and health issues	Carbon foot print	Adoption of green technology, energy conservation. Use of renewable energy

The globalization (expansion of markets) and free trade agreements can undermine community development at local, or regional level, and self reliance to meet basic human needs. Sustainable development should bring these three developmental processes, i.e., economic, social-community, and environmental into balance with each other. In view of this, sustainable development strategy should involve negotiation among the stakeholders involved in these processes (Figure 24(b)).

Once an action plan is agreed upon, the stakeholders have to take responsibility and leadership for implementation and accountability. In summary there should be a symbiotic relationship between different management systems as presented diagrammatically.

2.1.4 Sustainable Development Indicator for Industries

Measuring sustainability is not an easy task. Therefore, a concept of sustainable development indicator (SDI) has been introduced to assess measure and monitor sustainability of a process. For measuring sustainability of a development process, a useful way is to select and organize indicators in a pressure (cause), state (linking effects), and response (policy action) framework. See the table below for an example of the pressure-state-response framework. Indian Business Sector may adopt the similar **P-S-R** framework for selecting/ identifying SDI. (Table 12)

2.2 INDIA'S SUSTAINABLE DEVELOPMENT (SD) PRIORITIES

India's Ninth Plan recognized the integral link between rapid economic growth and the quality of life of the people and has set SD priorities. These are:

(i) Ensuring food and nutritional security; (ii) Providing the basic minimum services like safe drinking water, primary healthcare facilities, universal primary education, connectivity to all, (iii) Arresting the growth rate of population – increasing population has led to a number of interlinked issues; inequalities of income levels, low level of literacy, unemployment and ultimately poverty, (iv) ensuring environmental sustainability of the development process-Environment protection does not only involve prevention of pollution and degradation of natural resources, but also on integration with the overall development process and the well-being of people; (v) empowering of women and socially disadvantaged groups; (vi) promoting and developing people's participatory institutions (like Panchayati Raj); (vii) Strengthening efforts to build self-reliance (capacity building). Rapid urbanization has progressively declined essential services and the quality of life in urban areas. Therefore, synergy between environment, health and development needs to be specially recognized, as no development process leading to better quality of life can be sustained in a deteriorating environmental condition.

Poverty alleviation, economic and social development and environmental protection are overriding SD goals and priorities of India.

The present trend is that the human needs and aspirations like health, literacy, democratic values, women empowerment, and equity within and between generations are to be maintained. Recycle-reuse, waste management waste as a resource concept is being vigorously promoted. The concept gives importance to technology development and application. Sustainable development emphasizes economic, community, ecological development, environmental protection and making a balance between them.

2.2.1 Incentives for Adopting Sustainable Practices

(i) Financial gain – Pollution avoidance is less costly than pollution control
(ii) Stronger enforcement of environmental regulations
(iii) Layering of environmental regulations
(iv) Reduced risk of control costs from future domestic environmental requirements
(v) Reduced risk of control costs for meeting future international environmental standards
(vi) Boosts profits by substituting knowledge for material inputs
(vii) Reduces inputs to production (energy, water, materials) per unit output
(viii) Reduced dependence on external inputs insulates against price volatility
(ix) Spill-over benefits in terms of enhanced managerial and technical capacity
(x) New opportunities in "green markets"
(xi) The process having contributed to sustainable development is to be identified and promoted
(xii) Final users, especially in overseas markets, are interested in sustainability
(xiii) Potential for revenue growth in new markets for products and services
(xiv) Gain trust/ identify emerging markets by forging connections with communities
(xv) Enhance profitability by generating revenues from nature's services through ecosystem protection and restoration
(xvi) Offset degradation from other operations
(xvii) Use natural systems to reduce operating costs.

Former President Dr. APJ Abdul Kalam has proposed an environmental oath for every company and every individual and I quote; '(i) To promote a culture of environment friendliness, through recycling and conservation in my organization or company; (ii) to plant and nurture at least ten trees in my neighborhood; (iii) to keep my house and its surroundings clean and use products which are biodegradable to the extent possible; (iv) as I rise in my career, I will take the policy decision with respect of organizational processes which protect the environment and preserve biodiversity; (v) to encourage the use of renewable energy and use of captive power to the maximum extent possible; (vi) to plan all my future expansion in the organization using green building concepts with focus on energy and water efficiency; (vii) to spread the awareness about the need to preserve the environment in my peer group. Dr. Kalam comments that to meet the challenge of building sustainable environment, we have to find a confluence of technology, management, social science and policy'.

2.3 GREEN ECONOMY

The UNO Conference on Sustainable Development (UNCSD, Rio + 20) was held in June, 2012 in Brazil and has promoted a catchword '**Green Economy**' for sustainable development and poverty education. Besides sustainable development and poverty eradication, the focus was also on Institutional framework.

The objectives of the conference were: (i) to secure renewed political commitment for sustainable development; (ii) to assess the progress to date and identifying the remaining gaps in the implementation of the outcomes of major summits on sustainable development'; (iii) to address new and emerging challenges.

The UNEP has developed a working definition of green economy, which states that improved human well-being and social equity with significantly reducing environmental risks and ecological scarcities can be achieved by developing renewable energy technologies, energy efficient buildings and equipment, low-carbon public transport systems, clean energy vehicles, proper waste management with recycling facilities. Green investments will enhance new sectors and new technologies which will be the main resources for economic development and for the future growth.

The green economy is the pathway to achieving sustainable development and eradication of poverty. The environment is an 'enabler' of economic growth and societal well-being. Many terms, which are synonyms, are used to explain the concept of green economy. These terms are: ecological economics; environmental economics, welfare economics, Buddhist economics, etc.

2.3.1 Indicators of Green Economy

(i) Economic indicators; (ii) environmental indicators; and (iii) aggregate indicators of progress and human well-being. UNEP is collaborating with organizations for economic co-operation and development (OECD) and the World Bank to translate these indicators into action keeping the structure of the economy and natural resource endowment of the nations in view.

2.3.2 Prospects of Green Economy

1. Protecting and conserving ecosystems and biodiversity.
2. Strengthening the three pillars such as (i) economic development, (ii) social development & (ii) promoting environmental protection.
3. Discouraging unsustainable consumption and practising sustainable consumption. Green economy, productivity and sustainable consumption are mutually supportive and may require macro and micro interventions that may require change in policy and regulatory

framework, investments and business operations. This may induce behavioural change in the society.

4. Eradication of poverty. More than 70% of India's population lives in villages and about 50% of them depend upon biodiversity such as agriculture, forest products, animal husbandry, fishing and biodiversity based cottage industry for their livelihood. In view of this, biodiversity conservation and management to get value added products for poverty eradication is important. The type of economic growth as practised presently has resulted in high economic and social costs, especially for the poor. Economic wealth measured in terms of High Gross Domestic Product (GDP) is often linked to overexploitation of resources and causing environmental pollution. Green economy aims to increase the basic services and infrastructure for alleviating poverty and helping in the overall improvement of quality of life.
5. Green economy should generate employment. New avenues such as renewable energy, new building retrofits for energy efficiency, public transportation, organic agriculture and vermi-technology, reclamation of degraded lands and forests, recycling and reuse of waste materials, etc. These practices are expected to provide economic benefit, employment benefit and environmental benefits. For example, about 70,000 tonnes of plastic products are recycled in USA generating about 69 million dollars. In USA recycling of about 6.1 million tonnes of waste in five years has generated more than 1.6 billion dollars. Recycling of wastes instead of land filling or incinerating reduced about 4,12,000 tonnes of carbon dioxide emission (green house gas) (source: Paribesh Samachar, 2012).

2.3.3 Financial Incentive

Governments can adopt appropriate policies depending upon the capability of the country to promote green investment. The green economy policies may involve public-private partnerships as an economic instrument. This may involve public finance and fiscal measures, utilization of public expenditure on productive research and development, inclusion of environmental costs on goods and services, promoting green products and services, putting levies on pollution, and providing incentives on tax amount to industries for adopting green technology, strengthening legal framework.

Green economy will generate clean environment by minimizing waste generation, reuse, recycling, etc., provide security for getting clean water, renewable energy (energy security), change manufacturing philosophy, quality of transportation, and food security, etc.

CHAPTER 3

Environmental Management

3.1 DEFINITION

The process of getting things done effectively, efficiently, and involving concerned people. This is a simple definition. Effectiveness means doing the right thing to attain the goal in a specific time. Efficiency means developing relationship between inputs and outputs, minimizing resource costs, conserveing resources and doing things correctly in an eco-friendly manner.

In any organization/industrial set-up we have usually:

(i) First-Line Managers; direct day-to-day operations of employees.
(ii) Middle Level Managers: coordinators between first-line managers and top level managers.
(iii) Top level managers: Responsible for making decisions and carrying out organizational policies and directions and periodical reviewing.
(iv) Managing Director/Chairman: Monitoring, administrative control, national and international relations.

A manager (first and middle level) should develop: (i) conceptual skills, (ii) technical skills, (iii) interpersonal skills, (iv) environmental management skills. Management skills have become important in the context of globalization and sustainable development.

Environmental management is a process by which a development project can be made sustainable by ensuring its environmental compatibility.

This process commences from the planning stage of the project and is carried out throughout its implementation, operation and final stage.

(i) Establishment of an industry requires proper choice of site selection and technology at planning stage to keep the environmental damage within acceptable limit like minimum deforestation, displacement of people and pollution.
(ii) Similarly, care has to be taken to abate any environmental damages such as air, water and noise pollution, lack of proper sanitation and social problems due to migrant labour, etc., during the construction phase.
(iii) When the industry operates, all steps are required to be taken for prevention and control of air, water and soil pollution and hazardous waste disposal by technology control and installation of appropriate effluent/emission treatment plants.

(iv) Finally, the unavoidable solid waste and hazardous waste, hazardous chemicals generated from the industry (e.g., mining overburden and fly ash) has to be disposed of in an eco-friendly manner like properly rehabilitating the disposal site.

(v) Similar land rehabilitation is required when the industry is finally closed and dismantled after completion of its useful life (e.g., mine closure). Management systems are designed to enable the organization to upgrade technology, maximize its beneficial environmental effects and minimize adverse environmental effects. The International Standard Organization (ISO), a worldwide federation of National Standard Bodies of more than 110 countries, has developed environmental management systems.

A number of internationally recognized models for environmental management exist. These are termed ISO 9000 series of quality management standards and ISO 14000 series of standards for environmental management systems. The environmental management system should be integrated with the organization's other activities in order to get maximum benefit out of this management system. ISO 9000 emphasizes on quality management standards related to production, but ISO 14000 series encourages proactive environmental management and facilitates cooperation between industry and the regulatory agency. ISO 50000 series takes care of energy management systems. These management systems take a holistic view of the industry and environment and establish a framework for continual improvement.

These systems also encourage innovations at the facility level and bring about international awareness regarding the environmental performance of the industry. However, these systems improve the quality of management and, therefore, should be adopted by all industries, so that their environmental performance becomes much better than the existing performance. The industries should look for long-term profit-oriented goals. They must also spend a part of their profit on the upliftment of socio-economic conditions and health of the people in the area where such industries are operating. The industry is also obliged to provide finance for environmental restoration operating. The environmental laws, which have been enacted in India, provide a framework to achieve these goals. However, there are constraints in their implication, which can be solved by raising consciousness for sustainable development among people, industrial organizations, and government functionaries. The standard is applicable to any organization that wishes to:

1. implement and maintain an Environmental Management System (EMS);
2. satisfy and confirm with its stated environmental policy;
3. demonstrate such conformity to others by seeking certification of its EMS by an external agency; and
4. undertake self-determination and make a declaration of conformance with the existing standards.

3.2 CORPORATE ENVIRONMENT INDICATORS

The corporate environmental indicators to achieve sustainable development are represented in the Figure 25. These include environmental condition indicators, environmental performance indicators and environmental management indicators.

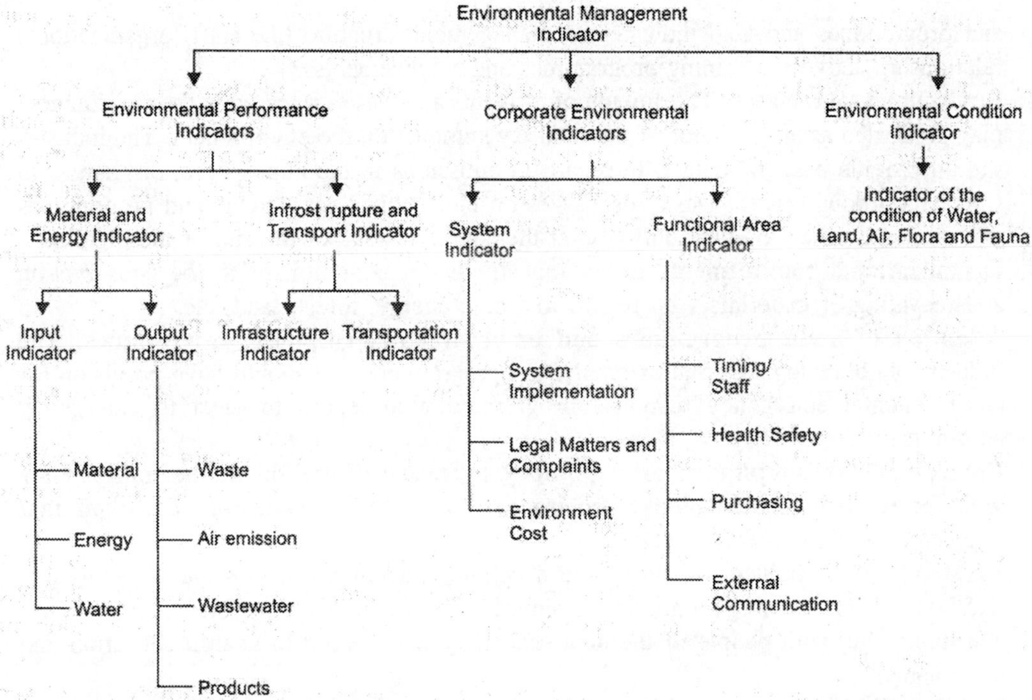

Figure 25. Corporate environmental indicators (from CII and ICC publications)

3.3 OBJECTIVE OF THE INDUSTRY

To attain sustainability the industry has to follow a green path keeping the corporate environment indicators in mind. Most of the companies' environmental programmes are driven by a strong set of corporate values. The International Chamber of Commerce (ICC) published in 1990 its business charter for sustainable development: "Principles for Environmental Management". In summary, these can be called the green path.

3.3.1 Green Path

An industry's environmental performance is increasingly viewed as an essential part of their national commitment to environmental protection for adoption of the green path. Each industry should have the following components in their environment management system. Green path for industries may have these components.

1. **Organizational profile:** Indicating the size of the organization like revenue generation, number of employees, major lines of activity, nature of environmental impact of the organizations operations.
2. **Environment policy:** Each industry should have its own environmental policy which should indicate the scope and applicability, constraints and goals.
3. **Environmental management:** Each industry should adopt a management system which should indicate organizational accountability for implementation of environmental policies

and programmes and also indicate the management structure like staff, organizational relationship activities, training programmes and achievements.

4. **Environmental releases:** The amount of effluents and wastes released in the environment may be treated as an indicator of the industry's impact on the environment. The industry should provide baseline data with regard to emissions in the atmosphere, discharges in water, hazardous wastes, waste discharges on land, objectives, targets and programmes and measures taken to abate pollution at the source instead of the end of the pipeline.
5. **Organizational commitment:** Every industry has a commitment to the conservation and recycling of materials with regard to water, energy, forest, land, etc.
6. **Adoption of audit programmes and environmental response programmes:** The industry should adopt internal/external audit programmes and should have provision for environmental emergency response programme with regard to meeting emergency commitments, etc.
7. **Environmental compliance to regulatory agencies:** There should be transparency with regard to implementation of environmental laws and regulations and reporting/interacting with regulatory agencies.
8. **R&D cell:** Each industry should have a cell for pursuing research and development (R&D) activities, training programmes, acquiring environmentally preferable technologies and interacting with people of the area especially with regard to health, education and environment.
9. **Excellence recognition:** Each industry should have a programme to reward their employees and their family members for excellence in their work with regard to environmental practices, resource conservation and R&D activities.
10. **Publication:** Each industry should have a publication cell. This cell should periodically highlight the activities of the industry, specially their achievements, quality of their products, nature of technology they use and their commitment to environmental compliance, particularly recent data on emissions, effluent release, and treatment facilities and solid and hazardous wastes generated and method of disposal. They may publish their contribution to corporate social responsibility, training facility etc.

Most leading companies' environmental programmes are based on a set of corporate values. Corporate environmental leadership will be sustained provided it translates into competitive advantage in business. The environmental forces are changing continuously and therefore, environmental management for sustainable development is important and need of the time.

3.4 LEGAL INSTRUMENT

The legal framework consisting of environmental laws is described in another chapter. The legal instrument is very important and the key aspects are the environmental impact assessment (EIA) and environmental management plan (EMP), which is described below.

3.4.1 Environmental Impact Assessment and Decision Making

Environmental impact assessment (EIA) is a requisite for deciding an environmentally sound project. EIA is a process designed to ensure that all potentially significant impacts are carefully assessed and taken into account in planning, designing, authorization and implementation of all relevant types of actions of a development project, which can be taken up to offer net economic and social benefits to the people and environmental protection. A project should be decided on the basis of a cost-benefit analysis, taking into consideration both tangible and intangible gains and losses. Till a decade or so before, environmental impact was not considered in deciding a project; only the techno-socio-economic feasibility was considered. Today, the techno-socio-economic feasibility is integrated with environmental compatibility to render any development project sustainable (Figs. 26 and 27). Environmental impact assessment (EIA) is a part of the decision-making process and should be carried out before a final decision is taken about a project. EIA should be carried out by a non-interest expert party in order to prepare a fair and unbiased report. The project proponents and those who oppose the project can be considered interested parties. The decision-making process using EIA tools consists of a sequence of different stages as detailed in Figure 26. The following steps should be followed in the planning and designing stage: (i) review the alternative ways of meeting the overall objective of the project; and (ii) examine the alternative locations for the proposed project, if the same is not site specific, e.g., mining project, hydroelectric project.

Study the alternative process designs, site layouts and other facilities of the proposed project. At this stage, the EIA study should be done along with technical and financial studies in order to arrive at an optional environmentally compatible alternative while accommodating the vital interests of the developer. However, detailed EIA study for all the alternatives may not be necessary and most of the alternatives can be eliminated by a rapid environmental screening (RES). Systematic EIA study should be done for only one or two final alternatives left after the rapid environmental screening. In this connection 14th September, 2006 notification of MOEF is very relevant.

3.4.2 What is EIA?

Environmental Impact Assessment is the process in which environmental factors are integrated into project planning and decision making so as to achieve ecologically sustainable development. Best practice EIA identifies environmental risks, lessens conflicts by promoting community participation, minimizes adverse environmental effects, informs decision makers, and helps lay the base for environmentally sound projects. Benefits of integrating EIA have been observed in all stages of a project, from exploration and planning, through construction, operations, decommissioning, and beyond site closure. EIA has been defined by Jain, Urban, Stacey (1977) in a simple yet convincing way as 'a study of probable changes in the various socio-economic and bio-physical characteristics and the environment which may result from a proposed or impending action'. Hagerty (1977) defines EIA in more precise terms as 'an activity that aims at establishing quantitative values for selected parameters which indicate the quality of environment before, during, and after the proposed activities'.

The United Nations Environment Programme (UNEP) in 1987, set certain goals and principles of EIA, and defined it as an examination, analysis, and assessment of planned activities with a view to ensure environmentally sound and sustainable development. The Rio declaration in 1992 has given emphasis to EIA (Principle No. 17) as a national instrument, which shall be undertaken for proposed activities that are likely to have a significant and adverse impact on the environment

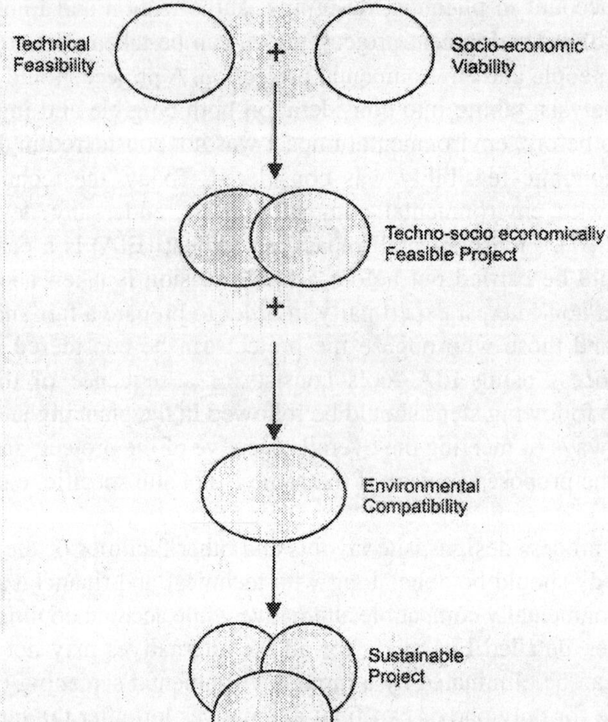

Figure 26. EIA sequences for decision making & conceptual framework for EMS (from Das and Mishra, 2001 & Dash and Dash, 2009)

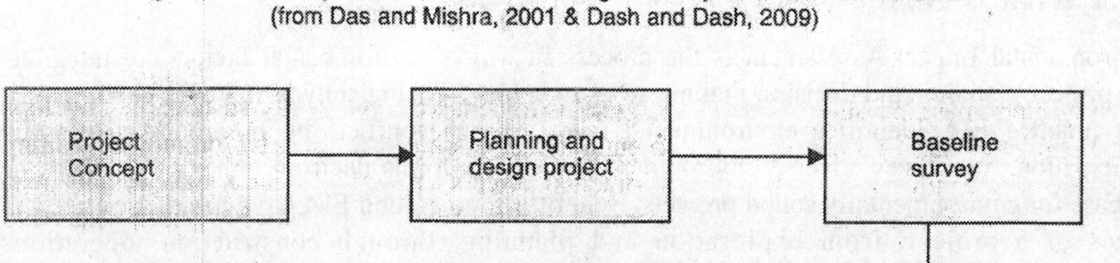

Figure 27. Sequence of project conception and processes.

and are subject to a decision of a competent national authority. In Agenda 21, Chapter 8 is entirely devoted to integrating environment and development in policy, planning and decision making processes, providing an effective legal and regulatory framework, making effective use of economic instruments and market and other incentives and establishing a system for integrated environmental and economic accounting.

The field of EIA was pioneered in the US by the formulation of the Natural Environmental Policy Act (NEPA) in 1969. Subsequently, a number of developing and developed countries such as Canada in 1973, Australia and New Zealand in 1974, Japan in 1981, the European Community in 1984, The Netherlands in 1986, and the UK in 1988, have enacted similar legislations at different times to conduct EIA. A lot of experiments have been going on throughout the world for the effective application of EIA to ensure environmentally sustainable development. The objectives of the article are to provide an overview of the generic and the World Bank EIA processes, methodologies developed over a period of time to assess the impacts, EIA guidelines and process as practised in different nations, issues involved in the process of implementation, and steps needed to strengthen the EIA capacity. In India the following processes are followed.

Project definition

During project identification and definition, the project proponent conducts feasibility studies, defines the usefulness of the study, considers alternatives, files a notice of intention to seek EIA clearance, and, ideally, initiates an inter-agency and public consultation process.

Screening

In the screening stage, the EIA agency consults the proponent and other agencies and public participants to determine the requirements of further studies. At this stage, the EIA agency determines whether the project may proceed as planned or if it needs to be subjected to an initial or complete EIA.

Scoping

The scoping stage, often merged with screening, deals with a more detailed plan of study for the project to identify major concerns and key impacts, and to decide assessment methods and models to be used. Agencies and public representatives concerned with the project or the project area are consulted.

Baseline data collection

Baseline data collection and analysis are involved from secondary sources and primary monitoring in the study area.

Identification of impact

Impact prediction and assessment are the most important of the technical processes. Since various methods and models are available, the process of selection of suitable models needs careful evaluation.

Alternative evaluation criteria

It will generally include a mixture of legally mandated criteria, technical/scientific criteria, and social acceptability criteria. Alternative sites and design processes should be critically examined to maximize the positive environmental impacts, socio-economic benefits and profitability, and minimize the temporary adverse impacts.

Management plan

Once the impacts are identified, the mitigation measures need to be defined. Project planning and the design process need to be flexible enough to adopt the modified basic project alternatives. But, in some cases, entirely new alternatives may be required. Where negative impacts cannot be eliminated, monitoring programmes may need to be developed to minimize adverse impacts.

Publication of EIA report

It is important to publish the full EIA report, which would be made available to the public for providing inputs.

Formal approval (with or without conditions)

The decision on the EIA report is put forward in a written record with conditions that the project proponent must comply with the provisions mentioned in the document.

Monitoring and compliance

Monitoring is an important aspect to ensure the compliance of provisions mentioned in the management plan. It not only provides confidence to workers, public agencies, and communities involved in dealing with negative impacts, but also gives useful feedback on the accuracy of the EIA's impact predictions.

Environmental Impact Assessment Methodology

A number of methodologies have been developed after the inception of the NEPA for evaluation and assessment of environmental impacts. Most of the methods suffer from excessive dependence on subjective judgments and are weak in predicting and quantifying the impact of the project on the environment, but the development of computer-based modeling techniques shows promise of bridging the existing gap. Some of the important methods developed over the period are discussed below.

Adhoc approach

This is the oldest and perhaps the crudest approach to EIA. The method provides very little guidance for assessing impacts on specific parameters beyond suggesting impacts on broad areas like impact on land, forests, population, water, wildlife, etc. It does not address secondary impacts.

Checklist

It is the updated version of the *ad hoc* approach in which specific areas of potential impacts are listed. Checklists are the lists of environmental attributes. The evaluator needs to tick against each environmental parameter for adverse, beneficial, or no effects due to proposed project activities. The method defines the parameters to be evaluated, but it is usually very large, very subjective, and provides little guidance that can aid in the decision-making process.

Matrix method

The method is attributed to Leopold *et al.* (1971). The method uses a matrix format to relate project actions and environmental components. The column of the matrix consists of 100 project actions (can be shortlisted as per requirement) against rows of the matrix of 88 environmental components (also can be shortlisted as per the project). If a project action is likely to make an impact on environmental components, the appropriate cell is scored for magnitude and importance of the impact (on an arbitrary scale). A +ve or – ve sign is provided for harmful or beneficial nature of the impact.

Row totals of the matrix reflect the total impact of all project actions on one environmental component, while the column totals reflect the impact of one project action on all components of the environment. The matrix total gives the total environmental impact.

One of the drawbacks of matrix approach is that it generally does not include secondary impacts. Also, the Leopold matrix is a non-mathematical matrix where true algebraic operations cannot be performed. A number of mathematical matrix methods have also been developed, namely, the Peterson's matrix, the component interaction matrix, etc., that try to address inclusion of secondary impacts and allow true algebraic operations.

Mathematical Matrices

The matrix was developed by Peterson, *et al.* (1974 - quoted by Sahoo, 2008)) and called the Peterson's Matrix. First, a matrix is formed to evaluate the effects of environmental action on the various physical components of the environment on a scale of +3 to -3. Another matrix is constructed to evaluate effects of the impacted physical components on human environment. Matrices are then multiplied to give a third matrix that brings out the effect of actions on the human environment. The production matrix is operated by a vector of relative weight of human impacts to result in a weighted vector of human impact. The weighted vector is then summed up to result in a total value of the project impact.

The approach has been criticized for too much of mathematical operations. It is also difficult to carry out the multiplication of matrices manually, and basic inputs to the matrix are still subjective.

Network approach

This approach links the project and its impacts in an easily understandable format. The network method aims at working from a list of project activities and establishes cause, condition, and effect relationships. Since the environmental system is dynamic and action impacting, certain environmental parameters can lead to a series of impacts on other environmental parameters.

The network method primarily addresses the need by defining a set of possible networks and allowing the user to identify impacts by selecting and tracing appropriate project actions. This approach has been identified as one of the best approaches for assessing higher-order impacts, although quantification of impacts is still subjective in nature.

Battlelle environmental evaluation system

This method has been identified as one of the most quantitative methods. In the Battlelle environmental evaluation system (BEES), 78 measurable environmental parameters are divided into four major categories of ecology, environmental pollution, aesthetics, and human interest. The first step includes the conversion of parametric estimates into an environmental quality (EQ) scale that ranges between 0 and 1, where 0 denotes extremely bad quality and 1 denotes very good quality. It is done using value function curves. The next step includes multiplication of EQ values with the respective parameter importance unit (PIU) values to obtain environmental impact units (EIU) for each parameter. Addition of EIU values provides a composite score. Total environmental impact is calculated by evaluating the expected future condition of the environmental quality with and without the project (Sahoo, 2008).

Computer-aided EIA

A number of computer-aided EIA methods have been developed in recent times. These basically link the multi-tasking software in a user-friendly manner to come up with an overall assessment system. A trend setting computer system for EIA has been developed by the US Army Construction Engineering Research Laboratory for predicting environmental impacts for army construction activities. The system integrates three sub-systems, namely: (1) the environmental impact computer system (EICS) to identify potential environmental impacts by relating army activities to environmental attributes, (2) the economic impact forecast system (EIFS) which provides quantitative estimates of regional economic impact of army actions based upon an extensive, diverse, interactive database, and (3) the computer-aided environmental legislative data system (CELDS) which stores abstracts of pertinent environmental legislation. In India, the National Environmental Engineering Research Institute (NEERI) has developed a computer-aided rapid EIA system using predictive models for a number of environmental parameters. The method divides the environment into various environmental components, namely, air, water, land, noise, biological, and socio-economic. Each environmental component is further divided into associated risks and each risk is further divided into measurable environmental parameters and predictors. Value function curves have been developed to convert measured values of environmental parameters into environmental quality on a scale between 0 and 1. The highlight of the method is the use of air, water, and noise models for prediction of environmental parameters. In recent times, Geographic Information Systems (GIS) has emerged as a very effective spatial analysis and presentation tool, enabling the identification of the impacted zones by using the overlay technique. Computer-based systems, however, are very expensive to run and maintain, and are, therefore, less frequently used in spite of all their merits.

Modeling approaches

A large number of mathematical models have been developed for the assessment and simulation of a number of environmental attributes like air quality, water quality, noise, and behaviour of biological systems. The approaches aim at modeling the environmental parameters for future prediction of impacts in quantitative terms. Key features of this approach include the ability to give the non-mathematical experts the capacity to model complex, and non-linear feedback systems. A major problem in the modeling approach to decision making is the scaling of judgment. Modeling the environment, as a whole is a resource-intensive and time-consuming procedure, which requires a significant level of expertise.

3.4.3 Environmental Impact Assessment Practice in India

The Ministry of Environment and Forests (MoEF), Government of India, under the Environmental (Protection) Act 1986, promulgated a notification on 27 January, 1994, making environmental clearance mandatory for expansion or modernization of any activity or for setting up new projects listed in Schedule-I of the notification. Till 1994, EIA clearance from the central government was an administrative requirement for big projects undertaken by the government or public sector undertakings.

After about a decade the EIA notification was completely reengineered in 2006. A new notification was issued under the EP Act, 1986 on 14th September 2006. EIA clearance from the central government is required for 8 categories of projects which can be broadly categorized under the following sectors:

(i) Mining and extractive industries and power generation,
(ii) Primary mineral processing,
(iii) Material production like metallurgical industries,
(iv) Material processing like petroleum refinery, etc.,
(v) Manufacturing and fabrication,
(vi) Service sectors,
(vii) Physical infrastructure and environmental services,
(viii) Construction and area development.

Under the recent notification the projects are designated as category A or category B projects on the basis of their size. Category A projects are required to obtain environmental clearance from Central Impact Assessment Authority after appraisal by a Central Expert Appraisal Committee and similarly category B projects will require Clearance from State Level Impact Assessment Authority after appraisal by the State Level Expert Appraisal Committee. For B category projects, EIA is not needed if in the opinion of the State Expert Appraisal Committee it falls within B1 category. The notification states that the requirement of EIA can be dispensed with by the impact assessment agency (EAA), which presently is under the MoEF. Environmental appraisal committees constituted by the MoEF for B1 category of projects. The MoEF has developed a generic structure for the preparation of EIA reports, however detail scooping is to be done by the Expert Appraisal Committee (either Central or State level depending upon the categories of the proposed project) on the basis of the questionnaires and checklists (Form-I). The State Pollution Control Boards (SPCB) in close coordination with the District Administration will conduct public hearing for the proposed project before the proposals are sent to the MoEF for obtaining environmental clearance. In the environmental clearance process, the documents to be submitted to the MoEF are project report, public hearing report, site clearance or site specific projects, an environmental appraisal questionnaire, the EIA/environmental management plan (EMP) report, risk analysis for projects involving hazard(ous) substances, and rehabilitation plans if more than 1000 people are likely to be displaced. Environmental impact assessment is an effective management tool which needs to be executed by recognizing project proponents with good environmental practices; strengthening institutional networking for proper implementation of EIA, emphasizing on information dissemination, education, communication, and training activities, and enforcing the EIA requirements strictly. The EIA process, by and large, has remained very subjective. There should be an increased stress on the development and incorporation of objective and quantitative techniques in EIA, which would contribute to the decision-making process. Screening and scoping, the most important parts of EIA, need to be certainly and effectively carried out to identify the environmental parameters that will be affected by development projects, and initiate dialogues with affected people for appraising the positive and negative features of the projects for effective public participation. It would facilitate to minimize future conflicts.

The EIA process could be simplified by improving the systems and procedures for processing documents, defining the appropriate methodology, introducing the component such as risk assessment, developing guidelines for various stages, providing guidelines for environmentally critical areas, and strengthening the coordination among central and state agencies, regional offices, and local governments in the implementation of EIA. The focus should be on capacity building to conduct EIAs by human resource development programmes for NGOs, (non-governmental organizations) local governments, and communities, improving standards of professional quality, preparation of environmental impact statement documents and developing an environmental information system. It is also important to introduce the environmental guarantee fund to generate funds to pay for damages caused by the project. The scope of EIA should be extended beyond the project levels to regional and strategic EIA to address policies, plans, and proposals for the regions and the projects. Some of the provisions of EIA document have not been adequately defined, for example the biodiversity (fauna and flora) enumeration. There is no mention of quantification of biodiversity, (diversity index, dominance index, evenness index, IVI values), enumeration level (species list, alpha, beta, etc. levels), threatened status region-wise etc. No importance is given to soil biodiversity in the site. This requires detailed study in immediate post-rains and in summer, by experts. Since the rural livelihood is biodiversity based and biodiversity conservation is a priority area as per the United Nations mandate, this aspect should get more scientific attention.

3.5 TECHNOLOGICAL INSTRUMENT

Science and technology plays on important role to prevent environmental degradation, to restore degraded ecosystems, and to control pollution and conserve resources.

Technology development and transfer and use are key to achieveing sustainable development.

3.5.1 Life Cycle Analysis

Life cycle assessment is a tool for evaluation of environmental consequences of a product across its entire life, i.e., looking at the resource, usages and release to the environment across all the stages involved. Life cycle assessment includes cradle-to-grave analysis of the products, that the industry makes with its environmental consequences. The cradle-to-grace principle means that all aspects of environmental impacts are considered from the acquisition of raw materials to the final disposal of the used products. Thus, life cycle assessment evaluates: (i) the environmental burdens associated with a product by identifying and quantifying energy and materials used and wastes released to the environment; (ii) the impact of these energy and material uses and releases on the environment; and (iii) the opportunity to effect environmental improvements (Figure 28).

Components in a product life cycle (1)

A complete life cycle assessment consists of: (a) Initiation with purpose and scope; (b) Inventory analysis for identification of opportunities for decreasing environmental releases, energy and raw

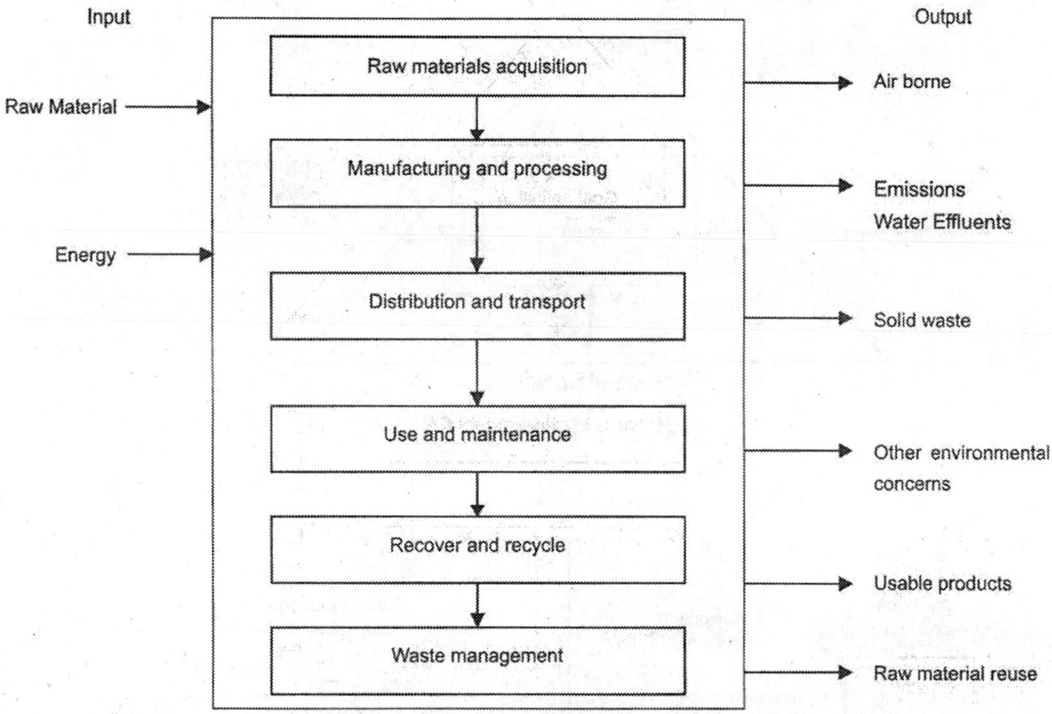

Figure 28(a). Life cycle assessment

material usage; (c) Impact analysis in relation to resource depletion, pollution, etc., and 1. Improvement analysis aimed at sustainable development for wider acceptance by people.

Figure 28(b). Components of LCA

3.5.2 Life Cycle Analysis for Aluminium, a Non-ferrous Metal Less Toxic than others of its Category-A Case Study

Processing aluminium took a giant leap forward with the advent of electricity. Aluminium is produced from alumina oxide. Bauxite ore is refined into alumina oxide. Alumina and electricity are combined in a cell with molten electrolyte called cryolite. Direct current is then passed from a carbon anode into the cryolite. This splits the alumina oxide into molten aluminium and carbon dioxide (green house gas). The molten aluminium is then collected from the bottom of the cell. Figures 29-31 show diagrammatically the technology and pollutants released and life cycle of bauxite and the pollutants released.

3.5.3 Technological Instrument for Pollution Control Methods

Industrialization has grown manifold and pollution from industries has also increased considerably. Due to the advancement of science and technology, it has been possible to control pollution to a large extent provided appropriate steps are taken. For sustainable development and due to

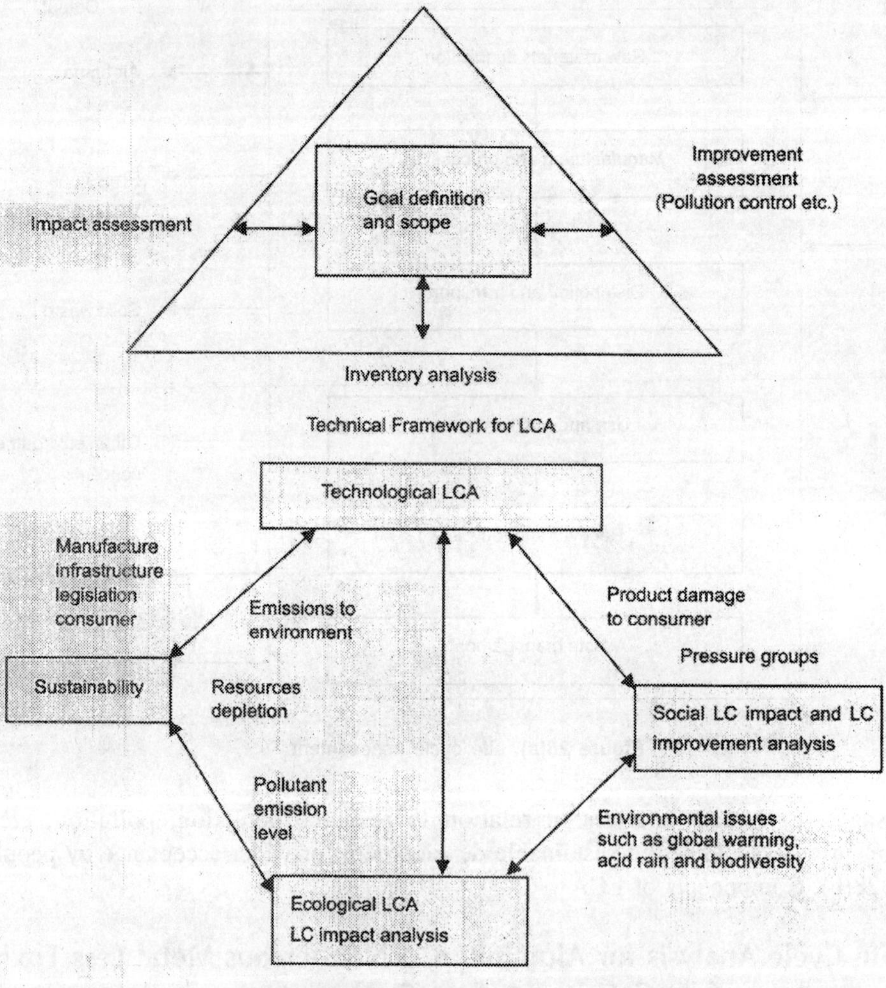

Figure 28(b), (c). Interaction between the three sections of life cycle assessment

technological advancement, it has been possible to utilize the waste of one production process as resource of another process to produce value added substances and to minimize pollution.

Raw material → Processing → Product + Waste—as resource for other processes.

Let us consider some mineral-based industries and bio-resource-based industries.

Mineral Based Industries
(i) Iron & Steel, (ii) Thermal Power, (iii) Aluminum, (iv) Ferro-Alloys, (v) Cement, (vi) Fertilizer
Biodiversity Based Industries: (i) Sugar (ii) Paper (ii) Brewery (iv) Furniture

Management Strategy involves the following:
(a) Quantity of waste produced in the primary process, (b) Streams where it can be used as resource (Thrust Areas for the State/Country), (c) Development of Secondary Industrial set up

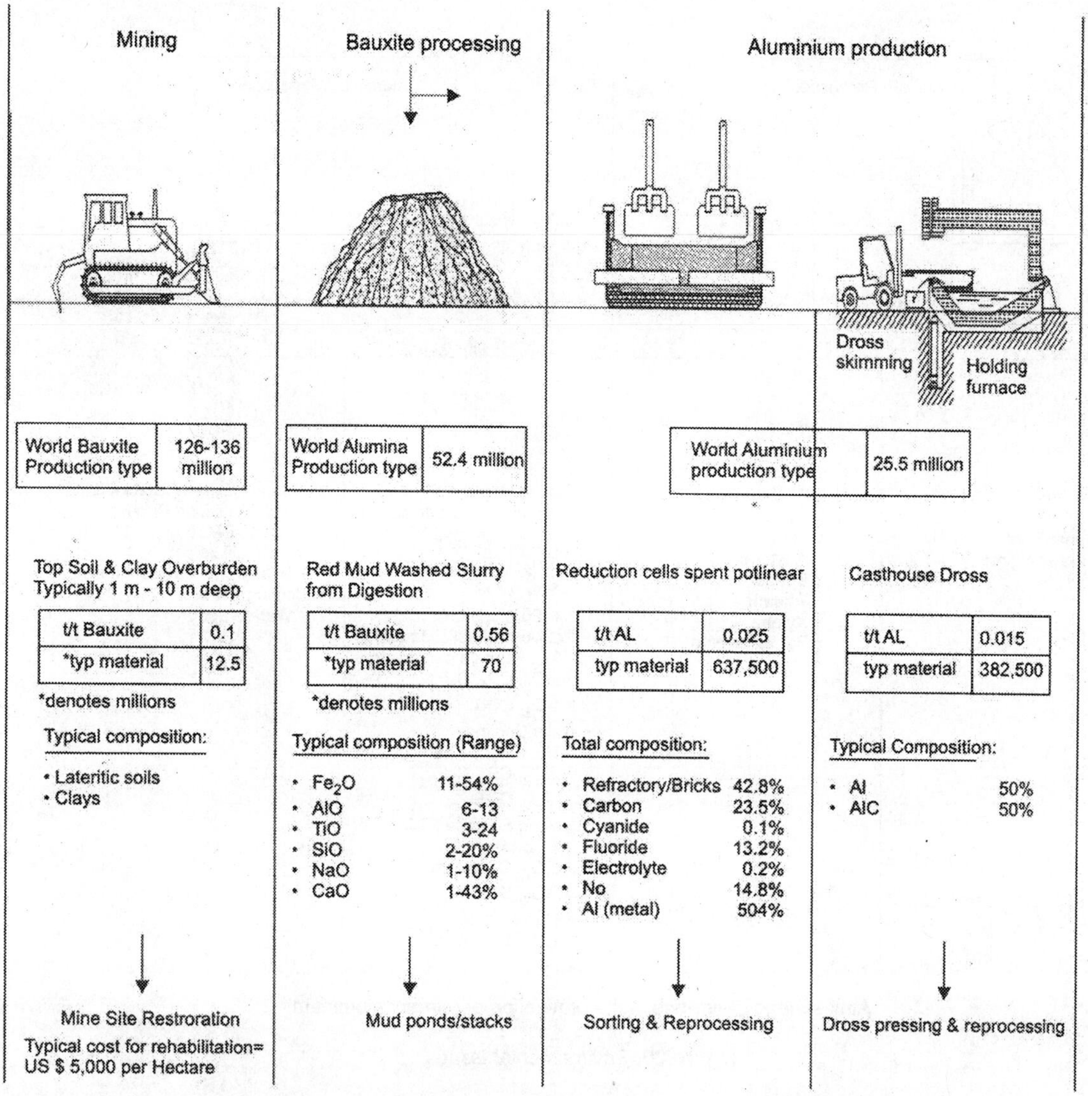

Solid waste-Bauxite Residue. Mining-Ground Water affected.

Figure 29. Environmental issues in aluminium production (from Er. S.K. Guru)

to produce products from waste, (d) Utilization potential of the state/country of these secondary products, (e) Investment Scenario

Air Pollutants

- Primary (major) types: (i) Oxides of Carbon, (ii) Oxides of Nitrogen, (iii) Oxides of Sulphur, (iv) Hydrocarbons, (v) Particulate matter and aerosols (dispersion of solid/liquid matter or particles.

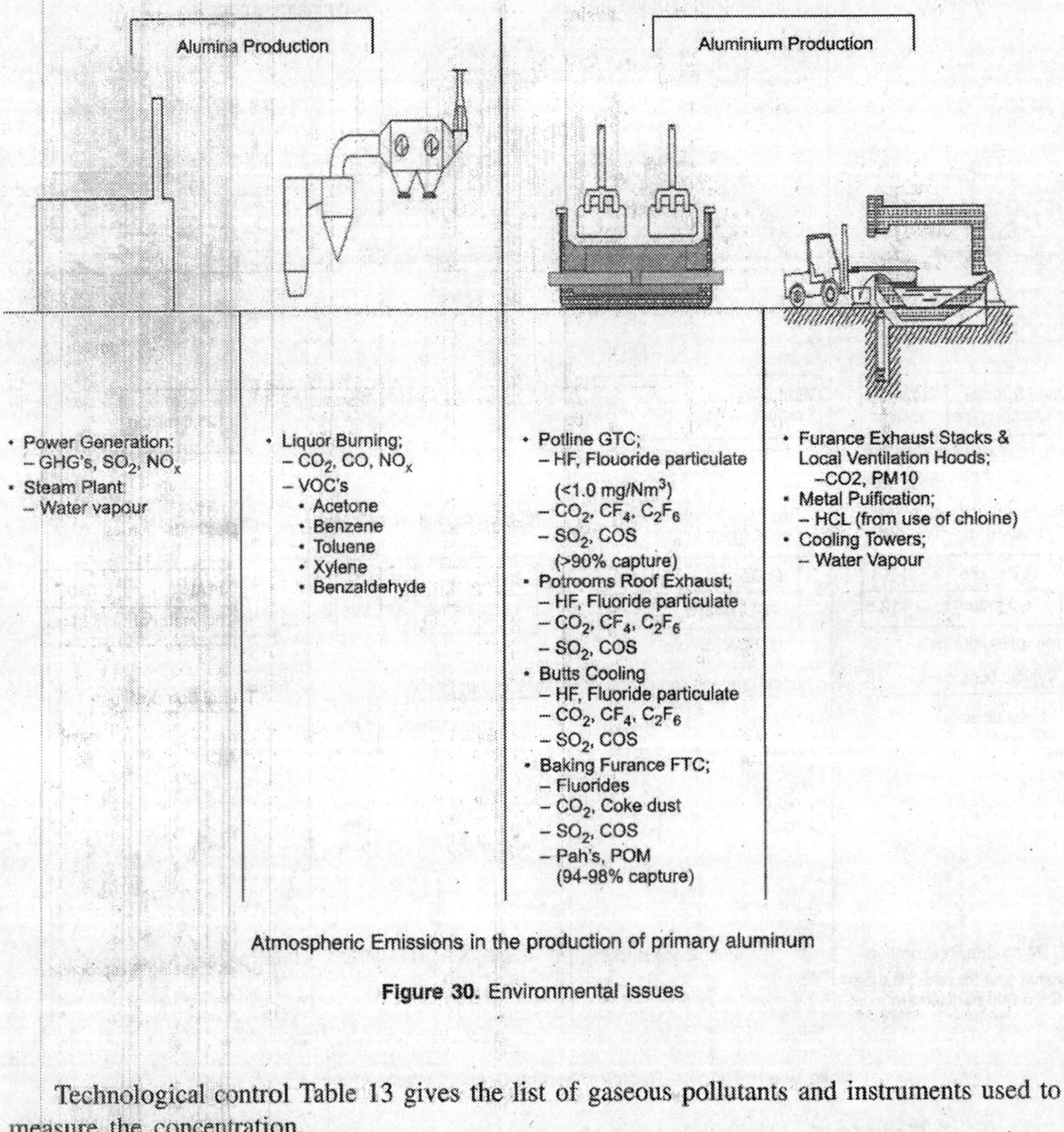

Atmospheric Emissions in the production of primary aluminum

Figure 30. Environmental issues

Technological control Table 13 gives the list of gaseous pollutants and instruments used to measure the concentration.

3.5.4 Control of Water Pollution

Turbidity is removed by: (i) settling, (ii) coagulation, (iii) filtration using alum/ double membrane reverse osmosis. Organic matter is removed by: (i) chlorination, (ii) coagulation, (iii) ordinary filtration, (iv) active carbon filtration, (v) scavenging anion exchanger. Oil is removed by: (i) coagulation with alum, (ii) physical barriers, (iii) organic solvents. Fluoride is removed by: (i) National Environmental Engineering Research Institute's (Nagpur) - Nalgonda technique:

Table 13. Gaseous Pollutants and List of Instruments Used to Measure the Pollutants

Gaseous pollutants	Instruments used to measure the concentration
CO (Carbon monoxide)	IR Spectrophotometer/Gas chromatography
SO_2 (Sulphur dioxide)	Spectrophotometer
NO_x (Oxides of nitrogen)	IR, chemiluminescence
Hydrocarbons	Gas liquid chromatography, IR
PAH (polycyclic hydrocarbons)	Gas liquid chromatography
Volatile particles	Gas liquid chromatography
Particulates; fluorides	Potentiometer
Silicates	Chromatography/ES
Sulphates	Electron spectroscopy (ES)
Particulates	

For As, Be, Cd, Cr, Fe, Mn, Pb, Hg, Zn:
Atomic absorption spectroscopy/Emission spectroscopy/spectrophotometer/X-ray fluorescence

For Se:
Spectrophotometer/X-ray Fluorescence/Neutron activation analysis

Control of Particulates
Gravity Settling Chamber for coarse particles Cyclone collector-particles of diameter 5 to 20 micron can be collected Electrostatic precipitators-small particles/aerosols can be collected Thermal precipitators for very fine aerosols Scrubbing (wet/dry)-by water, lime, alkali-removes liquid, solid, gas Impugners dry/wet)- collect particles of high velocity gas stream

Road side plantations for attenuating particulate matter, temperature, gas emissions & noise:
Plant Species: (in order of Tolerance):

Ficus religiosa, F. bengalinesis, F. glomerota,
Cassia tora, C.fistula, C.occidentalis, Albizzia lebbek, Nerium oleander, Zizyphus jujuba, Z.oenophila, Z. numularia, Azadirachta indica, Diospyros melanoxylon,Tamarindus indica, Mangifera indica, Syzygium cumini, Madhuca indica, Aegle marmelos, Phoenix regia, P.acauli, Butea monosperma, Tectona grandis, Dalbergia sissoo.

(a) by lime, and (b) lime bleaching powder + alum. Other techniques for fluoride removal are (c) reverse osmosis-double synthetic membrane, (iv) ion exchange technique, etc.

3.5.5 Case Study on Technological Instrument Required for Controlling Pollution for Sustainable Development:-Coal Based Thermal Power Plant

The major issues are: (i) air pollution, (ii) water pollution, (iii) solid waste pollution, (iv) thermal pollution, (v) noise pollution. Pollutants associated with coal burning are: (a) sulphur dioxide, (b) oxides of nitrogen, (c) carbon dioxide (d) particulate matter, and (e) ash. Application of technology can control these pollutants in such a way that the industry can maintain regulatory prescribed standard of emissions and effluents. These are described below: Air pollution control instruments: electrostatic precipitators, low NOX (oxides of nitrogen) burners, flue gas stack (gas that is emitted through the stack), dry ash extraction, etc.

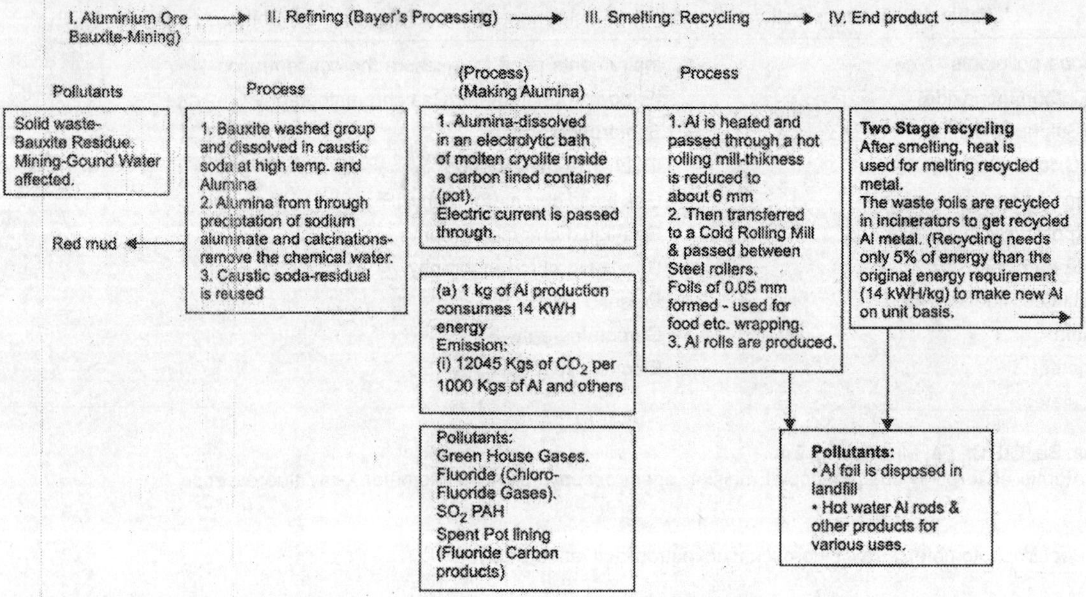

Figure 31. Life cycle analysis for aluminium (case study-summary)

Water pollution control instruments/technology

Coal/oil setting pits, ash dykes and disposal systems, ash water recycling system, effluent treatment plant (ETP).

Thermal pollution control technology

Cooling towers are provided for cooling the hot condenser cooling water in closed cycle condenser cooling water system. This helps in reduction in thermal pollution and conservation of fresh water.

Noise pollution control technology

The entire plant is so procured/installed that resultant noise level within premises remains within standard limits. Standard (World Bank) for industrial area – 70 dB max outside the project property boundary.

Air Pollution Control

The ash left behind after combustion of coal is arrested in high efficiency electrostatic precipitators (ESP) and particulate emission is controlled well within the stipulated norms. The ash collected in the ESP is disposed, mostly to ash ponds in slurry form. Dry ash collection and handling system are available. Emission standard of particulate matter (maximum) - 50 microgram per cubic metre can be maintained. Tall flue gas stack is provided for wide dispersion of gaseous emission (SO_2, NO_2, etc.) into atmosphere.

The prescribed stack height (in meters) is as follows:

500 MW and above - 275

200 MW and less than 500 MW - 220

Less than 200 MW - usually 130 and is

calculated using the following equation:

$H = 14 (Q) 0.3$

where H = stack height in m

and Q = emission rate of SO_2 in kg/hr

NO_2 emissions are controlled by provision of low NO_2 burners and by adopting best combustion practices and maintaining emission standards of World Bank

(In micrograms per cubic meter)

NO_2 : 100

SO_2 : 80

In coal and oil settling pits, coal dust and oil are removed from the effluents from coal handling plant, coal yard and fuel or oil handling areas before being discharged into effluent treatment plant (ETP).

Ash ponds are provided for ash disposal. Ash ponds are divided into lagoons and provided with garlanding arrangements for changeover of the ash slurry feed points for even filling of the pond and for effective of ash particles. Ash in slurry form is discharged into the lagoons where ash particles settled from the slurry and clear effluent water is discharged from ash ponds. Dry ash disposal is convenient. Dry ash has much higher utilization potential as listed below in ash based productsm e.g., (a) land reclamation, (b) structural land filling, (c) road making, (d) cement manufacturing, (e) bricks manufacturing, etc. (Figure 32).

Liquid Effluent Management

Neutralization pits are provided in water treatment plant (WTP) for pH correction of effluents before being discharged into effluent treatment plant (ETP) for further treatment and use.

Table 14. Ash Utilization - World Scenario

COUNTRY	GENERATION*	UTILISATION*	%
USA	71	22	31
CHINA	90	34	38
GERMANY	31	18	58
UK	12.5	6.1	49
AUSTRAILA	7.9	0.8	10
RUSSIA	62	21	34
JAPAN	7.3	5.0	68

* in Million tons.

Source: Seminar on Inter-Sectoral Co-operation in Fly Ash Management, 2005

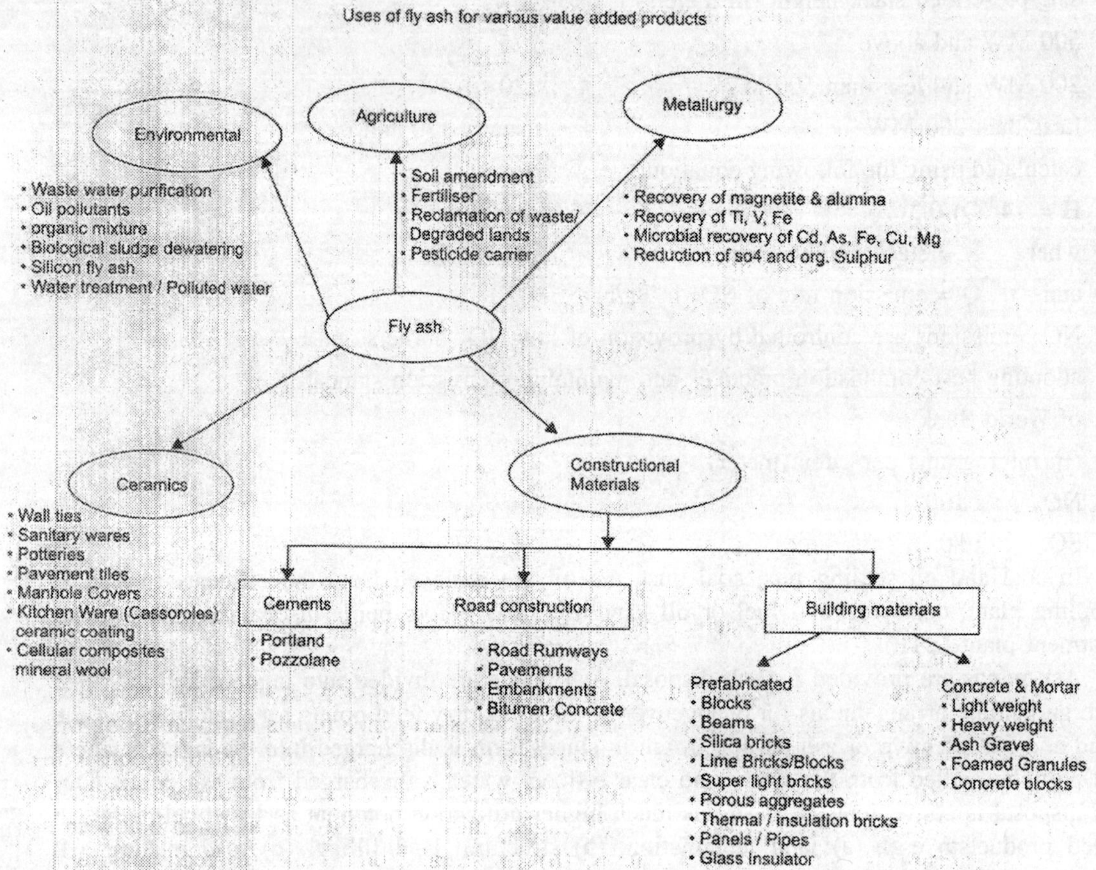

Figure 32. Fly ash utilization avenues

Table 15. Ash Generation-Indian Scenario

Year	Capacity in MW	Requirement of coal (million tons)	Ash generation (million tons)
1990	45,000	110	38
1995	54,000	200	75
2000	70,000	280	90
2010	98,000	300	110
2020	1,37,000	380	140

Source: Seminar on Inter-Sectoral Cooperation in Fly Ash Management

Sources of Liquid Effluents

Cooling tower blow down, boilers blow down power area service water waste, water treatment plant waste, demineralised (DM) plant, coal handling plant/ash handling plant waste, effluent from silo area.

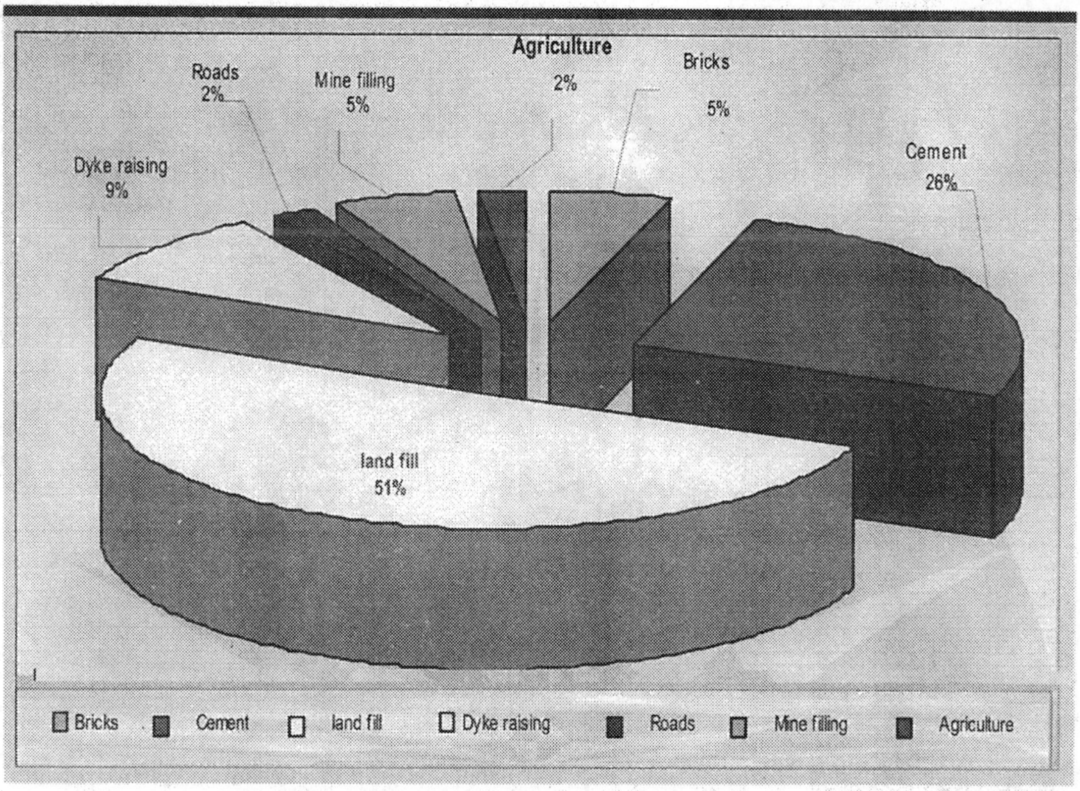

Figure 33. Ash utilization-Indian scenario (from Er. S.K. Guru)

Effluent Treatment Plant

The objective of industrial liquid effluent treatment plant (ETP) is to discharge clean effluent from the power plants to meet environmental standards and to reduce the intake of water. The scheme involves collection of various effluents and their appropriate treatment centrally and recirculation of the treated effluent for various plant uses.

3.6 MANAGERIAL INSTRUMENT

3.6.1 Environmental Management System-ISO 14000 Series

Environmental Management System (EMS) is a comprehensive, holistic management of the environment, which includes regulations, pollution prevention, resource consumption and ecological protection of the environment. EMS monitors environmental performance, similar to the way a financial management system monitors expenditure and income and enables regular checks of a company's financial performance. EMS integrates environmental management into a company's daily operations, long term planning and other management systems. It is the system to manage the environmental aspects arising out of the organisation's activities, products, and services. The

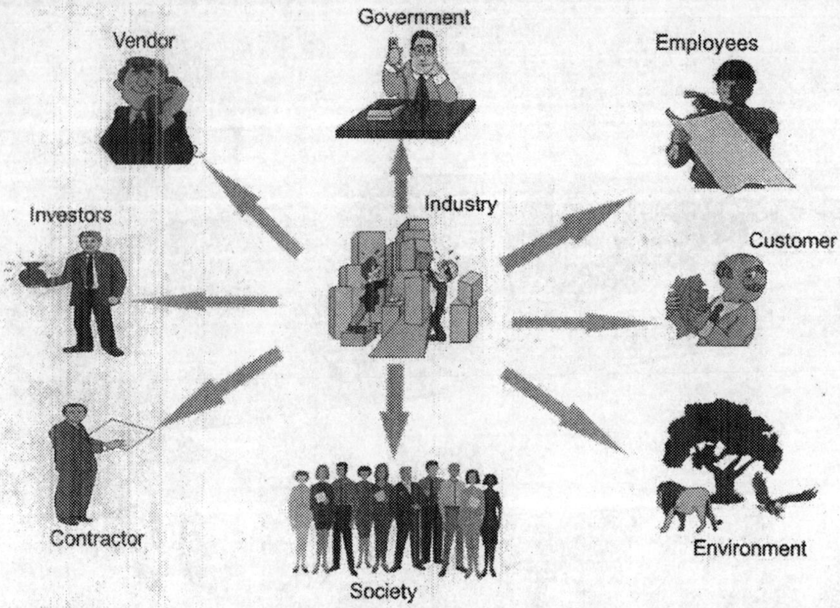

Figure 34. Industry and stakeholders (from Er. S.K. Guru)

objective is reducing adverse impacts and increase beneficial impacts to the satisfaction of all stakeholders/ interested parties (Figure 34).

3.6.2 Evolution of ISO 14000 Series

The International Organization for Standardization (ISO), a Geneva based independent organization established in 1947, is a worldwide federation of national standard bodies. India is the founder member of ISO. In 1991, ISO established a "Strategic Advisory Group on Environment" (SAGE) to study the feasibility of evolving uniform international standards on environmental management system. The SAGE, after studying various national standards, regulations and international conventions of EMS, recommended formation of an ISO technical committee dedicated to develop uniform international standards on environmental management systems. In 1992, United Nation Conference on Environment and Development (UNCED), also referred to as the Earth Summit held in Rio de Janeiro, considered how the world can move towards sustainable development and adopted Agenda 21, a "global consensus and political commitment at the highest level" on how governments, enterprisers and non-governmental organizations can cooperate to solve the crucial environmental problems which threaten human life and society. In 1993, on the recommendation of SAGE, a Technical Committee (ISO/TC/207) on Environmental Management was set up to develop ISO 14000 series of international standards on environmental management with the purpose to provide a systematic approach to the management of environmental issues. Canada was nominated to manage the secretarial work of TC 207. There are nearly 70 membe' countries and 40 liaison organizations participating in the work of TC 207. This committee is one of the largest of all the ISO technical committees. In 1996, the first set of five ISO 14000 series standards were brought out. The ISO 14000 series have addressed the following topics related to environmental management which are being developed by the six sub-committees as follows (Table 16).

Table 16. Environmental Management Standards

Sub Committees	Environmental Management Standards	Subjects	Nodal Country
SC1	ISO 14001 Series	Environmental Management System (EMS)	UK
SC2	ISO 14010 Series	Environmental Auditing (EA)	Netherlands
SC3	ISO 14020 Series	Environmental Auditing (EL)	Australia
SC4	ISO 14030 Series	Environmental Performance Evaluation (EPA)	USA
SC5	ISO 14040 Series	Life Cycle Assessment (LCA)	France
SC6	ISO 14050 Series	Terms and Definitions	Norway

India is a permanent member of sub-committees 1, 3 and 4. The Bureau of Indian Standards (BIS), being the national standard body, represents India in TC 207 and its various committees.

3.6.3 International Chamber of Commerce Charter

A separate appendix to ISO 14000 presents the International Chamber of Commerce Business Chapter for Sustainable Development. The key elements of the charter are the following:

(i) **Corporate Priority:** To recognize environmental management as among the highest corporate priorities and as a key determinant to sustainable development. To establish policies, programmes and practices for conducting operations in an environmentally sound manner.

(ii) **Integrated Management:** To integrate these policies, programmes and practices fully into each business as an essential element of management in all its functions.

(iii) **Process of Improvement:** To continue to improve policies, programmes and environmental performance, taking into account technical developments, scientific understanding, consumer needs and community expectations, with legal regulations as the starting point and to apply the same environmental criteria internationally.

(iv) **Employee Education:** To educate, train and motivate employees to conduct their activities in an environmentally responsible manner.

(v) **Prior Assessment:** To assess environmental impacts before starting a new activity or project and before decommissioning a facility or leaving a site.

(vi) **Product and Service:** To develop and provide products or services that have no undue environmental impact and are safe in their intended use, that are efficient in their consumption of energy and natural resources and that can be recycled, reused or disposed of safely.

(vii) **Customer Advice:** To advice and where relevant educate customers, distributors and the public in the safe use, transportation, storage and disposal of products provided and to apply similar considerations to the provisions of service.

(viii) **Facilities and Operations:** To develop, design and operate facilities and conduct activities taking into consideration the efficient use of energy and materials, the sustainable use of renewable resources, the minimization of adverse environmental impact and waste generation, and the safe and responsible disposal of residual wastes.

3.6.4 Need for Having an EMS and ISO-14001

Is compliance with environmental laws and regulations required for your organization? Does your organization want to improve environmental performance? Does your organization's activity constitute a potential environmental liability? Is lack of time and resources a deterrent for your organization to take charge of its environmental obligations? Do you know how your business objectives are related to environmental objectives? If answer to one or more of these questions is YES, Environmental Management System (EMS) will be helpful for your organization. ISO 14001 standards are applicable to an organization that wishes to implement, maintain and improve an environmental management system;

(i) Assure itself of its conformance with its stated environmental policy;
(ii) Demonstrate such conformance to others;
(iii) Seek certification/registration of its environmental management system by an external organization;
(iv) Make a self-determination and self-declaration of conformance with these International Standards.

An organization can be a company, corporation, firm, enterprise, authority or institution, or part or combination thereof, whether incorporated or not, public or private, that has its own functions and administration. For organizations with more than one operating unit, a single operating unit may be defined as an organization. The reasons for adopting ISO 14001 standards vary from case to case but according to Rene Vossenaar, UNCTAD Consultant, the main reasons for adoption of ISO 14001 certification by the enterprises are summarized below:

Improved management of environmental aspects: an EMS can provide a framework for continuous improvement of a company's management of the environmental aspects of its activities. Similarly, it may facilitate compliance with national and / or overseas environmental requirements.

Economic Benefits: An EMS may result in reduced cost of waste management and / or savings in consumption of energy and materials.

Trade Considerations: a company may seek ISO 14001 certification because it is perceived as a means to gain customer recognition, increase export competitiveness and strengthen market positions or as a means to avoid barriers to trade.

Corporate Image: a company may seek ISO 14001 certification with a view to improving corporate image among regulators, customers and the public. (Vossenaar, Rene., 1999. Presentation on ISO 14000 and trade MoEF-CUTS-UNCTAD Seminar on Strengthening Capacities for Trade and Environment Policy Integration in India. Jaipur, January, 1999).

3.6.5 What is ISO 14001?

This is the heart of 14000 Series. This is a framework for managing significant environmental aspects. This is a voluntary standard, designated for organizations, any size, anywhere. The emphasis is on pro-active and preventive approach.

3.6.6 Scope of ISO 14000 Standards

What ISO 14001 covers?

It enables an organization to formulate a policy and objectives taking into account legislative requirements and information about significant environmental impacts. It applies to those environmental aspects which the organization can control and over which it can be expected to have an influence. It does not itself state specific environmental performance criteria. Organizations of all kinds are increasingly concerned to achieve and demonstrate sound environmental performance by controlling the impact of their activities, products and services on the environment. Taking into account their environmental policy and objectives, they do so in the context of increasingly stringent legislation, the development of economic policies and other measures to foster environmental protection. A general growth of concern is from interested parties about environmental matters including sustainable development.

Doing business without a systematic management approach is economic doom and hence unacceptable. Providing quality protecting are nurturing the environment the keys. Doing it right the first time is crucial and getting your act together is essential. Listening to customers and other stakeholders is absolutely necessary and responding to society is mandatory.

What does ISO 14001 say regarding the benefits to an organization by implementing an effective environmental management system? Corporation and organization can protect human health and environment from the potential impact of its activities, products and services, assist in maintaining and improving the quality of the environment, meet customers' environmental expectations, maintain good public and community relations, satisfy investor criteria, improve access to capital, and provide insurance at reasonable cost. Further it may gain an enhanced image and market share, satisfy vendor certification criteria, improve cost control, limit liabilities, provide resource conservation, provide effective technology development and transfer, and develop confidence in interested parties (and share holders) and assure that policies, objectives and targets are met, emphasize on prevention, and ensure that reasonable care and regulatory compliance regularly occur, and system design includes continual improvement.

In summary, the benefits are compliance management, regulatory incentives, liability and risk reduction, improved access to insurance, improved access to lower-cost capital, improved process efficiency, improved environmental performance, reduced cost / increased revenues, improved customer / supplier relations, improved employee relations, creating green image among public, improved relations with other stakeholders, stepping-stone to sustainable development.

The different initiatives are waste minimization circles, clean technology and production initiatives, ISO 14001 certification, Green Rating, Eco-Labeling, Corporate Environmental Reporting, Environment Accounting, Green House Gas accounting. Figure 35 gives the flow sheet of ISO 14000 standards.

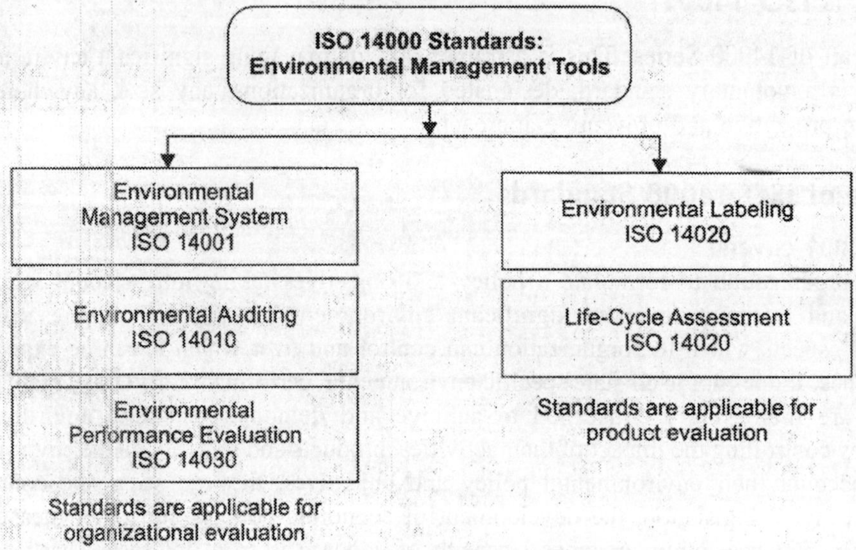

Figure 35. ISO 14000 Standards—Environmental management tools

ISO 14000 standards are environmental management tools to provide systematic approach to achieve environmental goals. These can be classified into two categories based on their focus

ISO 14001 EMS: Demin's PDCA Cycle (Figure 36).

The establishment of EMS, as per ISO 14000s based on "Deming's PDCA (Plan-DO-check-Act) Cycle" of quality management, as set out in ISO 9000. Figure 36 gives the flow sheet of the cycle.

According to Sohrab, Former Director, Bureau of Indian Standard (BIS), New Delhi, and ISO 14001 standards are designed on the following principles.

Principle 1: Understand all activities and processes being undertaken by the organization.

Principle 2: Identify potential aspects associated with the activities of the unit at all stages and determine their impact on the environment.

Principle 3: Determine processes/procedures/ operational steps that can be controlled to eliminate or minimize the likelihood of occurrence of the adverse impact.

Principle 4: Identify the regulatory requirements relating to them and establish target level(s) and tolerances, which must be met to ensure that operations affecting the environment are under control.

Principle 5: Establish a monitoring mechanism to ensure control of these aspects.

Principle 6: Establish corrective action to be taken when monitoring indicates that a particular aspect is not under control.

Principle 7: Establish a system for emergency preparation and for meeting such exigencies.

Principle 8: Establish procedures for verifications to confirm that the Environment Management System is working effectively in compliance with regulations and recording continual improvement.

ISO 14001 EMS: Demin PDCA cycle

The establishment of EMS, as per ISO 14001 standard, is based on "Deming's PDCA Cycle" of equality management, as set out in ISO 9000. It divides the organization's actions into four phases.

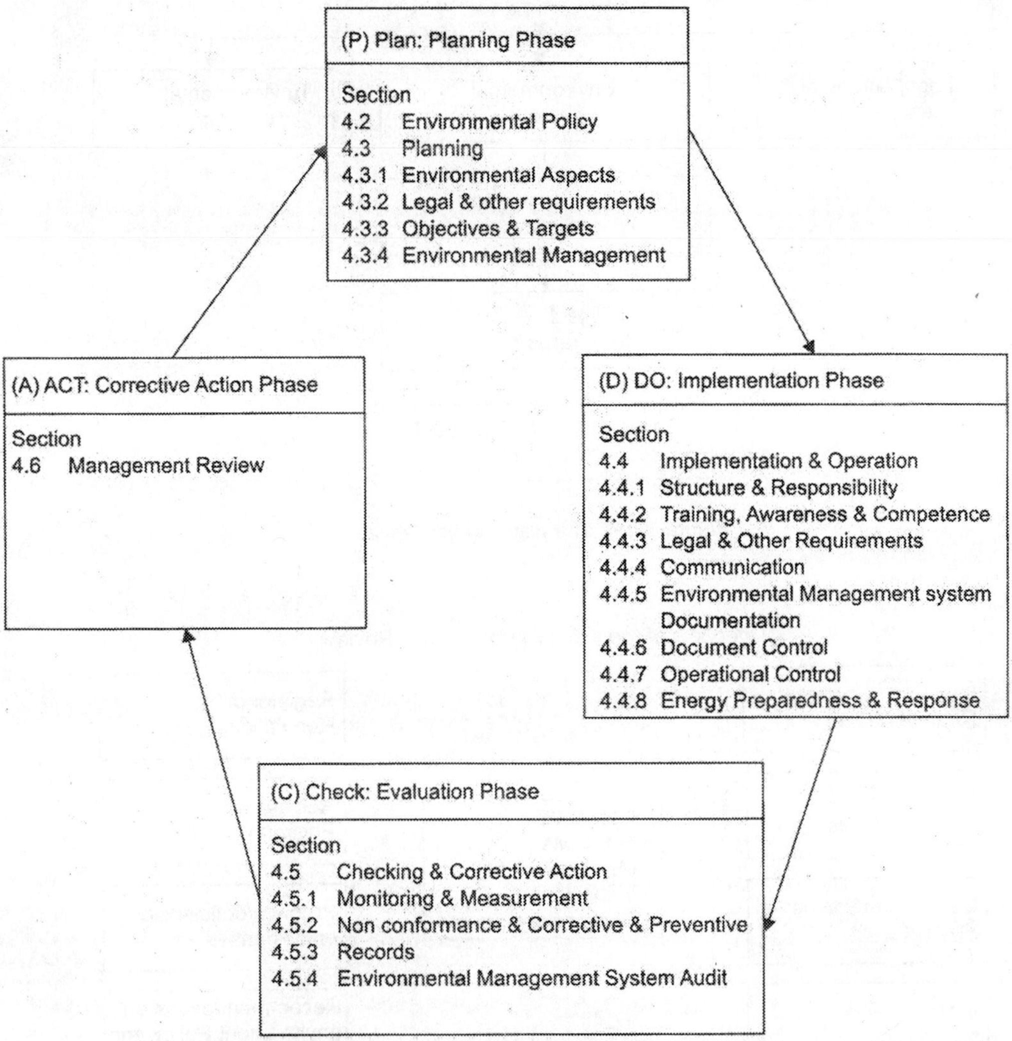

Figure 36. Demin's PDCA cycle (from Er. S.K. Guru)

Principle 9: Establish documentation concerning all procedures and record appropriate to these principles and their application.

Initial planning and review are very important for success of EMS. The planning and review flow sheets are given in Figure 37. The initial review will give the following points:

(i) Baseline for environmental management
(ii) Current and future legislative / regulatory requirements
(iii) Prioritisation of areas of significant risks

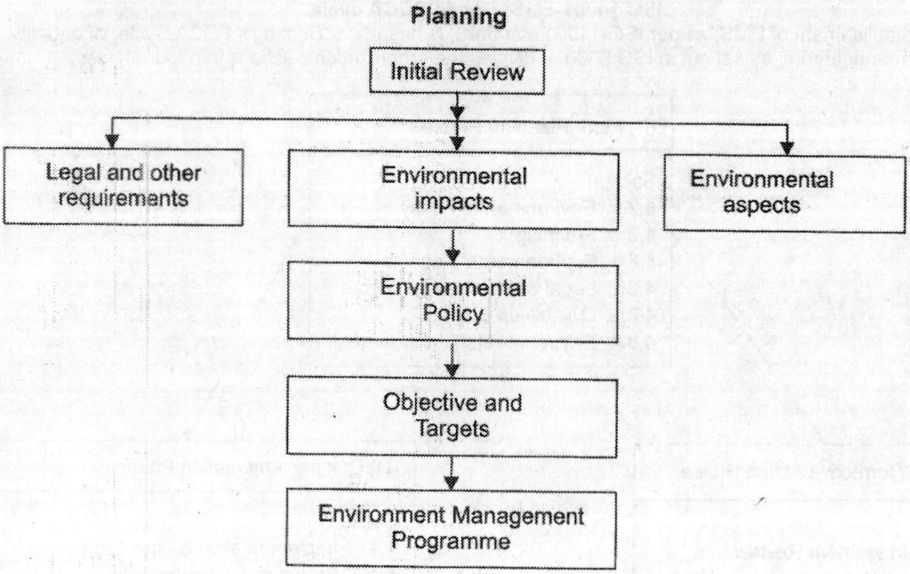

Figure 37(a). The planning flow sheet

Overview of the Initial Environmental Review

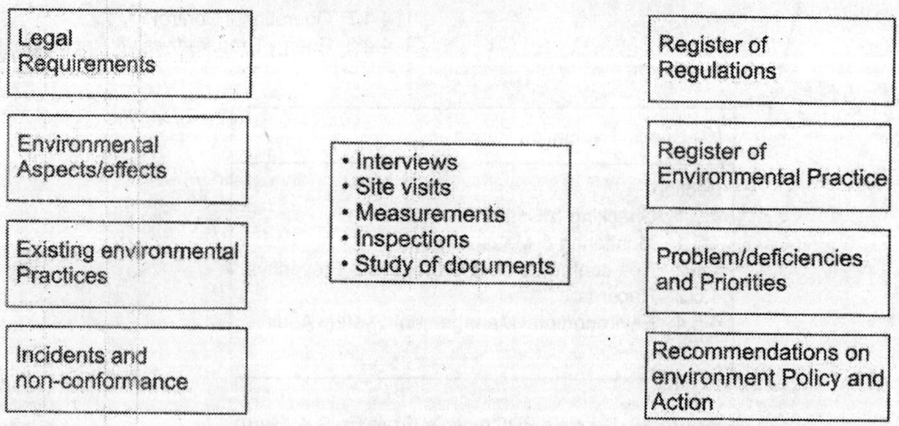

Figure 37(b). Overview of initial review flow sheet

(iv) Advance identification of potential problems
(v) Base for effective ongoing appraisal environmental performance.
(vi) Are perceived to be significant by public or customer.
(vii) Restrict future development of the company.

3.7 EMS CERTIFICATION

For organizations that sell their goods or services internationally, EMS certification could be a strong selling instrument in the global market. Organization that provides goods or services to government agencies may be granted 'preferred supplier status' if they implement an effective EMS. In view of this, EMS Certification may result in a competitive advantage for organizations that have achieved it. For good community relations, EMS certification may act as a vehicle to improve or maintain the public image. The requirements for ISO 14001 certification involves many steps namely: (i) identification of environmental aspects; (ii) initial environmental review; (iii) evaluation of significant environmental aspects and their impacts; (iv) framing environmental policy; (v) setting environmental objectives and targets; (vi) preparation of environmental programmes (EMP); (vii) preparation of EMS policy manual, EMS procedures and operational control procedures for all identified significant environmental aspects; (viii) preparation of environmental legal register; (ix) maintaining environmental records pertaining to all activities having environmental impacts; (x) environmental training and awareness; (xi) environmental communications; (xii) emergency preparedness and response; (xiii) environmental monitoring and measurement; (xiv) evaluation of compliance to legal and other requirements; (xv) non-conformity, corrective action and preventive action; (xvi) conducting internal EMS audit at periodic interval; (xvii) conductis management review at periodic interval; (xviii) conduc pre-certification audit by the certifying body and (xix) conducting certification audit and certification by the certifying body.

The details are given below in the flow sheets (Figures 38 and 39).

Besides, environmental management system also includes **occupational health survey assessment** (OHSAS-18001). After 1947, the industrial sector in India has grown multifold and there is a large population involved in industrial work. The health requirement of the population involved in industrial work involves diverse aspects of health problems depending upon the type of industry or the type of occupation. Occupational health has become more and more important at the workplace and occupational health has direct linkage with the business performance of the companies. The impact of occupational diseases in India is 4 to 6 percent of the turnover of the companies. Globally over two million people suffer from work related diseases and permanent or temporary disabilities. About six thousand people die every year from occupational injuries. World Bank estimates that about 2/3rd of the people suffering from occupational disabilities could be treated by adopting sound occupational health and safety programmes. In view of this, engineering controls, equipment designing in mining, ergonomic intervention in buildings, adoption of eye safety, adopting safety procedures to avoid falls in mining and falls from elevators, electrical accidents, periodical monitoring of hazardous gas leakage, etc., can play defying role in safety and prevention. Emergency preparedness and response is another key area.

In many countries, one of the unorganized sector concerns is the 'black lung' (coal workers pneumoconiosis), a serious lung disease caused by inhaling excessive quantity of coal dust. Various forms of pneumoconiosis are caused by inhaling dusts containing metallic and non metallic particles of aluminium, antimony, iron, barium, graphite, kaolin, mica, talc, etc. Therefore–occupational health survey is very important for taking remedial measures.

The requirements for OHSAS 18001 certification are: (i) gap analysis; (ii) identification of occupational health hazards; (iii) evaluation of significant OHS hazards and risks; (iv) framing

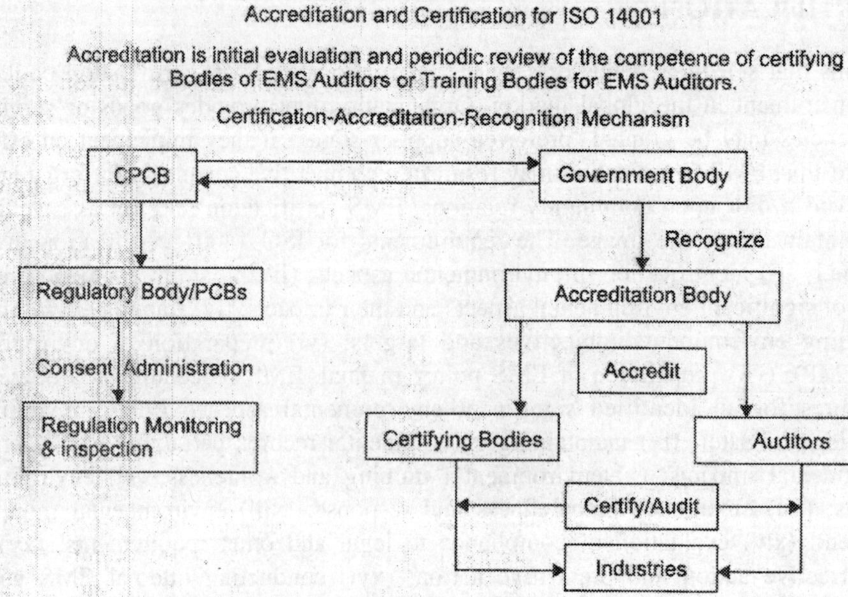

Figure 38. Flow sheet of EMS certification

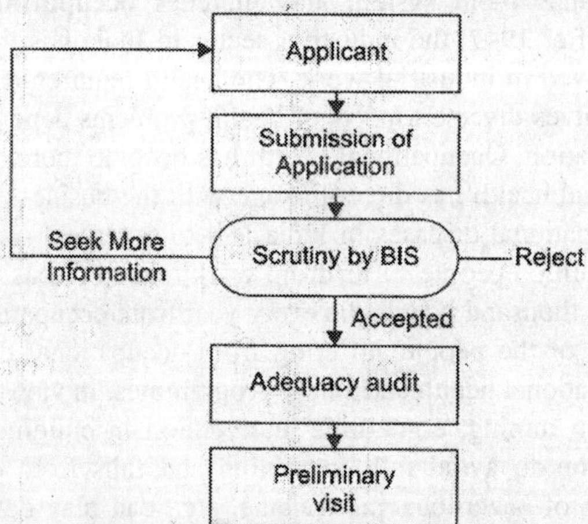

Figure 39. Process of EMS certification

OHS policy; (v) setting OHS objectives and targets; (vi) preparation of OHS management programme; (vii) preparation of OHS policy manual, occupational health survey manual (OHSM) procedures and operational control procedures for all identified significant hazards; (viii) preparation of OHS legal register; (ix) maintaining OHS records pertaining to all activities having environmental impact; (x) OHS training and awareness; (xi) OHS communication; (xii) emergency preparedness and response; (xiii) OHS monitoring and measurement; (xiv) evaluation of compliance to legal and other requirements; (xv) non-conformity, corrective action and preventive action; (xvi) conducting internal occupational survey-management; (xvii) conducting management review periodically; (xviii) conducting precertification audit by the certifying body and (xix) conducting certification audit and certification by the certification body.

3.7.1 Environmental Management Systems adopted Case Study

Hindalco-Hirakud Power: This is a coal-based thermal power plant.

About Hindalco Industries, Hirakud Power

This is a Captive Thermal Power Plant of 367.5 MW capacity with four units

First Thermal Power Plant deployed various systems as listed below:

(i) QMS (ISO-9001:2000) (ii) EMS (ISO-14001:2004), (iii) OH & S (OHSAS-18001:2007), WCM (World Class Manufacturing): Received many accolades to their credit

- Energy Award CII
- Best EHS award from CII
- British Sword of Honor in Safety
- Rajiv Gandhi Environmental Award for Cleaner Technology from Government of India.

Technology

- 1st Power Plant in India to adopt Clean Coal "CFBC Technology"
- Designed, Installed and Operating the high efficiency ESPs (> 99.9 % Efficiency)
- 1st Power Plant in India to opt for Complete Dry Ash (Both Bottom and Fly Ash) Collection, Handling and Disposal System.

Unique installation of Bag Filters at all Coal Transfer Points including Secondary Crusher House along with dust suppression and dust extraction systems.

(i) Review of its Process/Inputs/Outputs etc. through employee participation
(ii) Formulation of Environmental Policy related to its activities
(iii) Preparation of Initial Environmental Review (IER) through data collection (both Internal/External)
(iv) Identification of environmental aspects and impacts
(v) Identification of significant environmental aspects based on matrix system

Environment Management in Coal fired Thermal Power Plant: The Issues are listed point wise

The Major Environmental Issues are: (i) Air Pollution, (ii) Water Pollution, (iii) Solid waste Pollution, (iv) Thermal Pollution, and (v) Noise Pollution. The pollutants associated with coal burning are: Sulphur Dioxide, Oxides of Nitrogen, and Carbon dioxide and particulate matter.

Action Taken

(a) Air Pollution Control instruments are used to arrest air pollution. The instruments are: (Emission standard -World Bank, Particulate matter (max) - 50 micrograms per cubic metre): Electrostatic Precipitators, Low NOX burners, Flue gas stack, Dry ash extraction (b) Water pollution control is done by the industry by installing the following facilities: Coal/oil setting pits, Ash dykes and disposal systems, ash water recycling system, effluent treatment plant (ETP).

The ash left behind after combustion of coal is arrested in high efficiency electrostatic precipitators (ESP) and particulate emission is controlled well within the stipulated norms. The ash collected in the ESP is disposed, mostly to ash ponds in slurry form. Dry ash collection and handling systems have now been installed.

Flue Gas Stack

Stack height (in meters): Central Pollution Control stipulated guideline is given below.

- 500 MW and above - 275
- 200 MW and less than 500 MW - 220
- Less than 200 MW

$$H = 14\,(Q)^{0.3}$$

where H = stack height in m

and Q = emission rate of SO_2 in kg/hr

Tall flue gas stack as per the above guidelines is provided by Hindalco Industries, Hirakud for wide dispersion of gaseous emission (SO_2, NO_2 etc.) into atmosphere.

Low Knox Burners

KNO_x emissions are controlled by provision of low NO burners 22 The standard as mentioned below is maintained by adopting best combustion practices.

Emission standards – World Bank

(In micrograms per cubic meter)

NO : 100 2 SO : 80 2

Coal & Oil Settling Pits

In coal and oil settling pits, coal dust and oil are removed from the effluents from coal handling plant, coal yard and fuel oil handling areas before bing discharged into effluent treatment plant (ETP).

Ash Dykes and Ash Disposal System

Ash ponds are provided for ash disposal

Ash ponds are divided into lagoons and provided with garlanding arrangements for changeover of the ash slurry feed points for even filling of the pond and for effective disposal of ash particles.

Ash in slurry form is discharged into the lagoons where ash particles settle from the slurry and clear effluent water is discharged from ash ponds.

Dry Ash Extraction System has been installed

Dry ash is having much higher utilization potential in ash based products, e.g.,

- Land reclamation.
- Structural land filling.
- Road making.

- Cement manufacturing.
- Bricks manufacturing.

Neutralization Pits

- Neutralization pits are provided in water treatment plant (WTP) for pH correction of effluents before discharged into effluent treatment plant (ETP) for further treatment and use.

Source of liquid effluents generated by the Captive Power Plant

- Cooling tower blow down.
- Boiler- blow down.
- Power area service water waste.
- Water treatment plant waste.
- DM plant regeneration plant.
- Coal handling plant/ash handling plant waste.
- Effluent from silo area

Effluent Treatment Plant (ETP)

- The objective of industrial liquid effluent treatment plant (ETP) is to discharge clean effluent from the power plants to meet environmental standards and to reduce intae water requirement.
- The scheme involves collection of various effluents and their appropriate treatment centrally and recirculation of the treated effluent for various plant uses.

(c) Thermal Pollution Control

Thermal Pollution

- Cooling towers are provided for cooling the hot condenser cooling water in closed cycle condenser cooling water system. This helps in reduction in thermal pollution and conservation of fresh water.

(d) Noise Pollution Control

- The entire plant is so procured/installed that resultant noise level within the premises remains with in standard limits.

The standard for industrial area - 70 dB maximum outside the project property boundary. The industry meets this standard.

3.8 MANAGERIAL SYSTEM: ENVIRONMENTAL ACCOUNTING

Environmental costs and performance require attention for numerous reasons:

(i) Sound business decisions like good housekeeping, reduced operational costs, technology change, redesigning manufacturing process/products, etc., can reduce or eliminate environmental costs.
(ii) Generating revenue through waste utilization or transferable pollution allowances or even using clean technologies can reduce environmental costs.
(iii) By adopting improved environmental performance and benefits to human health and reduces environmental costs.
(iv) By designing preferable processes, products and services, environmental costs can be reduced.
(v) By adopting ISO 14001 standards and demonstrating environmental sound management and discipline will reduce environmental costs.

3.8.1 Classification of Costs

(i) Direct costs of materials and labour
(ii) Factory overhead or manufacturing costs other than material and labur cost
(iii) Sales
(iv) General and administrative overhead
(v) Research and development
(vi) Creating awareness among the employees and the immediate surroundings.

Environmental expenses may be classified in any or all of these categories. Costs incurred with implementation of environmental laws clearly come under environmental costs.

Costs of environmental remediation, pollution control equipment are both environmental costs. Sometimes, however, questions arise whether costs of adoption of clean technology can be considered environmental costs. But then, adopting clean technology industry may get other forms of incentives from regulating agencies and reduce the energy cost. Environmental accounting is a flexible tool and can be applied to:

(i) Production line (process change)
(ii) System line (waste management, energy use – lighting, packaging, etc.)
(iii) Product line (improving product quality, changing the product)
(iv) Facility improvement
(v) Corporate affiliation

Environmental accounting brings the environmental costs to the attention of corporate stakeholders who can be motivated to identify ways of reducing these costs and simultaneously improving environmental quality. Thus, environmental accounting is an important component of overall corporate environmental management, quality management and cost management.

3.9 MANAGERIAL SYSTEM: ENVIRONMENTAL AUDIT

Environmental audit is a basic management tool comprising systematic, documented, periodic and objective evaluation of an organization.

3.9.1 Definition of Environmental Audit

International Chamber of Commerce has defined environmental auditing as *a management tool comprising a systematic, documented, periodic and objective evaluation of how well environmental organization, management and equipment are performing with the aim of helping to regulate the environment by facilitating management control of environmental practices.*

3.9.2 Objectives of Environmental Audit

(i) Waste minimization
(ii) Waste utilization
(iii) Energy and resource conservation
(iv) Reduction of materials
(v) Improvement of environmental condition.

Establishing firm audit objectives is key to a successful environmental audit programme. The following factors are to be considered to establish audit objectives:

- Management concerns and motivation
- Type and size of the industry to be audited
- Regulatory compliance
- Level of environmental performance achieved
- Comparison with best practice environmental audit should be a combination of: (i) pollution audit, (ii) pollution prevention audit, (iii) waste minimization audit, and (iv) environmental management system audit.

The other important aspects are:

(i) Assessing the probable risks/hazards associated with the malfunctioning of the pollution control equipment, and evaluation of the adequacy of environmental plans and procedures
(ii) Assessing the scale of optimum utilization of the resources and evaluating the relative position and orientation of the company within and at national and international levels with regard to environmental safeguards, pollution minimization, etc.
(iii) Improving energy utilization.
(iv) Establishing performance baselines and evaluation of actual performance.
(v) Setting priorities and plans for future environmental establishments by analyzing the variances, shortcomings and plus points and corrective procedures.
(vi) Increasing the awareness of employees by educating them about their role and responsibility in protecting the environment.

3.9.3 Types of Environmental Audit

Environmental audit follows three basic stages such as pre-audit, site visit and post-audit and involves the following types of audits.

(i) Pre set-up audit
(ii) Impact assessment audit
(iii) Compliance audit

(iv) Evaluation of awareness
(v) Green audit

Pre-audit is a planning of the audit programme and site visit includes meeting with staff, inspection, examination of records, identifying the source of waste generation, existing pollution control measures, available monitoring facilities, etc. The post-audit activity involves a written assessment of the facilities compliance status, which also includes recommendation to correct deficiencies. The most important part is the active and meaningful participation of the industry personnel during the environmental audit so as to develop a meaningful environmental audit report.

3.9.4 Environmental Audit Practices in Industrialized Developed Countries

The environmental audit undertaken in the developed countries has basically two components:

1. Assessment—to determine pollution level, hazard identification, assessing energy conservation, etc.
2. Verification—evaluation of environmental policies and procedures including compliance status.

Range of audit objectives includes:

- Identifying the documents
- Improving overall environmental performance
- Better understanding and interpretation
- Increase of overall environmental awareness
- Accelerating overall development of EMS
- Improving environmental risk management system

Audit Methodology:

1. Pre-audit activity
   - Scheduling and selecting the audit team
   - Reviewing background information
   - Planning
2. On-site activity
   - Interviewing site personnel
   - Assessment of pollution level
   - Reviewing documents
3. Post-audit activity
   - Determining solution and assigning responsibility
   - Implementing corrective action and follow-up

3.9.5 Environmental Audit Practice in India

The environmental audit in India is termed as environmental statement, prepared in form-V since 1993 and submitted every year by the industries requiring consent under Section 25 of the Water (prevention and control of pollution) Act 1974 and under Section 21 of the Air Act 1981 and under the Hazardous Waste Rules 1989 issued under Environment (protection) Act of 1986.

Form –V for environmental statement:
The prescribed proforma has nine parts (A to I)

Part A: industry description, production capacity, etc.

Part B: water and raw material consumption per unit of product output.

Part C: pollution discharge to environment with reason of variation from prescribed standard.

Part D: hazardous waste from process and pollution control system.

Part E: solid waste from process and pollution control system indicating quantity recycled.

Part F: characteristics and composition of hazardous and solid wastes indicating disposal practice.

Part G: impact of pollution control measures on conservation of natural resources and cost of production.

Part H: additional/investment proposals for environmental protection and abatement of pollution.

Part I: other particulars related to improvement of the quality of the environment.

3.9.6 Benefits of Environmental Audit

The primary advantage is to help protect the environment and ensure adequate and proper compliance with regulatory agencies along with proper implementation of standards and company policy. It helps reduce social resistance, litigation and regulatory risk through an independent verification and provides a timely warning system to the management of the company to take remedial measures. It helps identify potential cost savings, energy conservation and waste minimization and utilization. It helps interchange of information between units of the same industry and even on a wider scale between similar industries.

It evaluates training programmes of the staff and their utility. It brings awareness of environmental policies between staff and generates an information base for disaster management.

The environmental audit has a great potential for resource conservation, waste minimization to achieve better productivity and improved environmental condition.

3.10 ENVIRONMENTAL MANAGEMENT: SUSTAINABLE MINING

Mining and mineral based industries are vital for the economic growth especially for developing countries such as India. The products from mining sector provide inputs for a host of other industries. The extent of utilization of mineral resources to generate value added products is an index of prosperity of any country and its people. Huge foreign investments flow to this sector. The importance of the sectorin Indian national economy andits impact on the environment, economy, ecology and society, are significant. No wonder, the sector also attracts attention and concern of all stake holders.

The way minerals are mined, processed and wastes disposed off can leave deep scars on the earth's surface and permanently damage the ecological and social systems. Naturally, these damages inhibit achievement of real and long term prosperity by the affected population. Scientific mineral survey in India was stated in 1851 by the Geological Survey of India. Geological mapping includes the search for mineral resources and the mapping has been completed for 98% of the total mappable areaof the country (SGAT, 2009).

India produces 89 minerals including four fuel minerals, 52 non-metallic minerals, 11 metallic minerals and 22 minor minerals. India stood as world's largest producer of mica blocks and mica splitting and ranked second in the production of chromites, third in coal and lignite, and barites; fifth in iron ore, sixth in bauxite and manganese ore, eleventh in aluminium and twelfth in crude steel in the world (IBM, 1999). With its contribution of about 16 percent in exports and 20 percent in imports, the mineral sector is an important component of India's foreign trade.

Between 1950 and 1991, mining displaced about 2.6 million people—note even 25 percent of these displaced have been rehabilitated. About 52 percent of these displaced were tribal. For every 1 percent that mining contributes to India's GDP, it displaces 3-4 times more people than all the development projects put together. Forest land diversion for mining has been going up. So has water use and air pollution in the mining hotspots. An estimated 1.64 lakh hectare of forest land has already been diverted for mining in the country. For instance, the forests in Burdwan have been decimated by mining. Iron ore mining in India used up 77 million tonnes of water in 2005-06, enough to meet the daily water needs of more than 3 million people. (Misra, 2008).

Mining of major minerals generated about 1.84 billion tonnes of waste in 2006, most of which has not been disposed of properly. Coal is the main mineral and every ton of coal extracted generates 3-4 tons or more of overburden.

Mining is being promoted in the country for the mineral resources for other industries and for generation of employment. The mining industry in India is gradually getting mechanized. Odisha, Jharkhand, Karnataka, Chhattisgarh and some other states are the main states where mining activities have drawn national attention.

3.10.1 Sustainability of Mining

Sustainability requires that human activity only utilizes nature's resources at a rate at which it can be replenished naturally. It is the ability to sustain a way of life indefinitely. It is the practical ability to satisfy the basic needs of today without compromising the ability of future generations to satisfy their needs.

Mining cannot be sustainable as per the Brundtland Commission's definition or truly environmentfriendly:

(i) Because all ore bodies are finite and non-renewable and

(ii) Because even the best managed mines leave "environmental footprints".

However, the principle of recycle, reuse, husbanding of resources as per actual need, application of proper technology, etc., form the basis of sustainability. Because of the development of technology, metals are now recyclable to a large extent. It is also a fact of life that mining and minerals are necessary for the existence of human civilization. The issue is not whether mining should be undertaken or not. Rather, it is about "how and how much" should be undertaken. It is about ensuring that mining is conducted in an environmentally and socially acceptable and environmentally friendly manner. Therefore, the key is *responsible mining for sustainable development*. This is only possible when the mineral deposits are explored thoroughly and their extraction and utilization strategy is planned centrally for a gradual transformation of the resource economy to a knowledge economy to produce value added products. The **three pillars of mining** sustainability are **environmental protection, increasing national economy** and **societal welfare**.

The 2005 World Summit in New York declared that actions on sustainability must involve cooperation across three sustainability "pillars" – environment, economy and society.

Environment Pillar: Impact on earth is being manifested through changes in the chemicals that are critical to life – water, oxygen, carbon and nitrogen. Mining affects it seriously, hence environmental friendly mining is important.

Economic Pillar: We can maintain and improve our standard of living by protecting both economy and the environment. Environmental taxes and incentives, carbon trading, etc., are the present market strategies. Sharing values is the key for sustainability.

Social Pillar: Although environmental, social and economic factors are closely interconnected, the areas having a strong social dimension are rehabilitation of displaced people due to mining and providing them alternate livelihood options, maintaing peace and security.

3.10.2 Mining Industry

The fixed location of the mineralized zone of interest imposes a constraint on all aspects of mining developments including the method of mining, location of mine facilities, requirements for new infrastructure and services (or conflict with existing infrastructure), and the suitability of waste management or disposal methods. This in turn, profoundly influences the environment, especially biodiversity, and water and air quality, also changes the livelihood options, and health impacts of mining developments, as well as the economic viability of developing a given mineralized zone.

Impact of the Mining Sector

On the positive side, if implemented responsibly, the mining industry creates employment, transfer of technology and skill sets, development of local infrastructure and services attract extractive and downstream investments that can create a multiplier effect in the local economy and augment the development process.

Waste from mining operations (i.e., waste from extraction and processing of mineral resources) is one of the largest waste streams to handle. It involves materials that are removed to gain access to the mineral resource, such as top soil, overburden and waste rock, as well as tailings remaining after minerals have been largely extracted from the ore. Some of these wastes are inert and hence not likely to represent a significant pollutant threat to the environment, save for smothering of river beds and possible collapse if stored in large quantities. However, other fractions, in particular those generated by the non-ferrous metal mining industry, may contain large quantities of dangerous substances, such as heavy metals. Through the extraction and subsequent mineral processing, metals and metal compounds tend to become chemically more available, which can result in the generation of acid or alkaline drainage. Moreover, the management of tailings is an intrinsically risky activity, often involving residual processing chemicals and elevated levels of metals. In many cases, tailings are stored on heaps or in large ponds, where they are retained by means of dams. The collapse of dams or heaps may have serious impacts on environment and human health and safety. Examples of this are the accidents in Aberfan (Wales, 1966), Stava (Italy, 1985), Aznalcóllar (Spain, 1998), Baia Mare and Baia Borsa (Romania, 2000). Other likely significant impacts relate to the physical footprints of waste disposal facilities and resulting loss of land productivity, effects on ecosystems, dust and erosion.

These impacts can have lasting environmental and socio-economic consequences and be extremely difficult and costly to address through remedial measures. Wastes from the mining and the mineral industries have, therefore, to be properly managed in order to ensure in particular the long-term stability of disposal facilities and to prevent or minimize any water and soil pollution arising from acid or alkaline drainage and leaching of heavy metals.

Promoting Sustainable Development

The role of mining in sustainable development is one issue that decision makers and resource managers have wrestled with for decades. With the development of their income-accounting tool, it can be attempted to show how mining activities, which have a finite life span, can be integrated with social and environmental concerns in a way that promotes long-term community development.

The approach adopted can place a monetary value on the effects of mining, such as air and water pollution, loss of forests, groundwater depletion, mineral resource use, and reduced agricultural productivity. It also takes into account the direct and indirect benefits to society. TERI used similar accounting practices to place values on the health and social costs of mining. To ensure the economic viability of communities after the resource has been exhausted, money would be set aside to finance human and community development. Considering the growing future needs and security of the supply of minerals, India needs to enhance its resource base considerably through various options including intensive exploration drive, improving the recovery and production from the existing resource base and ensuring supplies through imports. While technically robust approaches to managing and mitigating the environmental impacts of mining are well developed, socio-economic issues associated with mining present significant unresolved challenges. Policy initiatives are needed to meet the challenges.

Adoption and observation of the following mining laws is the first requirement to attain sustainable development. These laws are: (i) The Mines Act, 1952, (ii) The Mines and Minerals (Development and Regulation) Act, 1957, (iii) The Forest Conservation Act, 1980, amended in 1988, National Forest Policy, 1988, National Forest Policy, forest related Schedule Tribe Act, 2006, (iv) The Environment (Protection) Act, 1986. Besides the policy initiatives such as: (a) Recognizing people's right to say 'no' (mining should not take place without the consent of the people). The people must understand the disadvantages and advantages of mining in a particular place and the environmental problems and livelihood options associated with the area if mining does not happen or if mining is allowed; (b) Independent, impartial preparation of Environmental Impact Assessment (EIA) reports. (c) Disallowing mining in forests to the extent practicable. Fixing stringent conditions of compensatory aforestation in immediate vicinity to sustain forest cover. (d) Framing stronger and scientific mine closure regulations, (e) "Doing more with less" —a key to sustainable development. National policy on sustained availability of mineral resources for the future generation. For every mineral, a national target plan for mining keeping the present needs and future needs in mind, may be prepared and action should be taken accordingly. (f) Policy framework for value addition in the local area to ensure sustained economic prosperity.

Policies and guidelines must include

(a) Policy and procedures for environmental assessment, whereby potential impacts are taken into account in selecting, sizing, planning and designing projects. Government to prepare, implement and maintain environmental action plans.

(b) Policy to promote economically viable, environmentally sustainable and socially equitable water management.

(c) Policy to ensure that indigenous people benefit from development projects and the adverse effects are avoided or mitigated. Pragmatic policy and procedures towards displaced persons in projects involving involuntary resettlement. Policy on forest sector leading to reduced deforestation, enhanced environmental contribution of forests, promotion of aforestation, reducing poverty, and encouragement to economic development. Policy to support protection, maintenance, and rehabilitation of natural habitats.

In the light of the above discussions, it would be appropriate to have a discussion on the state of mining and mineral industry in states and the sustainability criteria. Odisha state has abundant reserves of coal, iron ore, bauxite, limestone, dolomite, manganese, chromites, etc. Jharsuguda and Angul (Talcher) districts having abundant coal reserves, have attracted massive investments in power, aluminium and steel (including sponge iron) sectors. Sundargarh, Keonjhar and Mayurbhanj districts have substantial limestone and dolomite, iron ore and manganese deposits that attracted lot of investment in mining, iron and steel sectors. The Jajpur Keonjhar-Dhenkanal districts have iron and chromite deposits and have seen a surge in mining activities along with the growth of iron and steel, ferro alloys industries.

Sustainable mining would lead to the following progressive benefits to the local population:

(i) Improvement of infrastructure and services resulting in local area development.

(ii) Restoration of the mined out area to its original natural state.

(iii) Improvement of skill sets of local population.

(iv) Employment generation.

(v) Opportunities for self-employment.

(vi) Growth of value added downstream production units.

(vii) Transition from resource economy to knowledge economy to take care of the needs of the area after the resources are exhausted.

The objective of mining the local resources, in a democracy, should be to develop the long term economy of the local area in a progressive manner and not to greedily exploit the innocent local population. It is high time for the intelligentsia, the industrial authorities, the trade unions and the governments to seriously consider and debate over the vital issues and prefer a sustainable development model of mineral development for long term benefit of the people.

Regulatory Framework for Environment-friendly Mining

Presently, in India many legislations deal with environmental pollution or degradation. However, three major comprehensive anti-pollution laws were enacted by the Parliament as part of environmental crusade which was launched with Stockholm Man and Environment Conference, organized by UNO in 1972. These laws are:

(i) Water (Prevention and Control of Pollution) Act, 1974,
(ii) Air (Prevention and Control of Pollution) Act, 1981,
(iii) Environment (Protection) Act, 1986.

These are enacted with a view to combat environmental degradation and restore clean environment. The water (PCP) Act, 1974 and Air (PCP) Act, 1981 create separate corporate bodies at centre as well as at state levels, namely Central Pollution Control Boards (CPCBs) and State Pollution Control Boards (SPCBs) to carry forward the legislative objective and to achieve the desired goal. Chapter (iii) and (iv) of Water and Air Acts respectively lay down the powers and functions of CPCB and SPCB. However, a glance over the relevant sections reveals that, in fact, the SPCB is the main regulatory agency under these Acts. Of the numerous tasks of SPCB, the following are the main ones:

(i) To plan a comprehensive programme for prevention, control or abatement of water and air pollution.
(ii) To collect and disseminate information relating to water and air pollution.
(iii) To give advice to the state government relating to any matter for prevention, control or abatement of pollution in water and air and regarding location of industrial establishments.

In addition to this SPCB also discharges three more important functions:

(a) Lay down, modify and annual standards of water and air quality.
(b) Inspect periodically the industrial and treatment plants.
(c) Revoke orders for discharge of pollutants into streams and atmosphere by taking into account the tolerance limit.

To carry out these functions, SPCBs have been vested with ample powers on them. Some of them are:

(i) To obtain information from the occupier of any industrial establishment about discharge of pollutants in water and atmosphere,
(ii) To enter any place to inspect to verify whether any notice or direction issued under the Act has been complied with or not,
(iii) To collect sample of effluents or emission for analysis. The results of such scientific analysis or investigation are admissible as evidence in judicial process,
(iv) To issue any direction (including closure) in case severe pollution is caused or envisaged to be caused,
(v) To prosecute the polluters in the court of law.

Besides, for new mines, EIA stipulations bring some eco-friendly actions. EIA clearance from the central government is required for 8 categories of projects which can be broadly categorized under the following sectors:

(i) Mining and extractive industries and power generation,
(ii) Primary mineral processing,
(iii) Material production like metallurgical industries,
(iv) Material processing like petroleum refinery, etc.

(v) Manufacturing and fabrication,
(vi) Service sectors,
(vii) Physical infrastructure and environmental services,
(viii) Construction and area development.

In the recent EIA notification (2006), the projects are designated as category A or category B projects on the basis of their size. Category A projects are required to obtain environmental clearance from Central Impact Assessment Authority after appraisal by a Central Expert Appraisal Committee and similarly category B projects require clearance from State level Impact Assessment Authority after appraisal by the State level Expert Appraisal Committee. For B category projects, EIA is not needed if in the opinion of the State Expert Appraisal Committee it falls within B1 category. The notification states that the requirement of EIA can be dispensed with by the impact assessment agency (IAA), which presently is under the MoEF. Environmental appraisal committees constituted by the MoEF for B1 category of projects.The MoEF has developed a generic structure for the preparation of EIA reports, however detail scooping is to be done by the Expert Appraisal Committee (either Central or State level depending upon the category of the proposed project) on the basis of the questionnaires and checklists (Form-I). The State Pollution Control Boards (SPCBs) in close coordination with the District Administration will conduct the public hearing for the proposed project before the proposals are sent to the MoEF for obtaining environmental clearance. In the environmental clearance process, the documents to be submitted to the MoEF are project report, the public hearing report, site clearance or site specific projects, an environmental appraisal questionnaire, the EIA/ Environmental Management Plan (EMP) Report, risk analysis for projects involving hazardous substances, and rehabilitation plans if more than 1000 people are likely to be displaced.

Role of SPCB in regulating environmental pollution

With the above powers and functions, SPCB carries out various strategies to regulate the process of industrialization, so that the environmental impact of the industrial/mining process remains minimal. The strategy of SPCB varies with the stages of industrial/mining process. For convenience these strategies have been broadly categorized as pre–establishment process, operating activity and post-operation phase activities.

Pre-establishment Phase

In pre-establishment phase SPCB carries out various functions to evaluate that the proposed industrial/mining activity at any place does not cause excessive pollution and it remains within the tolerance limit and also that the cumulative impact does not exceed to an extent that the damage is not reversible. This is based on "Precautionary Principle" of environmental law.

To ensure environmentally safe industrialization SPCB carries out the following functions:

(a) Preparation of comprehensive plans

SPCB carries out comprehensive environmental management plan for industrial or mining intensive regions. Depending upon the requirement SPCB prepares:

(a) Regional environmental management plans,
(b) Carrying capacity of an ecosystem/region study,

(c) Zoning Atlas,

(d) Environmental monitoring status report.

These studies indicate whether any particular type of mine can be established in a particular region or not. They also indicate the extent of mining that the region can sustain and provide an upper limit as "thus far and no further" for the process of industrialization. This can be considered a part of scientific mining or sustainable mining.

(b) Consent to Establish

Consent to establish is a process where the individual industry or mine proposed in an area is evaluated in detail for its likely environmental impact. In this process the proposed manufacturing process, pollution potential, adequacy of pollution control measures and soundness of environmental management practice is evaluated. In case it is found suitable SPCB stipulates adequate norms, prescribes proper management practices so that when the industry becomes operational, (consent is granted for operation) its environmental performance remains within the norms (Sahoo, 2011).

(c) Reclamation and Rehabilitation of Mines

Mineral Conservation and Development Rules, (MCDR) 1988, enacted in 2003 regulates the issue of reclamation and rehabilitation of mines. It has been made compulsory for every mine in the country to prepare progressive mine closure plan and final mine closure plan at the time of fresh grant or renewal of mining lease one year prior to the proposed closure of mine. Regional Controller of Mines, Indian Bureau of Mines (IBM) or the office authorized by the state government shall review and approve the plan. Besides, the rule 23F of MCDR stipulates that in case of failure to carry out reclamation and rehabilitation the surety amount of money.will be forfeited. The reclamation plan usually includes: (i) inside the mine, (ii) management of water body, (iii) management of roads, structures, etc., (iv) soil conservation measures, (v) plantations of trees, shrubs, and herbs keeping the soil quality and conditions, climate of the area. Post-mining land use is the defining factor for reclamation.

3.11 INDUSTRIAL SAFETY PRACTICES: DISASTER MANAGEMENT AND RISK ASSESSMENT ANALYSIS

The word disaster derives from the French word 'desastre' and Italian word 'diastro', which have originated from the Greek. The root of the word disaster ("badstar" in Greek) comes from an astrological theme in which the ancients used to refer to the destruction of a star as a disaster. World Health Organization (WHO) defines disaster as "any occurrence that causes damage, ecological disruption, loss of human life, deterioration of health and health services, on a scale sufficient to warrant an extraordinary response from outside the affected community or area". A disaster is an overwhelming ecological disruption occurring on a scale sufficient to require outside assistance. It is an event located in time and space which produces conditions whereby the continuity of structure and process of social units becomes problematic. In other words, a disaster is a seriously disrupting event or a series of events of abnormal activities.

Disasters can be natural or man-made. In the history of human evolution, many natural disasters such as droughts, floods, cyclones, landslides, earthquakes, volcanic eruptions, etc., have occurred and these natural disasters have caused immense loss to animals, plants, human life and their property. The frequency of occurrence and magnitude of damage have largely depended on climate change, tectonic movement of the earth and natural processes, which have not been well understood. Disasters are classified into: (i) geological such as earthquakes, volcanos eruptions, landslides, (ii) climatic such as cyclon, floods, droughts, etc., (iii) environmental fators such as deforestation desertification, etc., (iv) Epidemic like diseases, (v) technological or industrial such as Bhopal gas tragedy, etc.

Due to advancement of science and technology, it has been possible to predict climate change, occurrence of floods and volcanic eruptions, etc., and therefore remedial measures are taken to minimize loss of life and property. However, sometimes, prediction has failed causing colossal loss of human life and property.

India, after independence, has emerged as an industrial giant as many industries in metallurgy, petrochemicals, chemical food processing, railways-train, ship and aeroplane manufacturing and many other types of industries have come up since independence. This rapid growth of industries has involved utilizing, transporting, storing and disposing of resources, wastes and toxic chemicals.Therefore, technological or industrial disasters are becoming a frequent occurrence. Disasters, whether natural such as super cyclone which occurred in Odisha in 1999 and technological disasters like Bhopal methyl isocynate gas leak occured with negligible or no warning leaving behind a trail of suffering with huge loss of property and life, causing immense damage to the functioning of normal life. The role of district administration in natural and industrial disaster management is very important.

The industrial accidents have played a vital role in the economy of any country. According to an International Labour Organization (ILO) Report, every three minutes a worker dies somewhere in the world due to occupational injuries or illness, every second at least 4 workers are injured. India has one of the highest rates of industrial accidents. Over the last 30 years, nearly 36,000 workers have met with fatality and another 6.4 million were injured of industrial accidents. The industrial fatality in India is estimated to be 14 for every one lakh workers. This is 5 to 7 times higher than that prevailing in developed countries. This rate is 2 in case of Japan, 3 in case of the UK & the USA. Fatality rate in the unorganized sector, for which the statistics are not available, is many times higher than those prevailing in organized industry.

The subject matter of industrial safety and health have always been a matter of great concern for all of us, be it the governments, the managements or the unions. There has not only been a steady increase in the number of accidents, but also a rise in the accident rate. This leads us to a conclusion that, despite the bitter experiences like the Bhopal gas leakage in our own country, safety has not received its due importance yet. Textile, metallurgy, machinery manufacturing, chemicals and transport are most accident prone industries in the country.

Health and safety are definitely important concerns for industrial workers. We have seen many industrial injuries, fires and explosions taking place. Since accident prevention has been defined by management as an individual worker's responsibility, it is often a subject of employee involvement programmes. The most widespread employee involvement safety programmes are based on behaviour modification. These programmes use workers and supervisors to watch and document the behaviour of workers on safety observation forms. The goal is to reduce the (OSHA) recordable injury rate by changing the behaviour of workers. Companies selling these programmes include DuPont, Behavioural Science Technology (BST) and others. These programmes sometimes include the popular buzzwords: quality, cultural change, team work, jointness and empowerment. They promote union participation and sometimes include new full-time jobs for union representatives who help administer the programme. The union often creates a name for their local programme. Management may even agree not to use discipline when unsafe behaviour is observed.

International Labour Organization (ILO) has developed a powerful new programme for making fundamental improvements in health and safety. It is called the Triangle of Prevention Program (TOP). This is done by creating effective safety systems. A strong process safety management programme is one part of a systems approach to health and safety. Examples of safety systems include the safe design of processes and equipment, proper maintenance and inspection, and having effective procedures and training programmes.

3.11.1 Main Substances Causing Disaster

Five categories of substances cause major disasters. These are (i) flammable substances like gases and vapours such as LPG, ethylene, cyclohexane (hot), vinyl chloride, etc. The hazards are the fireballs including vapour cloud explosion (BLEVE), flash fire, pool fire, river of burning liquids, etc., (ii) highly reactive substances such as ammonium nitrate, sodium chlorate, which explodes if fire is involved, ethylene oxide, liquid oxygen and hydrogen, gunpowder, nitroglycerine, trinitrotoluene, RDX, etc., are highly explosive; (iii) toxic substances such as chlorine, sulphur dioxide, acid mist, toxic gas and vapour, methyl isocynate (MIC), dioxin, parathion, warfarin and phosgene are highly toxic to living systems; (iv) pathogens and mutagens which may cause diseases and mutations with short, long and very long effects; (v) radioactive isotopes have short, long, very long-term effects including genetic effects.

3.11.2 Accidents and Worker Error

When you read a newspaper account of an industrial accident it will almost always conclude that the cause of the accident was worker's error. In a society largely based on individualism the idea that worker mistakes are the primary cause of accidents rings true with most people. There is no denying that workers make mistakes. However, in every industrial accident there are almost always several management safety systems involved which may not be readily apparent.

The Center for Chemical Process Safety (CCPS), of the American Institute of Chemical Engineers is an industry sponsored publisher of widely used safety guidelines. They state that: "An axiom of incident investigation is that process safety incidents are the result of management system failure... Of course, many causes of incidents can be attributed ... to equipment breakdown or operator error. However, experienced incident investigators know that such specific failures are but the immediate causes of an incident and that underlying each such immediate cause is a management system failure, such as faulty design or inadequate training. It is from identifying the underlying causes that the most benefit is gained." (Technical Management of Chemical Process Safety, CCPS, pages 113-114).

"Rather than being the main instigators of an accident, operators tend to be the inheritors of system defects created by poor design, incorrect installation, faulty maintenance and bad management decisions. Their part is usually that of adding the final garnish to a lethal brew whose ingredients have already been long in the cooking." ("Preventing Accidents at Oil and Chemical Plants" by Najedin Meshkati, Chemical Safety November, 1990).

3.11.3 Basic Principles of Controlling Technological Hazards

The basic principles are: (i) avoidance of hazards occurring by using safer chemicals, if available and operating in lower pressure and temperature if possible, (ii) prevention of hazard by improving detection technology/procedure, regular maintenance, relief side layout, practicing mock drills, etc., periodically, (iii) taking steps to mitigate to reduce the impact by practicing on-site and off-site emergency plans.

Practical measures for controlling technological disasters can be as follows:

3.11.4 Safety is Downsized

Cost-cutting mania is sweeping through modern corporate houses. Spending on health and safety is not immune from the budget slashing axe. In the plants, corporate managers often tell workers that no expense will be spared in maintaining a safe workplace. Workers are told that safety is a win-win, non-adversarial issue which is in the mutual interests of both the management and the labour. Meanwhile, these same corporations are using their vast wealth to lobby the government to eliminate health and safety regulations and enforcement in the name of world competition and cost-cutting.

Corporate reengineering also has deadly consequences beyond the plant gate. It has even hit the medical care system. Sometime back, it was in the newspaper that one patient had the wrong leg amputated and another died when his respiratory machine was turned off by mistake. Clearly, doctors and nurses made serious errors, but these errors were set-up by a medical care system that is being downsized. This is a common occurrence in developing countries.

3.11.5 What is a Safe Workplace?

The dominant model of safety in the country says that an injury free workplace is a safe workplace. Therefore, a low frequency/severity rate of accident demonstrates that a workplace is safe. Having zero worker injuries is a worthy goal, but creating a safe workplace requires much more.

In 1994, an industrial unit in Ohio, USA, celebrated because of the fact that they had gone two million work hours without a lost work day injury. A major fire on the crude oil processing unit which had occurred during the award-winning period did not detract from the safety record. No one was seriously hurt in the fire. At a huge Texas plant, a release and fire caused hundreds of citizens living near the facility to seek medical treatment for possible exposure to hazardous materials. But since no workers were injured, the plant's safety record remained unblemished.

In the majority of potentially catastrophic chemical releases and fires there are no OSHA recordable injuries. Often the only thing that prevents fatalities and injuries is sheer luck. The wind direction was favourable or workers had just left the area before an explosion. When we measure safety by using the injury rate we get a very distorted view of actual safety conditions in industries. The primary theory used to explain the causes of industrial accidents is that mistakes by workers are responsible for virtually all accidents. This is the foundation on which health and safety programmes have been based for decades.

Therefore, the ultimate goal of corporate safety programmes and local union safety committees is generally the same, to have zero worker injuries. On safety attention focuses on finding ways to get unsafe workers to change their ways.

Workplace safety is measured by only one statistic, the OSHA (Occupational recordable rate. Based on this statistical yardstick, continuous process industries continue to be among the safest industries in the country and are getting safer. Many plants have celebrated working millions of hours without a lost work day accident. While all eyes are on the OSHA recordable rate, release of hazardous materials, fires, mechanical breakdowns and near misses are not included in the safety statistics.

Safety Systems: The Key to Fixing the Workplace

A safety system can be defined as the use of management programmes which proactively identify and eliminate or control hazards. This begins in the conceptual phase of process units and equipment and continues throughout the life of the process. Major safety systems include the following:

(i) Process and equipment design
(ii) Mitigation devices (relief valves, etc.)
(iii) Warning devices (alarms)
(iv) Mechanical integrity
(v) Procedures and training
(vi) Human factors.

All these systems are important in order to have a safer workplace. However, some systems are far more effective than others in their ability to maximize opportunities for prevention of disasters and injuries. The most important safety system is the design system. This is the only system in which primary protection takes place. For example, by designing a process to use lower pressures, temperatures and less toxic and reactive chemicals, the potential for disaster and injury has been effectively reduced by the use of inherently safer equipment and materials. Another example is the design and use of unique couplings for the connection of nitrogen, air, steam and other hoses. Good design techniques like the use of unique couplings are the most effective ways to eliminate the potential for accidents.

Changing worker behaviour is one of the least effective methods for accident prevention. Workers make occasional errors because they are humans. There is a natural error rate for even the most highly trained and drilled workforce. This is recognized whenever a process hazard analysis such as a HAZOP is performed. It is always assumed that if valves can be operated in the wrong order or at the wrong time then it will happen sometime. Therefore, the hazard analysis concerns itself with the design of a process where it will remain safe even when a worker makes a mistake. Examples of this concept include the use of relief valves, check valves, redundant controls and automatic shutdown systems.

Workers do have important responsibilities regarding health and safety. These include the responsibility to report all injuries and near misses no matter how many prizes and bonuses are offered for non-reporting. Workers have an obligation to question inadequate work permits, procedures and training and to demand that these are done properly. Workers have a responsibility not to be pressured to cut corners when management is in a hurry to get a job completed. They are responsible to demand that engineering controls are used whenever possible rather than PPE.

3.11.6 Preventing Catastrophes

In the corporate model of safety, a low injury rate equals a safe workplace. Therefore, preventing injuries in workplace prevents bigger incidents and disasters. This may not be the case always. The oil and chemical industries have very low OSHA recordable injury rates and their rates are getting even lower. At the same time, the number and seriousness of catastrophes in the industry has increased. An important safety concept used in writing workplace emergency response plans is that you always prepare for the most serious types of accidents. By doing this you are able to most effectively handle safely the entire range of incidents from minor to catastrophic.

By focusing on disaster prevention and creating strong safety systems, union members can most effectively prevent injuries and create a safer workplace.

Creating a truly safe workplace requires looking at industrial health and safety in a fundamentally new way. After all, our entire society is based on blaming the victim. When millions of people are thrown out of work by an inherently cyclical economic system, the individual worker is told to get out there and solve his problem by finding a new job. If he doesn't find a new job it is his fault. The best way to prevent industrial injuries, fires, explosions and hazardous material releases is by adopting and implementing safety practices at workplace by all level of employees.

Besides, hazard identification and characterization of potential release and providing information on the various hazardous substances handled by the unit are important to prevent hazards from occurring. Probability of occurrence of hazard analysis, consequence (impact) analysis, risk analysis, etc., are important to prevent the disaster from occurring. In order to minimize the impact and reduce the chemical accidents and health hazards, it is desirable to evaluate the assimilation capacity of the immediate environment and act accordingly. The assimilation capacity (carrying capacity) studies at ecosystem level or unit level are essential to minimize the impact. Health hazards caused by industrial emissions and effluent discharge along with occupational health problems are also important aspects of study and understanding.

3.11.7 Industrial Health Hazards and Environmental Management Model in Industrial Belts of North Odisha: A case study at Balasore

This study formed a part of D.Sc. thesis of Dr. Satyabrata Nanda, M.D., who worked under the author's guidance.

Balasore is a coastal town in northern part of Odisha. After 1947, many industries have been set up in Balasore. The major industries and the pollutants they release with or without treatment are listed below:

(i) Birla Rubber (Tyre) Industry—Pollutants: Oily sludge, zinc compound, sulphur, residue carbon from banbury, hazardous chemicals from discarded containers, scrap compound containing aromatic, napthamic, paraffin oil, paint containing silicon emulsions, waste of adhesive manufacturing unit, carbon empty packets, rejected rubber compounds, fabrics, cured tyres (scrap), cured flap and bladders, coal ash/cinder, etc.

(ii) Emami Paper Industry—Pollutants: Used oils, spent chemicals, corrosive waste arising from strong acids and bases, processed sludge containing adsorable halides (AOX), fly ash, plant sludge, etc.

(iii) Ori Plast-Plastic Industries—Pollutants: PVC scraps containing residue and stabilizer, sweeping/cleaning dust mixing, compounds, etc.

(iv) Balasore Alloys-Metallurgical—Air pollutants: Suspended particles, slag, particulate matter, etc. Used oil, flu gas cleaning, used batteries from the metal industries. The objective of the study was:

(a) To measure the health status of the population around industry (outside the premises), workers of the industry.
(b) To record the prevalence of the diseases in the villages under survey and for local, and national *comparison* of health status.
(c) It aimed at searching the *possible etiology* for the identified health hazards and to find out the relationship between industrial pollutants with that of identified health hazards.
(d) To ascertain the relationship between the occurrence of disease process with that of distance from industry.
(e) To develop a model which will address issues like health risk awareness, health risk assessment and health risk mitigation by involving the population, industry, government machineries and the volunteers working for the environment.

Methodology Adopted: Human population of all age groups living in villages surrounding the industries were taken as an experimental group and human population living in distant places from the industrial areas were taken as control keeping their socio-economic conditions in view. Both the groups were of more or less same socio-economic status.

Questionnaire survey, health record of the populations of the two groups from government and private sources, clinical study were adopted to get a clear picture of health conditions of people of the surrounding villages, from workers of the industries, and from distant places. The data were analyzed by the standard statistical methods. The methodology is given in a flow sheet (Figure 40).

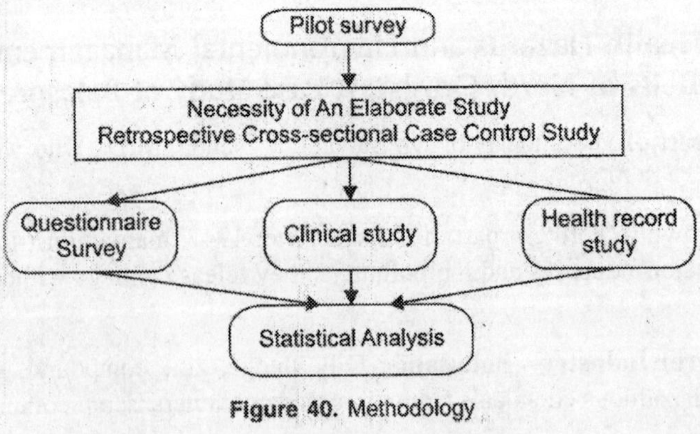

Figure 40. Methodology

Samples included: (i) Experimental Group (Industrial area), -12 villages and 14,346 Population, (ii) Control group (Non Industrial area)- 2 Villages and 2044 population. Survey conducted by- 4 skilled workers trained by the researchers with periodic checks and supervision. Questionnaire format comprised 3 sections each containing 8 questions of general type and pertaining to the living standard/earning profile and health statistics. Clinical study was made by a medical expert team comprising qualified doctor, health assistant, lab technician and female attendant. The data collected from the experimental group and from the control group are listed below:

- Experimental group (industrial area)
- 12 Nodal points
- 6298 respondents
- Control group (Non-industrial area)
- 2 Nodal points
- 399 respondents

Various studies like anthropometric, clinical, bio-chemical, pathological and special examinations like spirometry, electrocardiograph and radiology were carried out. Besides, data from health records of dispensaries of the industries concerned and records of operational health care unit of the areas under survey were collected and analyzed. The results of the survey show that the prevalence of skin diseases, respiratory diseases, hypertension and nutritional deficiency like anemia and malnutrition exists predominantly and the trend of occurrence of the diseases, especially skin diseases, respiratory diseases, and hypertension, etc., is more in the population residing around the industrial area. The data was statistically significant.

The present industries at Balasore were established with techno-economic consideration without adequate attention to environmental protection. The cumulative effect of the number of industries at a particular place is not being studied with the result that an industry or an industrial area over a period of time could cause significant damage to the surrounding environment and ecological features. The higher occurrence of skin diseases, respiratory problems, hypertension among population industrial estate and gradually declining while moving away from the industrial area raises the suspicion of an industrial impact. Industrial impact is due to higher concentration of allergens- like metallic dusts, oils, or some other chemicals, etc. Groundwater survey conducted around industrial estates of Balasore reveals incidences of high concentration of some heavy metals like nickel, chromium and cadmium. Chemical constituents in the effluents in few industries were found exceeding their respective tolerance limit for its discharge into inland surface water. Waste water of industries containing higher concentration of heavy metals above the permeable limits might have altered the nutritional value of vegetables grown and long run consumption of these may pose health hazards.

In control group the occurrences of diseases were less as evidenced by the questionnaire survey, clinical study and data from operational healthcare units. As the villages in this group were 20-25 km away from industry, chances of industrial impact were remote. The river Burhabalang separates the control group from the experimental group by taking its course adjacent to the villages in this group. The existence of river nullifies the industrial impact to some extent in distant places by the process of dilution. There might be some other socio-environmental pathology operating among the experimental group whose health hazards arise not only from intrinsic disorder of bodily structure and function, but also from environmental hazards related to industrialization and exposure to toxic substances. Health issues necessitate a Health Management Model and a model has been developed. The present model addresses the role of industry, that of government machinery, and non-government sectors working for environmental issues and the role of public/population at risk. This model works on Deming's cycle which is based on the poor message of continuum. Health risk awareness, health risk assessment and health risk mitigation are addressed in the model to all the sectors like industry, government and public practical utility of the study is very high in the sense that the study and model are based on the feedback of the executives of the industry which is incorporated to make it operational in practical situations. This user friendly model can be applicable to all other manufacturing organizations.

Health management model is expected to address the health management issues and define the role of industry, role of the government machineries/NGO's working in the area of environment and health management and the role of public for the mitigation of health risk.

Health management is an important activity in line with other activities required on day-to-day basis. It consists of three major elements:

(i) Health risk awareness: Hazardous substance exposure; awareness of public to health hazards caused by chemical, physical and environmental noxious agents; plans for communicating relevant timely information to ease public and allow quick action; effectiveness depends on habits and preferences of the target audience; skill of awareness and trusteeship are important considerations; crucial for health promotion and disease prevention; effective method of education to public; responding to enquiries; offering resources.

(ii) Health risk assessment: The various components in relation to human health risk assessment are some logical steps like identification of hazard; assessment of dose response; assessment of exposure; characterization of risk.

(iii) Health risk mitigation: One of the curative and preventive aspects is to intervene the usual sequence. Health promotion, specific protection, early diagnosis, treatment, disability limitation and rehabilitation are some of the important measures.

3.11.8 Technological Disaster Management: Breach of Ash Pond

Aluminium Company (NALCO), Angul, Odisha in December, 2000—A Case Study:
NALCO, a public sector enterprise, is one of the largest aluminium producing companing in India having a production capacity of 4.61 lakh metric tons per annum. The project is power intensive. A coal-based captive power plant (CPP) of 2000 MW has been installed to make itself self dependent in power supply for smooth operation. However, in the years 2000, NALCO had a production capacity of 2.2 lakh metric tons of aluminium and 720 MW of thermal power. The company has bauxite mines and alumina refinery at Damanjodi of, Koraput district of Odisha.

The CPP normally operated in 2000 at a load varying between 500 to 600 MW depending on the energy demand. For average generation of 500 MW, the plant consumed approximately 9000 metric tons of coal and generated about 4000 metric tons of fly ash and bottom ash. The ash was converted into slurry form with 40,000 KL of water pumped into the ash pond for settling.

The overflow from the ash pond was collected, treated in clarifier and recycled back for slurry making, hereby no water discharge was made outside.

Ash Pond

NALCO adopted three pond systems with two main ponds spanning 113 hectares each for settling of ash slurry and the third pond of 5 hectares served as a collection channel for overflows from the two large ponds. The third pond was located in between the two large ponds. For ash pond purpose, NALCO had 313 hectares of land at its disposal. All three ash ponds are made of earthen embankments and these embankments have undergone a vertical expansion to accommodate more and more ash. Besides, high quantity of fly ash was used as the core of embankment with soil cover.

In general practice, the capacity addition so created in a pond through raising of heights was put into service which catered to the requirements of two years and during the period the raising of dyke height of the other pond was undertaken so as make it ready by the time the former's capacity is exhausted. In this process, pond II was in service since August 2000 after the capacity of pond I was exhausted.

The Ash Pond Breakage Disaster

On 29th December 2000, engineers of the Civil Engineering Department of NALCO noticed unusual seepage on the foot of the embankment of the northern side of pond II. The engineers used sand bags, boulders and other materials to seal the seepage sites and the seepage could be brought down to manageable level by the night on that date.

On 30th December 2000, profuse seepage at the rock toe filter at intermediate height of the embankment of pond II over a very large stretch adjacent to the former seepage site was detected. Efforts were made to mobilize earthmoving equipment like tippers, shovels etc. to attend the problem as it required immediate redressal. During the said period, the total amount of slurry generated from the plant was diverted to pond I to reduce hydraulic load on pond II. But a small volume of slurry was fed to Pond II near the affected zone with the intention that slurry would choke the weak seepage zones and cracks and thus reduce the seepage. But further cracks appeared at higher levels of the embankment of pond II in the same area followed by soil slipping down along the slopes on the downstream side.

The situation created panic among the engineers and officers of NALCO and they immediately evacuated a part of impounded water of pond II. Since the overflow into pond III was unregulated, a small part of the embankment between pond II & III was dug and evacuation from pond II was accelerated. On 31st December, 2000 at about 10 am in the morning, the unregulated overflow increased and the excess discharge eroded the embankment of ponds II and III.

In the process the earthen embankments of ponds II and III were breached and the entire effluent of pond II and III gushed out along with enormous volume of ash (about 5 million tons) deposited in both the ponds. This disaster made the rivulet Nandira swell to unusual high levels and there was an overflow at both the banks of the rivulet, inundating habitation area, crop fields, causing excessive damage to property, drinking water source, fishery and cattle. Brahmani River banks were inundated from 10 metres to 100 metres at different places in the downstream. The area and the crop fields were flooded with fly ash. Fortunately there was no loss of human life but there was colossal loss of crop fields and fishery affecting the livelihood of the people and cattle.

Immediately after the breach, the regional office of the State Pollution Control Board was informed on Dec. 31, 2000 and the head office at Bhubaneswar was informed about the incident around noon on the same day. The regional officer inspected the site immediately to assess the initial impact of huge quantity of ash slurry on rivulet Nandira and on river Brahmani and the adjacent areas. Based on his preliminary report, two teams, one inspecting team and another scientific team to monitor the water quality and other aspects of the affected rivers, adjacent sites, crop fields, nearby wells, etc., were sent by the State Pollution Control Board during 3rd-5th January, 2001.

NALCO appointed a technical expert committee to find out the reasons of structural failure of the embankment and to assess the quantum of damage of the environment, property loss, etc.

Observation

The flooding was more severe near two adjacent villages, Tolakalundi and Dasanali where the ash flow was obstructed by the submersible causeway and meandering of rivulet Nandira at these places. The ash deposit on the rivulet bed was about 4 feet and ash deposit on the crop fields ranged from few millimeters to about a foot. The ash water made its way into village wells and village ponds near these two villages. Flood water containing ash entered into the residential areas of many villages and Talcher Thermal Power colony.

Though the flood discharge receded in a few hours, the decantation of water from the remaining ash in pond II was continuously oozing out carrying ash particles and made a stream of ash slurry discharge to the river Nandira. The water quality of the rivulet and river Brahmani few km downstream became worse, not suitable for animal and human use or use in agricultural field.

NALCO CPP operated at generation load of 460 MW and the entire ash was diverted to Pond I. Engineering care was taken to protect pond I.

Environmental Impact

The impact on land, vegetation, water quality in rivulet Nandira and river Brahmani, impact on air quality, on human health, on aquatic life, on land animals, on socio-economic conditions were studied, by a team of experts and the State Pollution Control Board appointed Geomin Consultants to study and suggest methods for restoring the water quality in rivulet Nandira.

The suspended solid content of river and rivulet water has gone up to about 5,650 mg/L in downstream and remained high throughout the downstream up to the Bay of Bengal. High concentrations of cadmium (~ 3 times higher than acceptable standard of 0.01mg/L) up to 50 km downstream of river were found. Aquatic biodiversity in the rivulet was completely wiped out and a few km downstream of the river Brahmani was also seriously affected. The situation continued for some time until the arrival of rains to flush everything into the sea. There was a huge impact on the livelihood of people as agricultural activity, fishery, grazing cattle on the field, collection of useable water from the well, and river, etc., could not be carried out for some time. NALCO and the government tried to address the issues.

Lessons Learned

The incident of ash pond breaching has raised serious questions about the safety of storing huge quantity of ash near water bodies and its environmental consequences. This was an eye opener to all thermal power plants practising wet disposal of ash. In addition, a quick response was expected from NALCO for restoring the ash management system to prevent consequential river water pollution having far reaching environmental consequences.

Vital information associated with industrial disaster should be made public and people at large should be made aware of the associated risk existing mitigation measures and preparedness measures, the public should adopt in case disaster happens. The role of district administration is very important to address public issues. In this case, NALCO should have taken precautionary measures after observing the seepage on 29 December, 200. More than 48 hours were available to bring the matter to the notice of the people of nearby villages.

Action Taken by SPCB

The State Pollution Control Board (SPCB) by using the power vested in them by the Water (Prevention and Control of Pollution) Act, 1974, directed NALCO to take emergency measures to remove the polluting matter from the rivulet, river, village wells, land, crop fields immediately in consultation with experts and SPCB; remedying or mitigating any pollution in the stream caused by ash slurry, and not to discharge any polluting matter outside/stream and to clean the drinking water source immediately. SPCB used the provisions of the clause 33A and provisions of Clause 32 (emergency measures in case of pollution of stream or well). NALCO has to shoulder the responsibility of cleaning up activities as per the 'Polluter Pays Principle' and SPCB used the provisions of clause 33 of the Water Act later.

On the direction of SPCB, NALCO cleaned the rivulet, the river bed, the crop fields, village wells, etc., and collected the ash and put it in ash pond I. NALCO supplied potable water to villagers till the village wells became usable and stream water was restored to its original quality. NALCO paid monetary compensation to villagers as per the assessment made by the district administration. All these remedial measures were taken in a record time of six months. SPCB also gave directions to NALCO to take permanent remedial measures.

3.11.9 Regulatory Measures

The Disaster Management Act, 2005 envisages proactive, holistic and integrated management of disaster with emphasis on prevention, preparedness and mitigation. These efforts are designed to minimize the losses to lives, livelihood and property and to conserve developmental gains. Prime minister is the chairman of Indian National Disaster Management Authority (NDMA).The chief minister / Lt Governor, as the case may be, is the chairman of State Disaster Management Authority. The fact that these authorities are being headed by the heads of governments themselves exhibits the national resolve to tackle the problem of disasters most seriously. The district collectors are the heads of district disaster management authorities and these bodies are co-chaired by the elected representatives of the districts. The Act largely addresses natural disasters. For technological/industrial disasters the district administration plays the most important role. The technical aspects are handled by the Director of Factories and Boilers, Central and State Pollution Control Boards, and other technical bodies.

3.12 CORPORATE SOCIAL RESPONSIBILITY

Industries try to adopt a holistic and inclusive business model, which is correlated to business performance covering economic, social and environmental protection in order to have competitive advantage. Industries are now expected to discharge their social obligation along with their share holders' wealth generation and maximization as they use societal and national resources. Industries are trying to develop mechanisms towards resource conservation to achieve sustainable development. Leading companies' environmental programmes centre on a set of strong corporate values. These values are (i) respect for people through development of good relations which are mutually beneficial for the stakeholders; (ii) respect for customers—the company's primary goal is to serve the customers; (iii) respect for shareholders—recognizing the risk they take and their role in company's welfare and customer interest; (iv) respect for the protection of environment by producing environment-friendly products and services and taking adequate pollution control measures; (v) respect for regulatory measures, environmental laws and intellectual honesty. Johnson and Johnson, company over 50 years ago, developed a corporate value system, which states that 'we must maintain in good order the property we are privileged to use, protecting the environment and natural resources'. Environmental leadership of companies will be sustained if it translates into competitive advantage (Kashmanian *et al.*, 2010).

3.12.1 Key Areas of Corporate Social Responsibility

It is generally accepted that there are four key areas: **(i)** encouraging community relations through human resource development like making charitable contributions for healthcare facilities, educational facilities, creating road communications, creating food for work for unskilled people of the locality, implementing reward programme for employees, creating scholarships for employees' children, etc., conserving resources, especially water, energy, trees and developing plantation programmes, etc., and sustaining them year after year. These steps help to develop trustworthiness, consumer goodwill and sustainable relationships with the community at large; **(ii)** creating training and development programmes and involving people in production and service sectors of the company; **(iii)** developing a cohesive global corporate social responsibility platform, which acknowledges success, measure success with international standards, and communicates the activities by using web-based human resources information system (HRIS), and **(iv)** protecting the environment by adopting green technology. Leading companies vigorously promote environmental performance while observing business value.

3.12.2 Social Commitment

The International Chamber of Commerce (ICC) published in 1990 its Business Charter for Sustainable Development: Principles of Environmental Management. These principles gave importance to environmental management in a broader social perspective and included corporate priorities, integrated management, product and services, customer interest and advice, contractors and suppliers, process of improvement, technology transfer, compliance to environmental regulations etc. The US Environmental Protection Agency (EPA) in 2004 created the Performance Track Corporate Leader designation as a method to recognize companies that are involved in achieving environmental excellence and leadership by promoting performance track at the facility level and developing facilities, programme, and green practices at the corporate level. (Kashmanian *et al.*, 2010).

Tata Steel Limited runs an 850-bed hospital and rural development projects in 800 villages around Jamshedpur with an expenditure of few million dollars annually in corporate social responsibility (CSR) programme.The Steel Authority of India (SAIL), a public sector organization spent few million dollars in CSR in 2009. Maruti Udyog and Bharat Petroleum were ranked as best companies for CSR in 2009 followed by Tata Motors and then Hero Honda.

NTPC, a public sector organization believes in growth with a human face, and pursuing people-centred development. NTPC is a socially committed organization and a socially responsible corporate citizen. It attaches great importance to discharging its overall social responsibilities to the community and the society at large where its projects and stations are located. Two mega thermal power plants are located in Kaniha and Talcher, Odisha and many more in other places of India.

In this regard Resettlement and Rehabilitation (R&R) programme becomes an area of sharp focus, a programme that addresses people affected directly or indirectly in the wake of the projects undertaken by NTPC. McDonalds has included nutritional information on packaging. McDonalds policy is to put nutritional information on its food packaging in restaurants in what it describes as a first for the fast food sector. The labeling, which uses simple icons and bar charts in an attempt to make information easily understandable, focuses on five key aspects thought by experts to be most meaningful in terms of nutrition - calories, protein, carbohydrates, fat and sodium. (Business Respect, Issue Number 87, dated 26 Oct. 2005). All multinational companies dealing with consumer goods provide vital information to consumers under corporate social responsibility. Industries generating hazardous wastes are now required to display information for public knowledge as per the direction of the Supreme Court of India.

3.12.3 Comprehensive Policy Framework

The Resettlement and Rehabilitation (R&R) policy aims at improving the overall economic status of Project Affected Persons (PAPs). This is achieved by providing opportunities in the fields of sustainable income, health, education, sanitation, communication and other such areas. Community development activities should be carried out in a transparent and participative manner. Each programme is based on specific local requirement and guided by extensive Socio-Economic Surveys (SES).

This helps meet the objective of ensuring that the Project Affected Persons (PAPs) improve or at least regain their previous standard of living. Efforts are made to adopt a holistic approach to community development. Thrust is also given on participation and consultation of stakeholders and setting up of institutional mechanisms like Public Information Centre (PIC), Village Development Advisory Committee (VDAC) etc.

The PAPs are systematically categorized on an individual basis, thereby bringing into its fold, agricultural landowners, agricultural and non-agricultural labourers, tribals, occupiers cultivating forest land, etc. The Resettlement and Rehabilitation programme is meticulously worked out for each PAP. The R&R policy options and entitlements include the following.

Resettlement

Developed alternate free house plot in resettlement colony with necessary infrastructure facilities or provisions for self-resettlement. Free transport arrangement for belongings and reusable material or suitable transport grant.

Infrastructure to be provided includes primary schools, dispensaries, panchayat ghars (house), drinking water wells/hand pumps, black top roads, drainage, Sulabh sauchalayas (clean toilet facilities) etc. and Suitable Resettlement Grant, etc.

Rehabilitation

"Land for land" on a 'willing buyer willing seller' basis is one option. Other rehabilitation options based on need and requirement. Capacity building programmes may include suitable rehabilitation grants, subsistence allowance, etc.

Other innovative measures include incentive purchase of land by the landless, etc.

Additional economic opportunities as per the need and requirement can be considered.

The rehabilitation process is attuned to the local conditions and the needs of the people. Facilitation for land on a 'willing buyer willing seller basis' is the main focus of rehabilitation. With an eye on long-term development, vocational training has been built into the rehabilitation process. The plans are implemented within a definite time frame and a specified budget.

There is sharp focus on all round socio-economic development of the community, which is why the efforts do not stop at the individual or family level redressal but take a holistic approach. Improving the roads, healthcare, education, vocational training, infrastructure development and sports are major activities. Apart from that various welfare and cultural activities are also taken up.

Implementation, monitoring and evaluation are important aspects of R & R policy. The Village Development Advisory Committee (VDAC) plays a key role in the implementation process. The basic objectives of the policy are:

- To avoid displacement wherever possible and minimize it exercising available options otherwise.
- To recognize voices of displaced communities emphasizing the needs of the indigenous communities and vulnerable sections.
- To ensure environmental sustainability through participatory and transparent process.
- To help guide the process of developing institutional mechanism for implementation, monitoring, conflict resolution and grievance redressal.

3.13 CORPORATE CULTURE: BUILDING A GLOBAL LEADERSHIP BRAND

Indian corporate has to think, act and compete globally and therefore, they are trying to create a culture that is conducive to promote global excellence. This requires more than a good product or service. Corporate excellence demands not only that every aspect of business be of high quality but also that every activity is changing and improving faster than the competition. Achieving corporate excellence is a journey and not a destination. More and more executives are now using social media to take the 'pulse of the company' and tap into the real time thoughts of employees and customers. Social media should be viewed as a creative tool as well as a listening post (Ashok Vemuri, Infosys Technologies, and 2010-SPAN). Technology development, keeping the modern trends and future developments in view is the key to develop global leadership. Besides customer satisfaction, trust, and their requirement play an important role in developing global leadership and brand security. Social commitment and philanthropic activity, public participation is also defining qualities of corporate social responsibility and to achieve leadership.

Leadership

Business leadership skills include the ability to drive innovation, identify new revenue sources, to spot talent worldwide and to develop solutions for the world's societal problems, from abating environmental degradation and pollution by using technology, to eradicate poverty, and to solve health problems such as malaria, dengue, TV, HIV/AIDS, etc. Corporates prefer to invest in efficient and effective organizations, who take social, cultural, health, and environmental initiatives.

The recent developments in India make one feel happy and these are:

Bharat Forge has the world's largest single location forging facility and its clients include Honda, Toyota and Volvo amongst others. India is the second largest tractor manufacturer in the world. Ford has just presented its Gold World Excellence award to India's Cooper Tyres. Hero Honda with about 2 million motorcycles a year is now the largest motorcycle manufacturer in the world.

Suzuki has decided to make India its manufacturing, export and research hub outside Japan. Hyundai India is set to become the global small car hub for the Korean giant and will produce 25,000 Santro cars to start with. The prestigious UK automaker, MG Rover is marketing 100,000 Indica cars in Europe under its own name, made by Tata – a feat no one would have even dreamt of just a decade ago. Aditya Birla group has presence in ten countries – China, Canada, Chile, Brazil, Australia, Egypt, Malaysia, Indonesia, Mexico and Thailand and the overseas business accounts for 30% of its turnover. Indian companies are now expanding their customer base by tapping not only Fortune 500 companies but also global 2000 companies. Not only in the area of business but also in the area of technology has India taken a big leap that makes it one of the forerunners in technological leadership too. Some points to bring to the limelight are: (i) Five Indian companies recently received the globally acclaimed Deming Prize for rigorous total quality management (TQM); (ii) fifteen of the world's major automobile makers are obtaining components from Indian companies.

Many Indian companies such as Tata, Ranbaxy, etc., are either buying or collaborating with foreign companies in diverse commodities like automobiles, tea, pharmaceuticals, mobile phones etc.

India has been self-reliant in its space programmes and is among the six countries who have launched their own satellites. India's INSAT is among the world's largest domestic satellite systems. ISRO has a very viable space programme. Further, India is among the 3 countries in the world that have built supercomputers on their own. India's leadership in computer technology has made its followers to establish their R&D labs in several locations in India. Texas Instruments, Oracle, Sun, i2, IBM, SAP, Philips, and HP have established their labs in places like Bangalore, Hyderabad, Mumbai and Pune.

Indian Human Resource

India has several inherent advantages for achieving and sustaining high rates of growth and integrates with the global economy as a dominant member. Some of them are: (i) large reservoir of skilled manpower with >787 million Indians in the age group below 35 years and > 181 million in the age group 25 to 35 years (2011 Census). India produces about 0.5 million engineers and technicians every year; (ii) India offers a vibrant market of young and vigour with about 55% of its population below 25 years of age; (iii) large and growing market of 1 billion people of whom about 250 million are middle class consumers with an organized and responsive capital market; (iv) strong hub for manufacturing components and services; (v) strong gross domestic product (GDP) growth; (vi) high forex reserves; (vii) growing exports; and (viii) infrastructure is being rapidly modernized to meet global challenges.

CHAPTER 4

Environmental Laws

4.1 INTERNATIONAL SCENE: ENVIRONMENTAL ISSUES

In the last century unprecedented deterioration of the environment occurred mainly due to industrialization and urbanization and loss of productive and wild habitats. Urbanization led to the discharge of high volumes of effluents and municipal sewage to water bodies and polluted the rivers and water bodies. Huge quantity of industrial emissions to the atmosphere created environmental pollution and health hazards.

The extent of deterioration can be judged by global warming, climate change, ozone depletion in stratosphere, acid rain, eutrophication, loss of habitat, vegetal cover and loss of biodiversity, excessive concentration of harmful chemicals and hazardous wastes in the environment and magnification of some toxic substances through food chain, growing risk of environmental accidents, and threat to life support systems. Concern over the state of the environment started building up since 1960s due to the decline in environmental quality and deterioration in living conditions. Science and technology could not solve the environmental problems so easily.

International Concern

UNO became concerned and was reflected at the UNO Conference on Human Environment held in Stockholm from 5th June to 12th June, 1972; Rio Conference, 1992; Review of Progress in Johannesburg, 2002 and the conference held at Rio de Janeiro (Brazil) in June 2012.

Government of India actively participated in the 1972 conference and follow-up conferences and strongly voiced concern and advocated for remedial measures.

Several measures were taken in India for environmental protection before the conference but there was no general legislation of a holistic manner to protect the environment.

4.2 INTERNATIONAL CONVENTIONS ON ENVIRONMENT: A HISTORICAL ACCOUNT

In July 1968, UNO Advisory Committee on Economic and Social Affairs recommended the organization of an International Conference on "Human Environment". The matter was taken up by the General Council and steps were taken to organize the conference in 1972.

UNO Conference on Human Environment was held at Stockholm from 5th June, 1972 for a week; Convention on the Prevention of Marine Pollution by Dumping of Wastes & Other Matter, London was held in 1972; World Climate Conference was held in 1979 in Montreal; Vienna Convention for the protection of the Ozone layer was held on 22nd March, 1985; Montreal Protocol on Substances that deplete the Ozone layer was held in 1987; Convention on the prior informed consent procedure for certain hazardous chemicals and pesticides in international trade was held at Rotterdam in 1988.

FAO International Code of Conduct on the distribution and use of pesticides, 1985, was held in 1985 at Rome. Brundtland Commission, 1983–1987 completed its report on "Our Common Future" and it was published in 1987. Convention on the Control of Trans Boundary Movements of Hazardous Wastes & their Disposal (Basel Convention, Switzerland) was held on 22nd March, 1989. UN Framework Convention on Climate Change was held on 9th May, 1992 at New York. These conventions were followed by the Earth Summit, which was held at Rio de Janeiro, Brazil on 5th June, 1992. The main topics were: (i) Sustainable Development (ii) Ozone Depletion (iii) Global Warming (iv) Biodiversity Conservation (v) Environmental Protection and the Concept of "Landscape Ecology" – Eco-cities etc. UNO Convention on the Law of the Sea was held in 1992. Climate Change conference in Kyoto, Japan is another landmark convention and produced a protocol called 'Kyoto Protocol, 1997' on climate change. Besides many conventions/conferences on many issues of the environment were held at different times and these are: Convention on the Conservation of Migratory Species of Wild Animals, 1979, Bonn; Convention on International Trade in Endangered Species of Wild Fauna & Flora (CITIES), 1973, Washington D.C.; Convention on Wetlands of International Importance especially as Waterfowl Habitat (Ramsar Convention), 1971, at Ramsar, Iran; FAO International Undertaking on Plant Genetic Resources Climate Control Conference at Bali, 2008; at Bonn, 2009; at Copenhagen, 2010 and at Cancun, Mexico, 2011, Johanesberg 2012 and at Rio + 20 in 2012 in Brazil.

4.3 INDIAN LAWS

In India the existing laws dealt directly or indirectly with several environmental issues like forest conservation, wildlife conservation, etc., but no general comprehensive law existed to deal with pollution prevention, control and abatement.

India had witnessed > 50 fold increase in the growth of industrial sector by 1970s and the increasing tendency of industrialization and urbanization is growing very fast. Earlier > 85% of people of India lived in villages while at present (2010), 72% people live in villages. Many urban centres have developed.

In the 42nd amendment to the Constitution, two articles were inserted and these have a direct bearing on the environment:

Article 48A: The state shall endeavour to protect and improve the environment and to safeguard the forests and wildlife of the country.

Article 51(g) of the Constitution states that: "It shall be the duty of every citizen of India to protect and improve the natural environment including forests, lakes, rivers and wildlife and to have compassion for living creatures."

Article 21: States that 'No person shall be deprived of his life or personal liberty except according to procedure established by law'.

The Apex court has interpreted this article to include the rights of a 'living environment congenial to human existence' while disposing the tannery case in 1996 and ordered for implementation of 'polluter pays' principle. Under Article 39A (42nd amendment) (equal justice & free legal aid), PIL was introduced.

Artcle 47: States that 'The state to ensure as its primary duty of (I) Raising standards of living of its people;

(ii) To increase the level of nutrition of the people and to bring improvement in public health.

4.3.1 Environmental Laws in India

1. General Enactments: Air Pollution

1. The Air (Prevention and Control of Pollution) Act, 1981, amended in 1987.
2. The Indian Boilers Act, 1923.
3. The Factories Act, 1948, amended in 1987.
4. The Industries (Development and Regulation) Act, 1951.
5. The Mines and Minerals (Regulation and Development) Act, 1947.
6. The Oriental Gas Company Act, 1857.
7. The Indian Explosives Act, 1884.
8. The Explosive Substance Act, 1908.
9. The Motor Vehicles Act, 1938, amended in 1988 and Rules, 1989.
10. The Inflammable Substances Act, 1952.
11. The Petroleum Act, 1934 and Rules, 1979.
12. The Environmental (Protection) Act, 1986.

2. Water Pollution

1. The River Boards Act, 1956.
2. The Merchant Shipping (Amendment) Act, 1987.
3. The Water (Prevention and Control of Pollution) Act, 1974, amended in 1988.
4. The Water (Prevention and Control of Pollution) Cess Act, 1977.
5. The North India Canal and Drainage Act, 1873.
6. The Indian Fisheries Act, 1897.
7. The Damodar Valley Corporation (Prevention of Pollution of Water) Regulation Act, 1948.
8. The Environment (Protection) Act, 1986.

3. Noise Pollution

1. The Environmental (Protection) Act, 1986.

4. Marine Pollution

1. The Shore Nuisance (Mumbai and Colaba) Act, 1953.
2. The Obstruction in Fairways Act, 1891.
3. The Indian Fisheries Act, 1897.
4. The Indian Ports Act, 1908.
5. The Major Port Trusts Act, 1963.
6. The Merchant Shipping (Amendment) Act, 1987.
7. The Territorial Waters, Continental Shelf, Exclusive Economic Zone, and other Maritime Zones Act, 1976.
8. The Coastguards Act, 1978.

5. Hazardous Substances

1. The Poison Act, 1919.
2. The Dangerous Drugs Act, 1930.
3. The Drugs and Cosmetics Act, 1940.
4. The Factories Act, 1948, amended in 1987.
5. The Prevention of Food Adulteration Act, 1954.
6. The Industries (Development and Regulation) Act, 1951.
7. The Insecticides Act, 1968.
8. The Environment (Protection) Act, 1986.
9. The Consumer (Protection) Act, 1986.

6. Radiation

1. The Atomic Energy Act, 1962.
2. Radiation Protection Rules, 1971.

7. Pesticides

1. The Insecticides Act, 1968.
2. The Factories Act, 1948.
3. The Poison Act, 1919.

8. Forest and Wildlife Conservation

1. The Indian Arms Act, 1978.
2. The Wildlife (Protection) Act, 1972.
3. The Indian Forests Act, 1927.
4. The Forest (Conservation) Act, 1980, amended in 1988.

9. Others

1. The Urban Land (Ceiling and Regulation) Act, 1976.

2. The Prevention of Food Adulteration Act, 1954.
3. The Ancient Monuments and Archaeological Sites and Remains Act, 1958.
4. The Slum Areas (Improvement and Clearance) Act, 1956.

The Rules are

1. The Petroleum Rules, 1975.
2. The Gas Cylinders Rules, 1981.
3. The Static and Mobile Pressure Vessels (Unfired) Rules, 1981.
4. The Explosives Rules, 1983.
5. The Indian Boilers Rules, 1956.
6. The Water (Prevention and Control of Pollution) Rules, 1982, amended in 1992.
7. The Air (Prevention and Control of Pollution) Rules, 1982, amended in 1992.
8. The Central Motor Vehicle Rules, 1989, amended in 1994.
9. The Environment Protection Rules, 1986.
10. The Hazardous Waste (Management & Handling) Rules, 1989, amended in 1999.
11. The Manufacture, Storage & Import of Hazardous Chemicals Rule, 1989, amended in 1994, 1998.
12. The Manufacture, Use, Import, Export, Storage of Hazardous Micro-organisms or Genetically Manipulated Organisms Rules, 1989.
13. The Public Liability Insurance Rules, 1991.
14. The Chemical Accidents (Emergency, Planning, Preparedness & Response) Rules, 1996.
15. The Biomedical Wastes (Management and Handling) Rules, 1998.

10. State Enactments

Water Pollution

1. The Orissa River Pollution Prevention Act, 1953.
2. The Maharashtra Prevention of Water Pollution Act, 1969.

Smoke Control

1. The Bengal Smoke Nuisance Act, 1905.
2. The Gujarat Smoke Nuisance Act, 1963.
3. The Bombay Smoke Nuisance Act, 1912.

Pest Control

1. The Andhra Pradesh Agricultural Pests and Diseases Act, 1919.
2. The Assam Agricultural Pests and Diseases Act, 1954.
3. The Uttar Pradesh Agricultural Diseases and Pests Act, 1954.
4. The Mysore Destructive Insects and Pests Act, 1917.
5. The Kerala Agricultural Pests and Diseases Act, 1958.

Land Utilization and Land Improvement

1. The Andhra Pradesh Improvement Scheme Act, 1949.

2. The Acquisition of Land for Flood Control and Prevention of Erosion Act, 1955.
3. The Bihar Waste Lands (Reclamation) Cultivation and Improvement Act, 1946.
4. The Delhi Restriction of Use of Land Act, 1964.
5. The Madhya Pradesh Nagar tatha Gram Nivesh Adhiniyam, 1973.
6. The Madhya Pradesh Gandhi Basti Kshetra (Sudhar tatha Nirmulan) Adhiniyam, 1976.
7. The Madhya Pradesh Town (Periphery) Control Act, 1960.
8. The Madhya Pradesh Regulation of Uses of Land Act, 1948.

Forest and Wildlife Conservation

1. The Madras Elephants Preservation Acts, 1873 and 1879.
2. The Nilgiris Game and Fish Preservation Act, 1879.
3. The Indian Arms Act, 1978.
4. The Wild Birds and Game Protection Act, 1887.
5. Notification in 1902 under the Sea Custom Act, 1878.
6. The Wild Birds and Animals Protection Act, 1912.
7. The Bengal Rhinoceros Protection Act, 1932.
8. The Punjab Wild Birds and Wild Animals Protection Act, 1933.
9. The Andhra Pradesh Forests Act, 1967.

Note: Further information on any of these can be obtained from the Central Pollution Control Board, New Delhi and from the Ministry of Forests and Environment, New Delhi.

4.4 FOREST CONSERVATION ACT, 1980

The Forest Conservation Act came into force in 1980. It is considered to be one of the most important legislations as far as conservation of forests is concerned. The main objective of the Act was the conservation of forests and matters connected therewith, which was completely ignored by the Indian Forest Act of 1927. The Forest Conservation Act was amended again in 1988-89. Some of the important objectives of the Act are:

- Imposition of restrictions on dereservation of forests
- Restriction on the use of forest land for non-forest purpose
- Conservation of the forest wealth
- Check further reforestation
- Maintenance of ecological balance

The Key Features of the Act

Role of the authorities: Punishments for the contravention of the provisions of the Act by the head of the departments or other concerned authorities. However, they are not liable to any punishment if proven that the offence was committed without their knowledge or that due diligence was exercised to prevent the commission of such offence.

Conversion of land from forest to non-forest purposes: The Act lays certain restrictions on diverting the use of land from forest to non-forest purpose, taking into account the interest of the nation as a whole. It requires the prior approval of the Central Government before doing so (See box: process of forest clearance).

As far as the implications of the Act are concerned, it has been able to regulate the diversion of the forest land for non-forest purposes (Table 17). The Government does allow the conversion/ diversion of the lands for developmental needs. The developmental needs may be irrigation

Table 17. Forest Clearance for Mining

Process of forest clearance for mining

When forest land is involved in any project, forest clearance needs to be sought from the Ministry of Environment and Forest prior to the environmental clearance itself. This is mandatory under the Forest Conservation Act, 1980. The steps specified in the Supreme Court order (Writ Petition No. 202 of 1995 (T. N. Godavarman Thirumulpad Vs Union of India), dated 4.8.2006 for seeking forest clearances and temporary working permit are as follows: 20

For forest clearance

A proposal seeking clearance under the Forest (Conservation) Act, 1980 needs to be filed (in case of renewal, the application has to be filed two years prior to the expiry of the mining lease).

If additional information is required, the State Government will ask for the same within 90 days after the receipt of the proposal by the mining company.

The state government will forward the proposal to the central government along with their recommendations within 9 months of the receipt of the proposal.

The central government (MoEF) will dispose of the application for grant of permission within four months of its receipt, under ordinary circumstances. If it is unable to do so, the special reasons for the same would need to be recorded explaining the delay.

For obtaining a Temporary Working Permit (TWP)

If the application is delayed at the MoEF level, the user agency or applicant can apply for grant of a TWP. In such cases it can apply to the state government in the proforma prescribed by MoEF with an advance copy to the MoEF. Such applications can be made any time after the expiry of 13 months from the date of filing of the proposal with the State Government but not later than 9 months prior to the expiry of the existing approval under the Forest Conservation Act.

In cases where lease/renewal was granted prior to 1980 and the lease period has not expired, the application shall be made at least 9 months prior to the expiry of lease period.

The proposal seeking TWP would be processed and forwarded by the state government to the MoEF within 3 months and the MoEF will place it before the Forest Advisory Committee (FAC).

If the state government fails to forward the application, the advance copy will be placed before the FAC. The FAC will allow for an opportunity to the state government and user agency to be heard before giving its final recommendations.

If the state government refuses to grant TWP (reasons to be recorded in writing), then FAC will give an opportunity to both the state government and the user agency to present their views and pass orders.

If no recommendation is received by the state government then the FAC will pass the appropriate orders after giving an opportunity to the state government to be heard. A few other directions were also provided by the court related to both forest clearances and TWPs. Some of these directives are as follows:

FAC will consider all proposals for forest clearances and TWPs. If it recommends grant of clearance or TWP, then MoEF will issue orders within 4 weeks, listing the terms including that of payment of Net Present Value of forest land diverted for non-forest use.

The decision on grant of forest clearance would need to be conveyed to the user agency before the expiry of TWP.

In case MoEF disagrees with the FAC recommendation, they will give it in writing to the FAC for consideration. If there continues to be a disagreement, then the Supreme Court may be approached.

In cases where FAC makes recommendation without state government inputs, the TWP will be effective only after the facts are confirmed by the state government. If there is a variance, the state government can refer it back to the MoEF. The MoEF, if so advised can suspend the TWP.

projects, railways, power projects, defence related, etc. To mitigate the ill effects of such diversion the government has come up with the concept of compensatory afforestation.

4.4.1 National Forest Policy, 1988

The Parliament in December 1988, passed the new forest policy, which was much more progressive than the earlier policies. Concept of community participation in the protection and maintenance of forests was the highlight of this policy. Some key features:

- Preservation and restoration of the ecological balance by environmental stability.
- Conservation of the natural heritage. 33% of India's land area to be forest (20% of urban centres to have tree cover).
- Fulfilling the basic requirements of the people dependent on forests like fuel, wood, fodder etc.
- Protecting the customary rights of the people who are dependent on the forests.
- The most important aspect of the policy was recognition of the relationship between the tribals and the forests. (The Scheduled Tribes & Other Traditional Forest Dwellers (Recognition of Forest Rights) Act, 2006.
- It encouraged public participation and involvement of women in the management of forests.
- It also encouraged a time bound afforestation programme. It extended certain rights including grazing rights and deals with shifting cultivation, forest based industries, forest extension, education and research, etc.
- An important development was the formalisation of the joint forest management.
- Programme, which involved the local people in the management of the forests.

Forest rights for forest dwellers (ecosystem people) have been a major concern and debate in India. Forestry in colonial India centred on commercial exploitation and revenue collection and therefore, did not recognise the rights of forest dwellers. There was no legislative framework for forest dwellers to meet their livelihood needs. This situation continued in Independent India as large tracts of forests were declared 'Reserved Forests', meaning no rights either existed before or would exist later and all those into resided in forests or claimed rights would be called encroachers (Table 18). This situation created incompatibility between forest conservation and livelihood.

4.4.2 Scheduled Tribes and Other Traditional Forest Dwellers Act (Recognition of Forest Rights), 2006

The Scheduled Tribes and Other Traditional Forest Dwellers (Recognition of Forest Rights) Act, 2006, is a key piece of forest legislation passed in India on December 18, 2006. It is also called the "Forest Rights Act", the "Tribal Rights Act", the "Tribal Bill", and the "Tribal Land Act." The law concerns the rights of forest dwelling communities to land and other resources, denied to them over decades as a result of the continuance of colonial forest laws in India. A little over one year after it was passed, the Act was notified on December 31, 2007. On January 1, 2008, this was followed by the notification of the rules framed by the Ministry of Tribal Affairs to supplement the procedural aspects of the Act.

Table 18. History of Forest Legislation

Year	Legislation/Control	Remarks
1807	East India Company acquired royalty rights over Teak	Locals were not allowed timber for domestic use. Conservation became the authority for teak felling and selling by executive order.
1846	Sanctioning Authority extended to all forests and forest produce	Locals including forest dwellers were not allowed extraction of timbers from all forests
1860	Company's sovereignty extended to total area of forest land. 1864-Imperial Forest Department was formed. Government control over forests and forestry was strengthened. The minor produce etc. became inaccessible to forest dwellers.	After 1857 sepoy mutiny (forest dwelling people provided safe hiding places to rebels) Company administration prohibited and withdrew all access rights and privileges to fuel, fodder and other minor produces.
1865, 1878, 1927	Series of Forest Acts promulgated in order to legitimize government control	1927 Act continued after independence as forest legislation. Rights of forest dwellers (Tribal people) were not recognised.
1947-1970	Commercial exploitation of forest land for mining, other industrial activities & for creating farmland for large peasantry class.	Forests were degraded, wildlife poaching rampant and became luxury activity of upper echelon of people.
1970-1988	1972-Wildlife protection Act was enacted, 1980-Forest Conservation Act was enacted.	The role of forest dwellers, tribals were not given importance and their rights were not recognised.
1988 onwards	1988, National Forest Policy was formulated. Forests were recognised as resource/local resource.	Participation of local forest protecting communities became mandatory in the regeneration of degraded forests.
1994 onwards, 1996 Panchayat Extension to Scheduled Areas Act, 2006-(PESA). The Scheduled Tribes & other traditional forest dwellers (Recognition of Forest Rights) Act enacted.	EIA document gave importance to forest resource conservation, importance to biosphere reserve, sanctuaries, public consultation, etc.	Formed part of EIA Generic Structure. PESA became significant after the 73rd constitutional Amendment (Gram Sabha/Village Assembly – authority to manage community resource) 2006 Act-provided forest rights (right to live and hold forest land under individual or common occupation for habitation, self-cultivation, for livelihood etc. upto maximum of 4 hectares of forest land. The act recognizes 'Community Forest Resource'. Problems Exist Settlement, Wildlife protection, wildlife movement corridor, forest conservation, etc.

The Act grants four types of rights:

- *Title rights*: i.e., ownership to land that is being farmed by tribals or forest dwellers as on December 13, 2005, subject to a maximum of 4 hectares; ownership is only for land that is actually being cultivated by the concerned family as on that date, meaning that no new lands are granted.
- *Use rights*: To minor forest produce (also including ownership), to grazing areas, to pastoralist routes, etc.
- *Relief and development rights*: To rehabilitation in case of illegal eviction or forced displacement and to basic amenities, subject to restrictions for forest protection.
- *Forest management rights*: To protect forests and wildlife.

Eligibility to get rights under the Act is confined to those who "primarily reside in forests" and who depend on forests and forest land for their livelihood. Further, either the claimant must be a member of the Scheduled Tribes scheduled in that area or must have been residing in the forest for 75 years.

Any treaty is only as effective as its weakest member, and the Ramsar Convention is no exception. If the world's threatened wetlands are to survive, the requirements of the convention must be taken more seriously by its present members—and more countries have to become signatories.

4.5 BIOLOGICAL DIVERSITY ACT, 2002

The Government of India, in 2002, enacted this piece of legislation. The introduction of the Biodiversity Act of India, however, is nothing but a reflection of an obligation that has been cast on India by the Convention on Biological Diversity, 1992 (CBD). It is designed as a complementary act that would go hand in hand with other legislations like the Wildlife Protection Act, Forest Conservation Act and Indian Forest Act, etc.

Objective of the Act

- Protection of India's rich biodiversity and associated knowledge from being used by foreign individuals and organisations without sharing the benefits arising out of such use.
- Conservation, sustainable use and equitable sharing of benefits.
- Promote at all levels good documentation of biological diversity, its uses and associated knowledge.
- Development of a well-designed Biodiversity Information System for India to serve as knowledge base.
- Establish a three-tier management system, i.e., a National Biodiversity Authority, State Level Biodiversity Boards and Local Level Biodiversity Management Committees.
- Check Biopiracy.
- The Biodiversity Act of 2002 stipulated setting up of a National Biodiversity Authority, State Biodiversity Board and Biodiversity Management Committee at the local level.
- The act also specifies offences and penalties. The court can take cognizance over the complaints under this Act only if the complaints go through the central government. The offences that are committed under this Act are cognizable i.e., the offender can be arrested without warrant and with non-bailable warrants. The penalties fixed by the Act have been fixed much higher than other Acts.
- The fine is one lakh rupees and in case of second offence it is two lakh rupees and for a continuing offence it is prescribed as two lakh rupees for each day of such disobedience or non-compliance. In case of commission of an offence by a company all those who are responsible for the management and conduct of the company will be held liable.

The Union Ministry of Environment and Forests (MoEF), India, passed the Biological Diversity Act, 2002, with an objective to regulate access to genetic resources and associated knowledge by foreign individuals and institutions and ensure equitable sharing of benefits arising out of resources and knowledge available in the country. In short, the Act is aimed to protect and regulate access to plant and animal genetic resources and traditional knowledge (TK). A three-tiered system of regulation is envisaged under the Biological Diversity Act, which consists of the National Biodiversity Authority (NBA) at the head, followed by State Biodiversity Boards (SBB) and local level Biodiversity Management Committees (BMC).

4.5.1 Biological Diversity Rules, 2004

After two years of the enactment of the Biodiversity Act, the government notified the Biodiversity Rules. The rules were formally notified in the official gazette on 15th April 2004. The Biodiversity Rules are the executive orders made by the government in order to carry out the purposes of the Act (Section 62) which states that:

Every rule made under this Act is to be placed in the Parliament for a period of thirty days and the houses can make changes in the rules (sec 62(3)).

The key features of the rule

The rules laid down procedures regarding the application to be made to have access to the biological resources and the traditional knowledge, situations when the application for access will be revoked or withdrawn, their Intellectual Property Rights protection, the procedures involved in the transfer of the research findings, the transfer of the access right to a third party etc.

The rules also dealt with the establishment of the Biodiversity Management Committees (BMCs) by the local bodies and their functions. The maintenance of the People's Biodiversity Register in consultation with the local people is one of the important functions of the BMC. The Register contained comprehensive information on availability and knowledge of local biological resources, their medicinal or any other use or any other traditional knowledge associated with them. The Act and the Rules set up the road map for National Biodiversity Fund, State Biodiversity Fund and Local Biodiversity Fund.

4.6 WILDLIFE CONSERVATION ACT

4.6.1. Wildlife Protection Act, 1972

The original Wildlife Act was enacted in the year 1972 and thereupon amended several times to further improve the objective of protection and the conservation of wildlife. The term 'wildlife' as per the Act means *'any animal, bees, butterflies, crustacean, fish and moths: aquatic or land vegetation which forms part of any habitat' {sec.2 (37)}.*

The Wildlife Protection Act aims at the protection of the components of biological diversity like wild animals, plants, birds, etc. It aims primarily at the maintenance of ecological and environmental security of the country as a whole. It is a comprehensive legislation dealing with the wildlife and the protection of the same effectively. The Act consists of 66 sections and 6 schedules. As the title of the Act suggests it mainly aimed at the protection of the wildlife but with the amendment to the Act 1991, specific species of plants were brought under the Act for protection. The main objectives of the Wildlife Protection Act are:

- The state government is given the power to declare the Sanctuaries/National Parks aimed at the protection of the wildlife.

- Conservation and protection of the flora and fauna of the protected areas.
- Regulation of the hunting of wild animals and birds.
- Regulation of possession, acquisition or transfer of, or trade in wild animals, animal articles and trophies and taxidermy, etc.
- Constitution of authorities to achieve the objectives of the Act.

4.6.2 Wildlife (Protection) Amendment Act, 2002

The Amendment has deleted a few sections and has inserted a few. The changes that were brought about in the Act were not too gigantic, but it did make considerable changes aiming towards the conservation of the wildlife in a better manner. It also tried to make a lot of cosmic changes. The 1972 Act had the concept of 'closed areas', which was completely deleted in the 2002 Amendment Act. Some features include:

- The hunting of the wild animals is prohibited by the Act, except in special situations. Protection of Plants: The Act not only deals with the aspect of wildlife protection, it also concentrates on the protection of the plants.
- Penalty and forfeiture of property derived from illegal trade or hunting.

4.7 THE WATER ACT, 1974

The Indian legal system provides four major sources of environmental laws for addressing water pollution. These are:

- The Water Act, 1974
- EP Act, 1986
- Public nuisance action against polluters,
- The common law—right of riparian owners to unpolluted waters.

The Water-Act (History)

To prevent water pollution, a committee was set up in 1962 to draw a draft enactment. The report was circulated to the state governments and considered by the central council of local self government (CCLF). A draft bill was prepared and considered in the joint session of Central Council of Local Self Government & 5th Conference of the State Ministers of Town and Country Planning held in 1965. In pursuance of the decision of the joint session, the draft bill was considered in detail by a committee of ministers of local self government from the states of Bihar, Madras, Maharasthra, Rajasthan, Haryana and West Bengal.

The central government examining the proceedings of these bodies came to the conclusion that the existing local provisions are neither adequate nor satisfactory and therefore, there is urgent need for introducing a comprehensive legislation. Since water is a state subject, the legislature of two or more states had to pass a resolution in pursuance of article 252 of the Constitution empowering the Parliament to pass necessary legislation. In view of this, such legislations on the subject were passed by the state legislature of Gujarat, Jammu Kashmir, Kerala, Haryana and Mysore. Finally, the Water (Prevention and Control of Pollution) Bill was passed by both Houses of Parliament and received the assent of the President on 23rd March,

1974 and led to the establishment of Pollution Control Boards. CPCB was established in September, 1974.

Provisions

The Water Act of 1974 represents one of India's first attempts to deal comprehensively with an environmental issue.

The Act was amended in 1988 to conform closely to the provisions of the Environment (Protection) Act, 1986. The Water Act is comprehensive in its coverage. It applies to streams, inland waters, subterranean waters and sea or tidal waters. Standards for the discharge of the effluents or the quality of receiving waters are not specified in the Act itself. Instead, the Act enables the CPCB & the State Boards to prescribe these standards. The Water Act regulates water pollution through a system of 'command and control'. The Water Act provides for a permit system or consent procedure for operation of industries to prevent and control pollution.

A person must obtain consent from the State Board before taking steps to establish any industry, operation or process, any treatment or disposal system or any extension or addition to such a system. The important provisions are listed below:

Definitions

Items (a) to (k): (a)-(c)-Definition of Boards & Member (including chairman as a member),(d) **Occupier**- In relation to any factory or premises, means the person who has control over the affairs of the factory or the premises and includes, in relation any substance, the person in possession of the substance. (dd) **'Outlet'** - includes any conduit pipe or channel, open or closed, carrying sewage or trade effluent or any other holding arrangement which causes, or is likely to cause pollution.

'Pollution' means such contamination of water or such alteration of the (i) physical, chemical or biological properties of water or (ii) such discharge of any sewage or trade effluent or any other liquid, gaseous or solid substance into water (whether directly or indirectly) as may, or is likely to create a nuisance or render such water harmful or injurious to public health or safety or to domestic, commercial, industrial, agricultural or other legitimate use, or to the life and health of animals or plants or aquatic organisms.

'Sewage effluent' means effluent from any sewerage system or sewage disposal works and includes sullage from open drains.

'Sewer' means any conduit pipe or channel, open or closed, carrying sewage or trade effluent.

'Stream' includes: (i) river, (ii) water course (whether flowing or for the time being dry), (iii) inland water (whether natural or artificial), (iv) subterranean waters, (v) sea or tidal waters to such extent or as the case may be, to such point as the state government, by notification in the Gazette, specify in this behalf.

'Trade Effluent' includes any liquid, gaseous or solid substance, discharged from any premises used for carrying on any (industry, operation or process or treatment and disposal system), other than domestic sewage.

Constitution of Boards

Central Board: 17 members including: (a) a full time chairman - being a person having special knowledge or practical experience in respect of matters relating to environmental protection or a person having knowledge and experience in administrating institutions dealing with the matters aforesaid, to be nominated by the central government. The Gazette notification of Government of India date 30 November 2012 stipulates the qualification of the Chairman. A person having an M.Sc. related to the environment or an Bachelor of Engineering related to the environment with special knowledge and 15 years of experience related to environment al protection, pollution abatement-related to water pollution and air pollution with an over all of 25 years of experience, are required. (b) five officials to be nominated by government to represent the government; (c) five nominated by Govt. from amongst the members of the state boards (2 shall be from state local authority); (d) 3 non-officials nominated by the government to represent the interests of agriculture, fishery, industry trade or any other; (e) 2 persons to represent the companies or corporations owned by the central government; (f) a full time member secretary, possessing qualification, knowledge and experience of scientific, engineering, or management aspects of pollution control to be appointed by the government. The Gazette notification of 22nd November 2012 stipulates the qualification of the member secretary. A person having more or less similar qualification with 12 years experience is requiresd. However an Ph.D. degree in science or an M.Tech degree has been mentioned as the desirable qualification.

Central Board shall be a body corporate

State Boards

1. A full time chairman - qualification as cited above.
2. Not exceeding 5 members to be nominated by the state government to represent that govt.
3. Not exceeding 5 members to be nominated from local authorities functioning in the state.
4. Not exceeding 3 members nominated by the government to represent the interests of agriculture, fishery, industry, trade or any other.
5. Two persons to represent companies or corporations owned /controlled or managed by state government.
6. A full time member secretary with qualifications as mentioned earlier.

Term of Office—Three years from the date of nomination, provided that a member shall, notwithstanding the expiration of his term, continue to hold office until his successor enters upon his office.

The term of office of the person under 2 and 5 will cease as soon as he/she ceases to hold office under the government.

Disqualification to become a member

No person shall be a member: (a) any time adjudged insolvent or has suspended payment of his debts or has compounded with his creditors; (b) unsound mind (declared by a competent court); (c) & (d) convicted of an offence – If government is of opinion that it involves moral turpitude, or convicted under this act; (e) directly or indirectly has share or interest in an industry; (f) salaried officer of any company; (g) has abused his office.

Removal of a member requires giving reasonable opportunity to him to explain—if removed will not be eligible for further nomination.

Meetings

A Board shall meet at least once in every three months—rules and procedures are to be prescribed. Chairman can convene urgent meeting. Clause 9 - Constitution of Committees 10. Temporary Association of Persons with Board with particular purposes Board delegate does it power to the Chairman from time to time Board or its chairman may delegate power to member secretary.

Power and Functions of the Central Board

Section 16. Main function of CPCB to promote cleanliness of streams and wells in different areas of the states and advise central government on prevention and control of water pollution. Coordinate the activities of State Boards and resolve disputes among them. Provide technical assistance and guidance to the State Boards, carry out and sponsor investigations and research relating to problems of water pollution and prevention, control or abatement of water pollution.

Training of persons.

Organization of comprehensive programme through mass media to prevent and control water pollution.

Collection of samples and publication of technical and statistical data relating to water pollution and to decribing measures to prevent water pollution to preparing codes or guides relating to treatment and disposal of sewage, trade effluents, etc., and dissemination information on these matters.

Laying down standards for a stream or well, modifying in consultation with state government.

To plan and cause to be executed a nationwide programme for the prevention, control and abatement of water pollution and perform such other functions as may be prescribed. The Board may establish or recognize lab/labs to enable the board to perform its functions efficiently.

Section 17. Functions of the State Boards; same the line of CPCB pertaining to a particular state **Fifteen functions.**

Section 18. In the performance of its functions: (i) the CPCB shall be bound by directions of the central government: (ii) a State Board shall be bound by directions of the state government, subject to certain contingencies (central government has overriding power as per clause 18 section 19-33 provisions deal with prevention and control of water pollution.

19. Power of state government to restrict application of the Act to certain areas.

20. Power to obtain information - The State Board can collect information, conduct survey, give directions to any person, to prevent and control water pollution.

21. Power to take samples of effluents and procedures (1, 2, 3, 4 & 5).

Admissibility of sample: The sample must be lifted in accordance with the provisions of Section 21 of the Act when only its analysis could be admissible evidence, Delhi Bottling Co. Pvt. Ltd. Versus CPCB, AIR 1986,152.

22. Deals with reports of the result of analysis of samples taken under Section 21 and Section 22. The concerned Board analyst is bound to analyze the sample and submit a report to the concerned Board. The concerned Board is required to send the report to the occupier or his agent. In case of discrepancies in the result of different laboratories- Section 51 (central water

lab) & 52 (state water lab.) will prevail. Section 23. Power of entry and inspection - Any person empowered by the Board can enter into the premises of an industry to collect samples.

Section 24. Prohibition on the use of stream or well for disposal of polluting matter, etc. (3 clauses).

Section 25. Restrictions on new outlets and new discharges - Consent Administration by the Board.

Section 26. Provision regarding existing discharge of sewage or trade effluent.

Section 27. Refusal or withdrawal of consent by state Board.

Section 28. Appeal - Appellate Authority.

Section 29. Revision - State government may call for the records and revise the procedure – recently done for sitting criteria for stone crushers.

Revision lies against an order which has been made by the State Board under Section 25, 26 or 27, to the state government. No period of limitation is prescribed for filing a revision application. Revision is not a right given to a party but is only a power conferred on the authority, which that authority may or may not exercise on the facts and circumstances of the case (Balkishan v. Union of India (1994), 3 SLJ (CAT) 440). Sections 30 & 31. Power of state Board to carry out certain work and furnishing of information to state Board and other agencies in certain cases.

Section 32 - Emergency measures in case of pollution of stream or well (a) removing that matter from the steam etc. (NALCO-Ash pond breach case study described in this book) (b) Remedying or mitigating any pollution (c) Issuing orders immediately restraining or prohibiting the person from discharging, etc.

Section 33 - Power of Board to make application to Courts for restraining pollution of water in streams or wells.

Section 33A - Power of the Board to give Directions - the closure, prohibition, or regulation of any industry, operation or process or (b) the stoppage or regulation of supply of electricity, water or any other service.

Chapter VI Funds, Accounts and Audit Sections 34-40

- Chapter VII: Penalties & Procedure : Sections 41-50
- 41-Failure to comply (under Sections 20, 32, 33 or 33A) shall on conviction, be punishable with imprisonment up to 3 months or with fine up to ten thousand rupees or both and in case failure continues, with an additional fine of upto 5 thousand rupees for every day till the failure continues (under Section 20).
- Under Sections 32, 33 or 33A, on conviction, be punishable for not less than 1 ½ years and upto six years and with fine and in case the failure continues, with an additional fine upto five thousand rupees per day till the matter is complied. If compliance is not done for one year, the prison term may extend to not less than 2 years and upto 7 years.
- Section 42 - Penalty for certain Acts.
- Sections - 43 & 44. Penalty for contravention of provisions of Sections 24, 25, 26 same as under sections 32, 33 or 33A.
- Section 45. Enhanced penalty after previous conviction under section 24, 25, 26 minimum 2 years and upto 6 years.

- Section 46. Publication of names of offenders.
- Section 47. Offences by companies.
- Section 48. Offences by government departments.
- Section 49. Cognizance of offences.
- No court inferior to that of a Metropolitan Magistrate or a Judicial Magistrate of the First Class shall try any offence punishable under this Act. Notwithstanding anything contained in Section 29 of the code of Criminal Procedure, 1973 (2 of 1974), it shall be lawful for the Judicial Magistrate/Metropolitan Magistrate (I class) to award punishment for a term exceeding 2 years and a fine exceeding two thousand rupees).
- Sections 51-64. Miscellaneous Section 58. Bar of Jurisdiction- No civil court shall have jurisdiction to entertain any suit or proceeding in respect of any matter which an appellate authority is empowered and no injunction shall be granted by any court or other authority.

Legal Implications of Non-compliance

Section 24 - (i) Prohibits discharge or flow of any polluting water into any stream or well or sewer or on land and (ii) not to impede flow of water of any stream which is likely to aggravate pollution due to other causes or of their consequences.

- Exemption: If such act is done with proper consent for constructions like bridge, repairs etc., for public welfare.
- The contravention of the above provision is punishable under Section 43 of the Act with imprisonment for a term not less than one and half years and may extend up to six years and fine.

Section 25 - Restricts establishment of any industry, operation or process or any treatment and disposal system or extension or addition thereto which may discharge sewage or trade effluent into stream, well, sewer or on land without prior consent of the State Board.

Section 26 - This section makes it obligatory for every existing industry to apply for and obtain consent under Subsection 2 of Section 25 in respect of every outlet for discharge of any sewage or trade effluent. Violation of any of the above provision, i.e., Sections 25 & 26 is punishable under Section 44 of the Act, i.e. imprisonment for a term not less than two years and may extend up to six years and with fine.

Section 27 - The Board has the right to refuse the consent or withdraw the consent already granted under Sections 25 or 26 of the Act. It can also be for non-compliance of the conditions imposed under the consent.

Section 47 - Offences by Companies - Every person who, at the time of the offence committed, was in charge and was responsible to the company, for conduct of business of the company, as well as the company shall be deemed to be guilty of the offence and shall be liable to be proceeded against provided that nothing will render such person liable to punishment if he proves that the offence was committed without his knowledge or that he exercised all due diligence to prevent the commission of such offence. If it is proved that the offence has been committed with the consent or connivance of or is attributable to any neglect on the part of the Director, Manager, Secretary or other officer of the company, shall be deemed to be guilty and liable to be prosecuted and punished.

Section 33A: Authorizes Board to issue directions in writing to any person, office o who shall be bound to comply with such directions.

Power to issue directions includes to direct: (a) the closure, prohibition or regulation industry, operation or process; or (b) the stoppage or regulation of supply of electricity, wate any other serviced.

Section 45A provides that whoever contravenes any provision of the Act or fails to comply with any direction given thereunder for which no specific penalty has been provided shall be punishable with imprisonment of three months and also a fine up to Rs.10,000/- or both and if contravention or failure continues, a further fine of Rs. 5000/- for each day of such continuance.

Section 42 prescribes penalty for any act contrary to the provisions of the Act or intervening with the property of the State Board or meter or gauze or other measuring and monitoring devices will be punishable with the imprisonment of three months or with fine upto Rs.10,000/- or both.

4.8 THE WATER CESS ACT, 1977; CESS RULES, 1978

This Act provides for the levy and collection of cess on water consumed by Schedule I industries.

The Cess Act aims to augment the resources of the Central Board and the State Boards for the prevention and control of water pollution. The industries specified in the schedule to the Act (are to affix meters and submit returns/ reports of consumption in prescribed forms to the Central Board.There is a provision for 25% rebate for industries, which install a plant for the treatment of trade effluents.

Crediting proceeds of cess to Consolidated Fund of India & application thereof, power of entry, interest payable for delay in payment of cess, penalty for nonpayment of cess in time, recovery, appeals to appellate authority, penalty, etc.

Rules: Standards of the meters and places where they are to be fixed. Appeals to the committee - chairman & others.

4.9 THE AIR ACT, 1981

The Air Act was enacted in 1981 under Article 253 of the Constitution of India, which gives power to the central government to make laws to implement decisions taken at international conferences.

The Act represents the implementation of the decisions made at the United Nations Conference on human environment held at Stockholm in 1972.

The Air Act provides power to State Boards for the protection of environment. With increasing industrialization and tendency of cluster /aggregate in few areas, the problem of air pollution has been felt. The problem is acute in densely populated areas. The presence of various pollutants discharged through industrial emissions and from certain human activities connected with traffic, domestic fuel use, heating, incineration, refuse, etc., has a detrimental effect on the health of people and on biodiversity. Air does not have boundaries; pollutants released at one place are carried to distant places and create health problems.

Provisions

- Sections 1 & 2 deal with preliminaries, definitions (chapter I),
- Sections 3 to 15 deal with the constitution of Pollution Control Boards, terms and conditions of service of members, constitution of committees, member secretary & officers and delegation of powers (Chapter II) - more or less same as in Water Act.

Definitions

- 'Air pollutant' means any solid, liquid or gaseous substance (including noise) present in the atmosphere in such concentration as may be or tend to be injurious to human beings or other living creatures or plants or property or environment.
- 'Automobile' means any vehicle powered either by internal combustion engine or by any method of generating power to drive such vehicle by burning fuel.
- 'Approved fuel' means any fuel approved by the State Board for the purpose of this Act.

Provisions

- Section 16 - Functions of the CPCB
- Section 17 - Functions of the SPCB
- Section 18 - Power to give directions
- Section 19 - Declaration of restricted areas
- Section 20 - Powers to give instructions for ensuring standards for emission from automobiles
- Section 21 - Restrictions on use of certain industrial plants
- Section 22 - Industries not to allow emission of air pollutants beyond the standard laid down by the State Board.
- Section 22A - Power of Board to move the court for restricting from causing air pollution by industry / persons
- Section 23 - Information to SPCB
- Section 24 - Power of Entry
- Section 25 - Power to obtain information
- Section 26 - Power to take samples of air or emissions and procedures
- Section 27 - Reports of the results of analysis
- Sections 28-30 - State air lab., analysis, reports of analysis
- Section 31 - Appeals - appellate authority
- Section 31A - Power to give direction for closure, prohibition or regulation of any industry
- Section 32 to 36 - Funds, accounts and audit
- Sections 37 to 46 - Penal provisions
- Sections 47-54 - Miscellaneous

The Air Rules, 1983

- There are 17 rules to deal with preliminary, definitions, procedures for transaction of business of the Boards and Committees, Budget, etc.
- 1983 for Union Territories
- Important notifications

Legal Implications of Non-compliance

Section 21 - Provides that without previous consent of the State Board no person shall establish or operate any industrial plant in an air pollution control area.

Note: In Odisha the entire state has been declared as air pollution control area.

Section 22 - No person operating any industrial plant in any air pollution control area shall discharge or cause or permit to be discharged emission of any air pollutant in excess of the standards laid down by the State Board.

Section 31A - Authorizes the Board to issue directions in writing to any person/officer or authority that shall be bound to comply with such directions. The Board to issue directions: (a) the closure, prohibition or regulation of any industry, operation or process; or (b) the stoppage or regulation of supply of electricity, water or any other service. Failure to comply with the provisions has been made punishable under Section 37 of the Act.

Section 37 - Provides that person failing to comply with the provisions of Sections 21 or 22 or 31, shall, in respect of each such failure, be punishable with imprisonment which shall not be less than for a term of one year and six months but may extend to six years and fine and in case the failure continues an additional fine of Rs. 5000/- for every day of such continuance after conviction of first such failure. It is further provided that if contravention continues beyond a period of one year after the date of conviction, offender shall be punishable for an imprisonment of term not less than two years and be extended to seven years with fine.

Sections 38 & 39—Provide for any other violation of the provisions of the Act or on failure to intimate the occurrence of the emission of air pollutants into the atmosphere in excess of the standards or apprehension of such occurrence or giving any false statement in any material particularly for obtaining consent u/s 21 or giving any other false information to Board has been made punishable with the imprisonment for a term which may extend to three months or fine upto Rs.10,000 or both.

Section 40 - contains the provision to deal with offences of companies which are similar to section 47 of the Water Pollution Act.

4.10 THE APPELLATE AUTHORITY

The Appellate Authority is constituted under Section 28 of the Water Act, 1974; Section 31 of the Air Act, 1981, Rule 13 of the Biomedical Wastes Rules, 1998 under EP Act, 1986.

The Appellate Authorities (AA) - for water, air and biomedical wastes are functioning since Nov. 5, 2005 in Odisha. ~ 80 appeals under the Air and Water Acts have been filed so far (till March, 2010) and ~75 of them have been disposed of. By interpreting case laws of different courts in India, the AA has expanded its scope and jurisdiction by allowing any affected party to file appeal even though he/she is not a party to the order of the Board, thereby all litigations against the order of the Board are now being adjudicated by the AA.

Air Act, 1981—Section 31, 21—Operation of sponge iron plant-appeal-locus stand of petitioner held, any person can file appeal against any order passed by the State Board, if he is aggrieved by that order, even if he/she is not a party to it. (Sankar Oram vs. MS, SPCB, 2008)

4.11 THE ENVIRONMENT PROTECTION ACT, 1986

In the wake of the Bhopal Gas Tragedy in 1984, the Government of India enacted the Environment (Protection) Act of 1986.The Act is an umbrella legislation designed to provide a framework for central government coordination of the various central and state authorities established under the Water (Prevention and Control of Pollution) Act, 1974 and Air (Prevention and Control of Pollution) Act, 1981. The EPACT envisages filling up gaps in the legislative protection to the environment. The main thrust of the Act is to make top management responsible for compliance with provisions of environmental laws: Liability and prosecution; statutory provision to empower executive to issue notification, directions, standards and regulations for compliance to meet the required contingencies; private citizens empowered to file cases against violation of environmental laws against industries after notice to authority; punishments and penalties made more stringent; powers conferred on enforcement agencies to effect closure of polluting industries. By 1992 amendment, industries have to furnish annual environment statement to regulatory bodies and observe self-discipline.

Section 2

Deals with the definition of different terms:

Environment - Includes water, air and land and the interrelationship which exists between water, air, land and human beings and other living creatures, plants, micro-organisms and property. [Section 2(b)]

Environmental Pollutants

Any solid, liquid, or gaseous substance present in such concentration as may be or may tend to be injurious to the environment. [Section 2(c)]

Hazardous substances

Any substance or preparation which, by reason of its chemical or physicochemical properties or handling, is liable to cause harm to human beings, other living creatures, plants, microorganisms, property or the environment. [Section 2 (e)]

Occupier

In relation to any factory or premises, an occupier means a person who has control over the affairs of the factory or the premises and includes in relation to any substance, the person in possession of the substances. [Section 2 (f)]

Section 3 (1)

Powers to and functions of the central government

- To set new national standards for the quality of the environment (ambient standards), as well as standards for controlling emissions and effluent discharges.
- To regulate industrial locations.
- To prescribe procedures for managing hazardous wastes.

- To establish safeguards for preventing accidents; and to collect and disseminate information regarding environmental pollution.

Section 4 Appointment of officers and their powers and functions

Section 5 Power to issue directions (similar to section 33A of WA-1974, section-31A of Air Act, 1981).

Under Section 5, the central government is empowered to issue directions in writing to any person, officer, or any authority and such person, officer or authority shall be bound to comply with such directions. The power to give directions under this Section includes the power to direct (a) the closure, prohibition or regulation of any industry, operation or process; or (b) stoppage or regulation of the supply of electricity or water or any other service. The power is delegated to State Government / SPCB.

This is an important section as it empowers the government to give directions for preservation of ecological order, social harmony, pollution free environment and bring awareness on environmental conservation through media and press, etc. Reference may be made to (i) Dahanu Taluka Environment Protection Group vs. Bombay Suburban Electricity Supply Company Ltd (1991)-2.S.C.C.539.

The Supreme Court of India gave direction to make environment a compulsory subject in schools and colleges in a graded system (M.C. Mehta vs. Union of India A.I.R. 1992 S.C.382)

Section 6 - Rules to regulate environmental pollution.

MoEF is responsible for making rules to implement the EPA and has adopted industry specific standards for effluent discharge and emissions for 24 designated industries.

Section 7 - This section expressly states that those persons who are carrying on industry, operations, etc., are not to allow emission or discharge of environmental pollutants in excess of the standards.

Section 8 - Persons handling hazardous substances to comply with procedure.

Section 9 - Furnishing of information in certain cases

In cases where discharge of environmental pollutants occurs in excess of the prescribed standards, or there is an apprehension of this occurring due to an accident or some other unforeseen event, then the person who is in charge at that particular time is responsible for preventing environmental pollution due to the said discharge.

It is the responsibility of the person to intimate the occurrence of the discharge to the CPCB/SPCB, and provide all possible assistance to the regulatory agencies to counter the ill effects of the discharge. All expenses incurred by the regulatory agency in undertaking remedial measures may be recovered from the polluter. In Indian Council for Environ-legal Action vs. Union of India (Supreme Court, 1996), the court held that the central government has the power under Sections 3 and 5 of the EPA to levy and recover the cost of the remedial measures. The polluter pays principle was also held to be applicable and Sections 3 and 5 of the EPA were held to empower the central government to give directions and take measures for giving effect to this principle.

Section 10: Power of search and entry.

The EP Act empowers authorized officers to enter, at all reasonable times, any place, or premises for determining the infringement of standards and procedures set under the Act, and for testing any equipment, industrial plant, record, register or document or any other material object for determining offences under the EPA.

A willful delay or an obstruction of such an inspection is an offence and the person in charge is liable for prosecution.

Section 11 - Power to take samples.

Power to take samples of air, water, soil or any other substance from the factory premises. The person taking the sample is to serve a notice to the occupier or his agent in charge of the place and then, in the presence of the occupier or his agent, place the sample in a container and seal it. The sample containers are to be signed and sealed by both the occupier and the person taking the sample. Collected samples are to be sent without delay to the environment laboratories.

Section 12 - Environmental laboratories.

The samples collected are to be sent to notified laboratories for analysis. Government analysts with specific qualifications are appointed under Section 13.

The functions of environmental laboratories and the qualifications of government analysts are described in the Environment (Protection) Rules, 1986.

The following are empowered to enter and search the premises and take samples of air, water, soil or any other substance from a thermal power plant as per the provisions of Sections 10 and 11:

- Director (Pollution Control)
- SPCB and the officers empowered by the State Board under Sections 21 and 23 of the Water (Prevention and Control of Pollution) Act, 1974 or under Section 24 of the Air (Prevention and Control of Pollution) Act, 1981.
- CPCB and any officer empowered under Section 23 of the Water (Prevention and Control of Pollution) Act, 1974 or under Section 24 of the Air (Prevention and Control of Pollution) Act, 1981.

Section 14 - Evidence

A document, which is a report signed by a government analyst, can be used as evidence for any proceedings under the EPA.

Section 15 - Penal provision

EPA provides for punishment with imprisonment for a term which may extend to five years or with a fine which may extend to one lakh rupees, or with both.

In case the contravention continues, there may be an additional fine of Rs. 5000 for each day of the contravention.

If the contravention continues beyond a period of one year after the date of conviction, the offender is punishable with imprisonment for a term which may extend to seven years.

Section 16 - Offence by a company

When an offence under this Act has been committed by a company, then every person directly in charge of and responsible to the company at the time of the offence, shall be deemed to be guilty of the offence, unless he or she proves that the offence was committed without their knowledge or that they exercised due diligence to prevent the offence.

Section 17 - Offence by Government department

In case a Government department has committed an offence under this Act, then the head of the department is deemed guilty unless he or she proves that the offence was committed without their knowledge or that they exercised due diligence to prevent the offence. Any other person other than the head of the department, who has consented to the offence or was in connivance, or neglected their duties in preventing the offence, shall also be guilty under the Act.

Section 18 - Protection of action done in good faith.

No suit, prosecution, or other legal proceedings lie against the government or any officer or employee of the government or any authority constituted under this Act, or any member, officer or employee of such an authority, in respect of anything which is done in good faith in pursuance of this Act, Rules made under the Act and orders and directions issued under this Act.

Section 19 - Cognizance of offences (citizen's suit).

A court can take cognizance of an offence only on a complaint made by the central government, or any authority or officer authorized or by any person who has given notice of not less than 60 days to the central government, or any authority or officer authorized.

This citizen's suit section appears to give significant powers to the citizens to enforce the EPA. However, under the EPA, only government officers have the power of sample collection, which may be produced as evidence during proceedings. This particular aspect seems to weaken the Section.

Section 22 - Bar of jurisdiction.

No civil court has the jurisdiction to entertain any suit, or proceedings in respect of anything done, action taken, or order or direction issued by the central government or any other authority or officer in pursuance of any power conferred by or in relation to its or his /her function under the Act.

Section 23 - Powers to delegate.

The central government can delegate its functions (as specified in Section 3 of the Act).

Section 24 - Effect of other laws - (i) Subject to the provisions of subsection (2), the provisions of this Act and rules or orders made therein shall have effect not withstanding anything inconsistent therewith contained in any enactment other than this Act, (2) Where any act or omission constitutes an offence punishable under this Act and also under any other Act then the offender found guilty of such offence shall be liable to be punished under the other Act and not under this Act.

Section 25 - Power to make rules - The central government may, by notification in the Official Gazette make rules for carrying out the purpose of this Act. (2) In particular, and without prejudice to the generality of the foregoing power, such rules may provide for all or any of the ten following matters: (a) the standards for discharge and emissions of environmental pollutants under Section 7, (b) procedure for handling of hazardous substances under Section 8 (c) matters of subsection (1) of section 9, (d) manner of taking samples of air, water, soil or other substances for analysis as dealt with under subsection (1) of Section 11, (e) manner of serving the analysis report under clause (a) of subsection (3) of Section 11, (f) the functions of environmental laboratories, procedure of submission of samples to those laboratories, form of laboratory report, fees payable for such report and other matters for good functioning of laboratories under subsection (2) of Section 12, (g) the qualification of government analyst as under Section 13, (h) the manner of serving the notice of the offence and intention to make a complaint to the central government as under clause (b) of section 19, (i) the authority or officer to whom any report, statistics, returns, accounts and other information shall be furnished as under Section 20, (j) any other matter which is required or may be prescribed by the central government.

26. Rules made under this Act to be laid before Parliament. The procedure and time period have been prescribed.

Additional Provisions: Environment (Protection) Act, 1986 and Rules 1986

- Notifications issued under the Act
- EP ACT- Hazardous Waste (Management & Handling) Rules, 1989; recent amendment in 2008-Hazardous Material (Management, Handling & Transboundary Movement). The following are the important provisions of the Rules. The Amended Rules (2008) include seven chapters containing 26 clauses, seven schedules and fifteen prescribed forms. There are guidelines and regulations for the features.
- The manufacture, Storage and Import of Hazardous Chemicals Rules,1989.
- The Bio-Medical Waste (Management and Handling) Rules,1998.
- The Plastics Manufacture, Sale and Usage Rules,1999.
- The Noise Pollution (Regulation and Control) Rules, 2000.
- The Municipal Solid Wastes (Management and Handling) Rules, 2000.
- The Batteries (Management and Handling) Rules, 2001.
- Coastal Regulation Zone Notification (1991).
- Dhanu Taluka Notification (1991).
- Doon Valley Notification (1989).
- Revdanda Creek Notification (1989).
- Disposal of Fly Ash Notification (1999).
- Taj Trapezium Notification (1998).
- Ash Content Notification (1997).
- The Environment Impact Assessment Notification (1994) and as amended in 1997, 2006, 2009, & 2011.
- Under EIA Notification, 1994, section 2 stipulates requirement of prior environmental clearance (EC) for all new projects or activities listed in the Schedule to this notification and for expansion and modernization of existing projects listed in the Schedule to this notification. This is reiterated in Section 7 of EIA Notification.

4.11.1 Environmental Impact Assessment (EIA), 1994

Until January 27, 1994, obtaining environmental clearance from MoEF was only an administrative requirement intended for mega projects undertaken by the government or public sector undertakings. Public hearing provision was part of the EIA.

The EIA notification of Sept. 14, 2006, makes EIA statutory for 40 items (A & B category) under 8 projects/activities (Schedule of the notification). There will be a Central Expert Appraisal Committee for all projects included under MOEF (A category) & a state level EIA authority for B category projects. Further Amendments were made in 1997, 2006 and 2011.

The salient provisions of the notification are as follows:

All projects listed under Schedule are required to obtain environmental clearance (EC) from the MoEF/state government. Projects that fall under 'A' category need clearance from the MoEF.

All development projects, whether under Schedule or not, if they are to be located in certain notified ecologically sensitive or fragile areas, will have to obtain clearance from MoEF. Industrial projects are further required to obtain a LoI (letter of intent) from the Ministry of Industry, and a NOC (no objection certificate) from the SPCB and the State Forest Department if the location involves forest land.

Once the NOC is obtained, the LOI is converted to an industrial licence by the State authorities. However, if the project falls under Schedule of the EIA notification, (A-category) it must obtain an environmental clearance from the MOEF. In all cases an application seeking prior EC shall be made in the prescribed Form-1 and with a pre-feasibility project report except that, in case of construction projects or activities in addition to Form-1 and the supplementary Form-1A, a copy of the conceptual plan shall be provided instead of the pre-feasibility report.

Form 1A includes the checklist of environmental impacts such as: (i) Land Environment (photograph and nine aspects; (ii) Water Environment (14 aspects); (iii) Vegetation (3 aspects); (iv) Fauna (3 items); (v) Air Environment (6 items); (vi) Aesthetics (4 items); (vii) Socio-Economic Aspects (3 items); (viii) Building Materials (4 items); (ix) Energy Conservation (13 items); (x) Environment Management Plan. Environmental Clearance(EC) will have four stages: (i) Screening, (for A, B1 & B2 categories), (ii) Scoping for A and B1 category of projects, (iii) Public Consultation (for A and B1 categories—except building, township etc. Defence, Expansion of Roads & Highways, modernization of irrigation projects and B2 category projects), (iv) Appraisal (detailed scrutiny by EAC or State level EAC). The EIA report that is submitted after the site clearance contains the following. (i) Description of site, site map, (ii) land requirements, no objection certificate from State Forest Department if forest land is involved, (iii) Rehabilitation plan for displaced people, (iv) Consent to establish from SPCB (regarding effluents and emissions), (v) Report on impacts on the environment during construction, (vi) Collection of ambient air quality and meteorological data, (vii) Report on hydrology and water quality, (viii) Report on occupational safety and health, (ix) Details of transport and handling of raw material, (x) Report of impact on sensitive territory.

EIA generic structure includes the following: (i) Introduction—purpose of the report, identification of project and project proponent, brief description, scope of study as per term of reference (TOR); (ii) Project description; (iii) Description of the Environment-study area, components and methodology, baseline for valued environmental components as identified in the scope, base maps of all environmental components; (iv) Anticipated environmental impacts and mitigation measures; (v) Analysis of alternatives (Technology and Site); (vi) Environmental Monitoring Programme; (vii) Additional studies (Public Consultation, Risk assessment, Social Impact Assessment; R&R Action Plans; (viii) Project Benefits; (ix) Environmental Cost-Benefit Analysis; (x) EMP; (xi) Summary & Conclusion (This will constitute the summary of the EIA report); (xii) Disclosure of Consultants engaged.

The EIA document is designed: (i) to impose certain restrictions and prohibitions on some projects or activities and expansion and modernization of existing capacity of projects/ activities, (ii) to seek public consultation from stakeholders, (iii) to incorporate necessary environmental safeguards through Environment Management Programme by assessing the impacts at planning stage itself through a transparent process involving consultation of public and relevant experts.

The general conditions of EIA notification: (i) any project or activity specified in category B will be treated as category A, if located or in part within 10 km from the boundary of (a) protected areas notified under the Wildlife (Protection) Act, 1972, (b) critically polluted areas as notified by CPCB from time to time, (c) notified ecosensitive areas, (d) interstate boundary and international boundaries.

4.11.2 EIA Case Studies

Impacts of mining

(i) Impacts on Land, (Figure, 41-46)—Changes in topography and land scenario, change of land - use pattern, changes in drainage pattern, changes in top soil composition by run off from overburden dumps, damage to archeological / religious monuments, (ii) Impacts on water regime, (iii) Impacts on Atmosphere, (iv) Impacts on Ecology, (iv) Impacts on Society.

Impact on Atmosphere

The impact can be summarized as: (i) Increase in temperature in the area due to industrial activity and decrease in vegetation, (ii) High Suspended Particulate Matter (SPM) levels due to vehicle movement and other operations, (iii) Drilling and blasting contribute to explosive fumes, (iv) Increase in oxides of nitrogen, hydrocarbons, carbon monoxide and lead levels due to diesel equipment, generators, vehicle movement, etc., (v) Increase in ambient noise. Figures 47-50 show the activities in the mining area and dust generation.

Impact on water sources

The possible impact can be (i) Changes in surface and groundwater regime (ii) Removal of surface water bodies (iii) Damage of all aquifers above the mineral deposits (iv) Depletion of

Figure 41. Shows the impact on land (physical disturbance) from Er. S.K. Guru)

Figure 42. Disturbance to landscape (from Er. S.K. Guru)

Figure 43. Waste rock disposal

Figure 44. Erosion of waste dumps

Figure 45. Left out voids

Figure 46. Subsidence due to mining (from Er. S.K. Guru)

Figure 47. Surface mining and suspended particulate matter

Figure 48. Dust generation in coal mining quarry

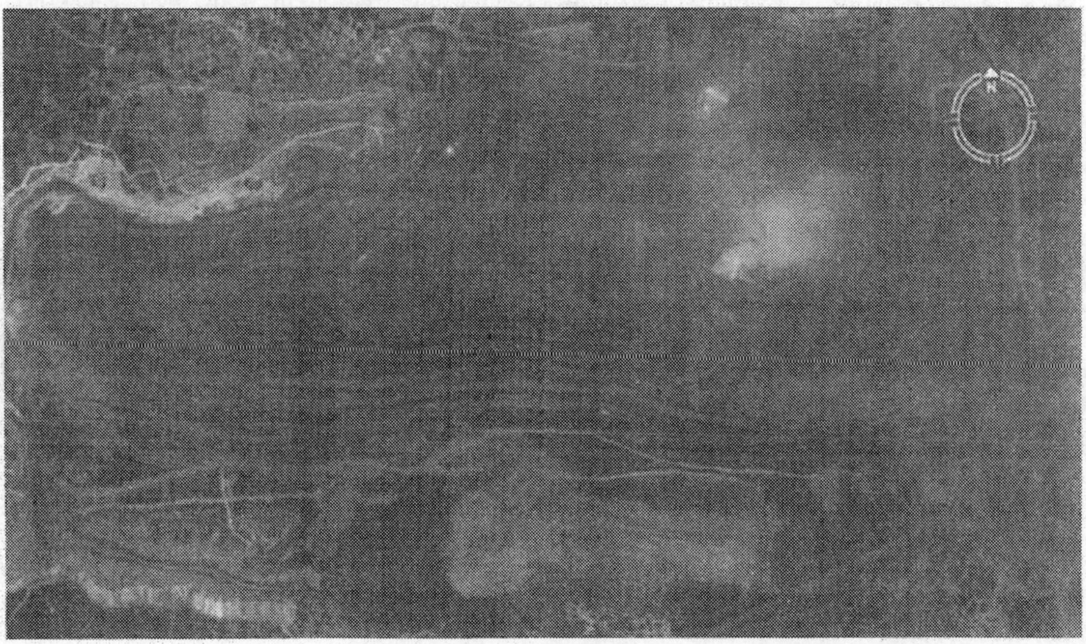

Figure 49. Emissions from mine fire

Figure 50. Gaseous emissions due to blasting

Ground Water - Pumping of high pressure aquifers, below the minerals deposits: (v) Pollution of surface water bodies due to runoff from mines, leaching from dumps, and beneficiation activities. Besides, mineral deposits rich with pyrites/sulfides leach acidic water to the water bodies and on closure of the mine, open pits act as water bodies and recharge groundwater table. Figures 51-52 show the impact on water bodies.

Impact on Ecology

The impact is caused due to removal of vegetation, which affects fauna; pollution of water bodies, which affects aquatic ecology; high fugitive emissions and release of other gaseous emissions, which retards the growth of vegetation; and by noise pollution due to blasting and subsequent vibration, which drives away wild animals. Besides, bioaccumulation of heavy metals may happen through the food chain. (Figures 53-54)

Impact on Society

The mining activities will create employment opportunities, economic upliftment, development of infrastructure facilities such as healthcare, education facilities for local people, and secondary business opportunities etc. The negative impact can be displacement of people, loss of livelihood, changes in population, increase in cost of living, economic disparity and frustration among lower income groups, water scarcity, and health impact due to deterioration in environmental quality.

Who requires an EIA? The following require an Environmental Impact Assessment Study. (Figures 55-58): (i) A new mine, (ii) Mine intending to increase production, (iii) Mine intending to

Figure 51. Acidic and metal bearing soil and water

Figure 52. Acid drainage due to mining

Figure 53. Bioaccumulation

Figure 54. Cumulative impact

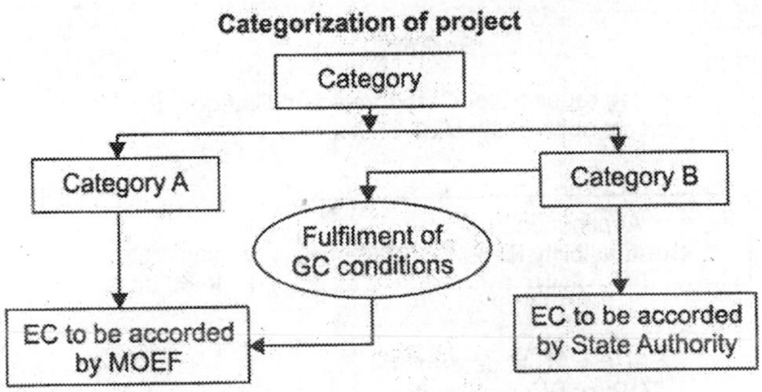

Figure 55. Project categorization and processes

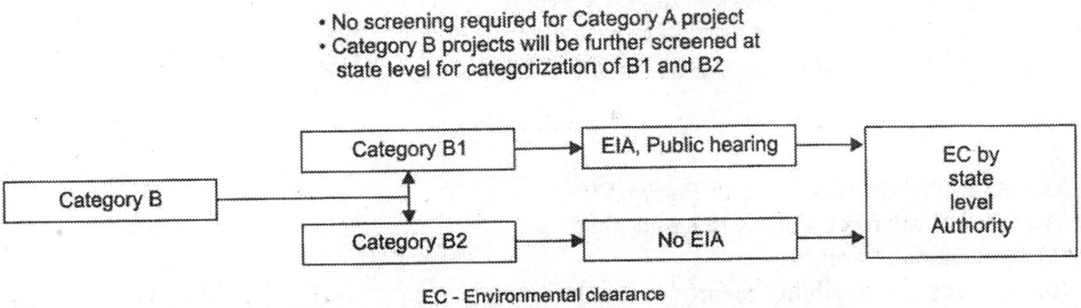

Figure 56. Screening

increase lease area, (iv) While renewing lease after 1994, (v) Inclusion of beneficiation process Figures 55 and 56 show the categorization of projects and screening procedure.

Features of Category A Projects:

- Non-coal mining e” 50 ha lease area
- Coal mining e”150 ha lease area
- Mineral beneficiation e” 0.1 MTPA
- Coal beneficiation e” 0.10 MTPA

(vi) Slurry pipeline passing through certain areas.

- Slurry pipelines passing through national parks/sanctuaries/coral reefs/ecologically sensitive area

Features of Category B Projects

- Non-coal mines <50 ha e” 5 ha
- Coal mines <150 ha e” 5 ha
- Mineral beneficiation < 0.1 MTPA
- Coal beneficiation < 1.0 MTPA

Projects of Category A or Category B cannot be allowed to be established in situations narrated below:

(i) Inter-state boundaries (ii) International boundaries (iii) within 10 km of protected areas as per Water Act, 1974 (iv) Eco-sensitive areas as per EP Act, 1986 (v) Critically polluted areas.

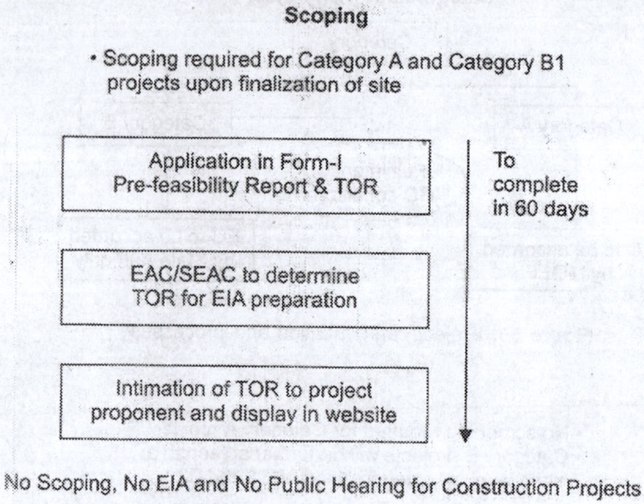

Figure 57: Screening Chart

The screening chart is given in Figure 57

The term of reference (TOR) is based on:

(a) Application in Form I
(b) Based on pre-feasibility report
(c) Mining Plan
(d) Site Map and Plan
(e) Proposed term of reference

Information on the following aspects is required by the Regulatory Agency.

- Proposed activity
- Use of natural resources - source, quantity
- Use, storage, transportation and handling of materials
- Solid waste generation and disposal methods
- Release of air pollutants, and pollution abatement equipment and efficiency
- Noise, vibration, light, heat and control of the pollution
- Risk of contamination of land and water and plan to mitigate risk
- Risk of accident and mitigation plan
- Cumulative impact and neutralization plan
- Environmental sensitivity

Public Hearing (Figure 58) requirements are listed below and Figure 58 shows the steps involved.

- Required for project requiring Environmental Clearance
- EIA / EMP circulated widely
- Public Notice issued
- Public opinion communicated to the Regulatory Agency

The application processing procedure is listed in Figures 59-60.

Figure 59-60 The currently practiced procedure in India is listed below.

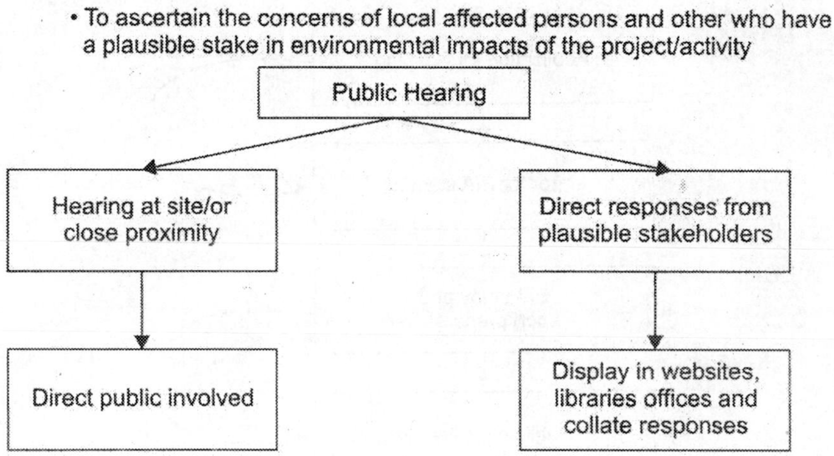

Figure 58. Public consultation process

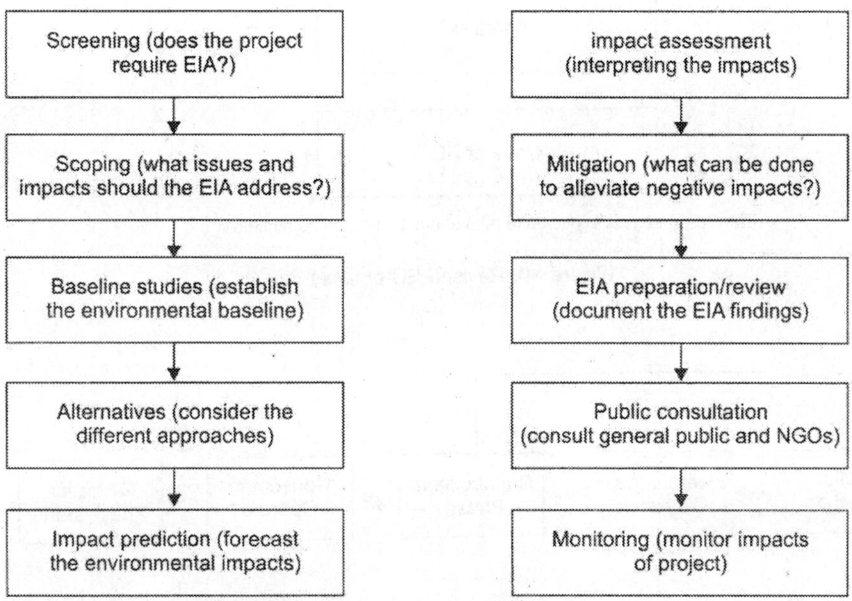

Figure 59. Application processing procedure

The public disclosure procedure is as follows:

- Proceedings of public hearing to be displayed at panchayat, zilla parishad and collectorate.
- SPCB to display on its website. (SPCB—State Pollution Control Board)
- Category A project to notify it in two local dailies.
- Category B to intimate on clearance in newspaper.
- MoEF and SEIAA to display clearance on their website. (SEIAA—State Environment Impact Assessment Authority)
- Proponent to submit copies to local bodies and relevant offices of Govt.

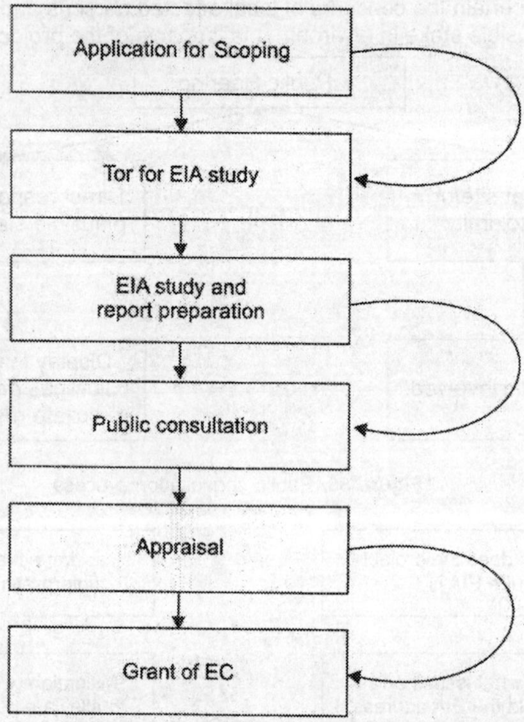

The EC process is expected to take about 11-12 months minimum

Figure 60. Revised EC process

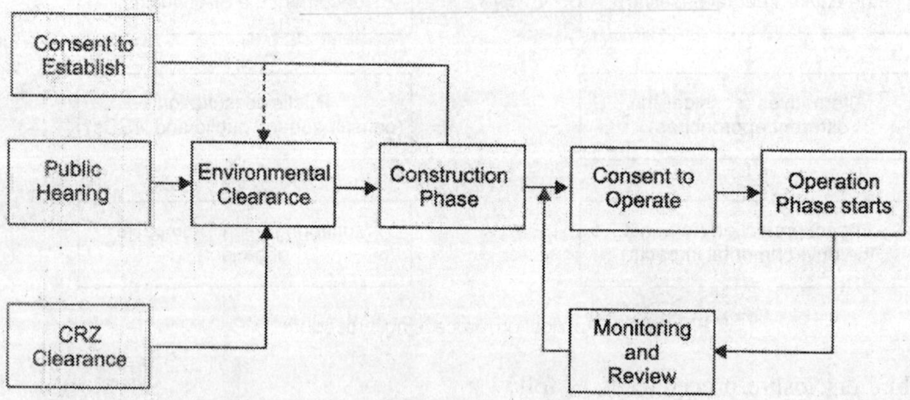

Figure 61. Regulatory framework (operational phase)

After the operational phase the following aspects are important:

- Six-monthly compliance report.
- Public display of self-monitoring result.
- Physical verification by MoEF / SPCB.

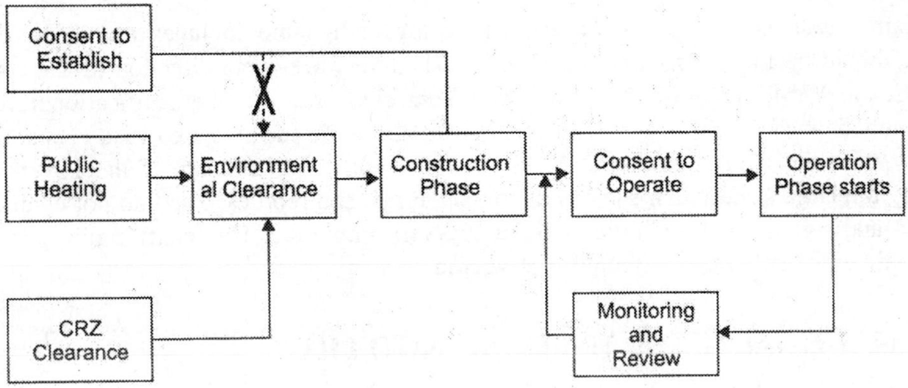

Figure 62. Regulatory framework

4.11.3 EP ACT: A Critique

Section 19 (citizen's suit provision) of the Act seemingly gives the public significant powers to enforce the Act. However, only government officials are given the power under the Act to collect samples needed as evidence. In addition, during the sixty days notice period required for the government to decide whether to proceed against the alleged isolator, the offending industry has time to clean up and prepare itself for collection of samples. Section 24 of the Environment (Protection) Act, 1986 is one of its controversial provisions. Generally, more recent legislation, which conflicts with the previous legislation, supersedes the previous legislation. Standards established under the EPA are also dealt with under the Water Act and the Air Act.

In case of a violation, both under the EPA and Water Act or Air Act, the penal provisions of the Water Act or the Air Act would usually apply. The high penalties provided in the Act are, therefore, illusionary for those violations where Water Act and Air Act also apply. In the case Research Foundation for Science Technology and National Resource Policy versus Union of India, the direction of Supreme Court of India is important.

Selected local residents should be appointed as wardens for environmental surveillance, particularly to take note of illegal dumping of hazardous wastes. Access to public records with the environment protection authorities should be freely allowed to the public, as the right to a healthy environment has been defined as part of the Right to Life under Article 21 of the Constitution. Relevant important information should be displayed on notice boards and newspapers and communicated through radio, television and the Internet. The court decisions stipulate that all industries, involved in hazardous chemicals and generating hazardous wastes display online update outside the factory gate, on quantity and nature of hazardous chemicals being used in the plant, as well as water and air emissions and solid wastes generated within the factory premises. If such data is not made available, the unit should be asked to show cause or even be asked to close down. Relevant information should be displayed on notice boards and newspapers and communicated through radio, television and the Internet. Besides, the informers and "whistle-blowers" within, industry, who provide information, should be protected and strict confidentiality about them maintained.

Third party audit of hazardous wastes, where the audit team includes members of the community, should be made a routine practice. This is a very welcome direction of the court.

Under EIA and EMP the flora (vegetation) and fauna enumeration and quantification have not been adequately defined. The forest departments may not have the adequate expertise to enumerate and quantify the flora (trees, shrubs, herbs, etc). The wildlife departments of the government usually study the large sized fauna such as mammals, birds, and reptiles. They do not enumerate invertebrates and soil fauna, which are ecologically very important. University biology faculty and individual biodiversity experts should be involved.

4.12 THE NATIONAL GREEN TRIBUNAL (NGT) BILL

This bill was signed by the minister of Forests and Environment on 29th July, 2009 and listed as Bill no. 63 of 2009 dated July, 2009 and adopted by the Indian Parliament in 2010.

4.12.1 Purpose of the Bill

The bill is aimed to provide for the establishment of a National Green Tribunal (NCT) for the effective and expeditious disposal of cases relating to environmental protection and conservation of forests and other natural resources including enforcement of any legal right relating to environment and giving relief and compensation for damages to persons and property and for matters connected therewith or incidental thereto.

The bill has been prepared and placed before the Indian Parliament for enactment on the basis of the preamble that the UNO Conference on the Human Environment held at Stockholm in June,1972. It called upon the states to take appropriate steps for the protection and improvement of the human environment, and on the basis of the decision at the UNO Conference on Environment and Development held at Rio de Janeiro in June,1992, called upon the states to provide effective access to judicial and administrative proceedings including to redress and remedy and to develop national laws regarding the liability and compensation for the victims of pollution and other environmental damages. This bill also refers to the judicial pronouncement in India that the right to healthy environment has been construed as a part of the right to life under Article 21 of the Constitution. It is considered expedient to implement the decisions taken at the aforesaid conferences and to have an NGT in view of the multidisciplinary issues relating to the environment. The National Environment Tribunal Act, 1995, which had a very limited mandate and was not established, and the National Environment Appellate Authority Act, 1997 has a limited workload because of the narrow scope of jurisdiction and therefore, the Supreme Court requested the Law Commission of India to consider the need for constitution of specialized environmental courts having both original and appellate jurisdiction relating to environmental laws. The final outcome is the Green Tribunal Bill and enactment of the NGT Act.

4.12.2 Arrangement of Clauses

The bill consists of five chapters; Chapter 1 includes the short title and commencement and definitions; Chapter 2 includes the establishment of the Tribunal; Chapter 3 includes the jurisdiction, powers and proceedings of the tribunal; Chapter 4 includes the penalty provision; Chapter 5 includes miscellaneous matters such as bar of jurisdiction, cognizance of offences, power of amendments, repeal and savings, and followed by provisions of Schedule I, Schedule II and Schedule III.

4.12.3 Salient Features

This Act may be called the National Green Tribunal Act, 2009.

In the context of this Act, accident, chairperson, environment, expert member, handling, hazardous substance, injury judicial member, etc. have been defined.

Besides the words and expressions used in this Act but not defined herein and defined in the Water Act, 1974; the Water Cess Act, 1977; the Forest Act, 1980; the Air Act, 1981, the Environment (Protection) Act, 1986; the Public Liability Insurance Act,1991 and the Biological Diversity Act, 2002 and other Acts relating to the environment shall have the meaning, respectively assigned to them in those Acts.

The National Green Tribunal shall consist of: (a) a full time chairperson: (b) judicial members, (c) expert members.

Qualification of Chairperson and Members

A person who has not been a judge of Supreme Court of India or Chief Justice of a High Court cannot be the chairperson. A person who is or has been a judge of the High Court shall be qualified to be appointed as a judicial member.

An expert member shall have a Master of Science degree in Physical or Life Sciences with a Doctorate degree or Master of Engineering or Master of Technology and with an experience of 15 years in the relevant field including five years' practical experience in the field of environment and forests including pollution control, hazardous substance management, environmental impact assessment, climate change management, biological diversity management and forest conservation in a reputed national level institution or has administrative experience of fifteen years including an experience of five years in dealing with environmental matters in the central or a state government or in a reputed national or state level institution. The Chairperson and the judicial and expert members shall not hold any other office during their tenure as such and they also shall not, for a period of one year from the date on which they cease to hold office, accept any employment in, or connected with the management or administration of, any person who has been a party to a proceeding before the Tribunal under this Act. However, this will not apply for appointment under central or state governments or local authority or any statutory authority or any corporation established by or under any Central, State or Provincial Act or a government company as defined in section 617 of the Companies Act, 1956.

The central government shall appoint the Chairperson in consultation with the Chief Justice of India, and appoint other members on the recommendations of such selection committee and in such manner as may be prescribed. The Chairperson or judicial member who is or has been a judge in the Supreme Court shall not hold office after he has attained the age of seventy years. In case a person, who has been the Chief Justice of a High Court, has been appointed as Chairperson or judicial member of the Tribunal, he shall not hold office after he has attained the age of sixty-seven years. Judicial members who have been a judge of the High Court shall not hold office after the age of sixty-seven years. No expert member shall hold office after he has attained the age of sixty-five years.

The Chairperson and members can resign from their office by serving notice in writing under their hand addressed to the central government. There are conditions attached to removal of the Chairperson, and members of the Tribunal by the central government.

Power of the Tribunal

The Tribunal shall have jurisdiction over all civil cases where a substantial question relating to environment (including enforcement of any legal right relating to environment), is involved and such question arises out of the implementation of the enactment specified in Schedule I.

Relief, Compensation and Restitution

The Tribunal, may by an order, provide: (a) relief and compensation to the victims of pollution and other environmental damage arising under the enactment specified in Scheduled I (including accident occurring while handling any hazardous substance); (b) for restitution of property damaged; (c) for restitution of the environment for such area or areas as the Tribunal may think fit.

The relief, compensation and restitution of property and environment referred to above shall be in addition to the relief paid or payable under the Public Liability Insurance Act, 1991. No application shall be entertained after a period of five years from the date on which the cause for such compensation or relief first arose. The Tribunal if satisfied that the applicant was prevented by sufficient cause from filling the application within the said period, can allow another sixty days for filing of application.

The Tribunal will have appellate jurisdiction. The details have been prescribed.

The Tribunal shall not be bound by the procedure laid dawn by the code of Civil Procedure, 1908 but shall be guided by the principles of natural justice. The Tribunal shall also not be bound by the rules of evidence contained in the Indian Evidence Act, 1872. The Tribunal shall have, for the purposes of discharging its functions under this Act, the same powers as are vested in a civil court under the code of Civil Procedures, 1908 while trying a suit, in respect of matters mentioned in this Act.

All proceedings before the Tribunal shall be deemed to be judicial proceedings within the meaning of sections 193, 219 and 228 for the purpose of section 196 of the Indian Penal Code and the Tribunal shall be deemed to be a civil court for the purpose of section 195 and chapter XXVI of the Code of Criminal Procedure, 1973.

The decision of the Tribunal by majority of its members shall be binding. Every order of the Tribunal under this Act shall be final.

In Chapter IV penalty for failure to comply with Orders of Tribunal have been prescribed. The penalty prescribed is stricter than that prescribed under the Water Act, Air Act and EP Act. Whoever fails to comply with any order or award or decision of the Tribunal under this Act, shall be punishable with imprisonment for a term which may extend to three years, or with fine which may extend to ten crore rupees or with both and in case the failure or contravention continues, with additional fine which may extend to twenty-five thousand rupees for every day during which such failure or contravention continues after conviction for the first such failure or contravention. The penalty is more severe in case a company fails to comply with any order or award or decision of the Tribunal under this Act. The fine may extend to twenty-five crore rupees and in case the failure or contravention continues, with additional fine which may extend to rupees one lakh for every day of non-compliance.

Chapter V deals with bar jurisdiction, cognizance of offences, etc.

No civil court shall have the jurisdiction to entertain any appeal in respect of any matter, which the Tribunal is empowered to determine under its appellate jurisdiction. Provisions for protection of action taken in good faith have been stipulated. The Act will have overriding effect.

The Chairperson, judicial and expert members and other employees of the Tribunal shall be deemed to be public servants within the meaning of Section 21 of the Indian Penal Code.

Article 37(1) of chapter V stipulates that The National Environment Tribunal Act, 1995 and the National Environment Appellate Authority Act, 1997 are hereby repealed (hereinafter referred to as repealed Act). The persons appointed to various positions shall vacate their respective offices and no such chairperson, vice-chairperson and every other person appointed as member shall be entitled to claim any compensation for the premature termination of the term of his office or of any contract of service. Some other provisions to pending matters have been made.

Schedule I includes the provisions of seven Acts: The Water Act, 1974; The Water Cess Act, 1977; The Forest Act, 1980; The Air Act, 1981; The Environment (Protection) Act, 1986; The Public Liability Insurance Act, 1991; The Biological Diversity Act, 2002.

Schedule II includes heads under which compensation or relief for damage may be cleared (14 items).

Schedule III includes Amendment (Insertion of new 33 B to the Water (Prevention and Control of Pollution) Act, 1974 & Appeal to National Green Tribunal; Amendment of Section 13 and insertion of new Section 13A under Water (Prevention and Control of Pollution) Cess Act, 1977; Amendment to the Forest (Conservation) Act, 1980; Insertion of new Section 2A & Appeal to National Green Tribunal (NGT), Amendment to the Air (Prevention and Control of Pollution) Act, 1981 and insertion of new section 31B and Appeal to NGT, Amendment to the Environment (Protection) Act, 1986; Insertion of new section 5A & Appeal to NGT; Amendments to the Biological Diversity Act, 2002; Amendment of Section 52, insertion of new Section 52A; and Appeal to NGT.

CHAPTER 5

Waste Management

5.1 MUNICIPAL SOLID WASTE (MSW)

The urban population in India is increasing rapidly without proportionate increase in housing and other infrastructure facilities. This has led to serious insanitary conditions. One of the main causes of insanitation is the grossly inadequate management of the urban/municipal solid waste (garbage).

5.1.1 Impact of Improper Management of Urban Solid Waste (USW)/MSW

Urban solid waste/municipal solid waste can itself be hazardous or may produce secondary hazards by combination with other materials or could be hazardous by reason of location, handling and disposal. The adverse impact of improper management of MSW is broadly as follows. Flies and insects breed on rotting garbage and can be disease vectors (malaria, dengue, dysentery, diarrhoea, etc.). Rats thrive on garbage and can transmit diseases like plague, murine, typhus, leptospirosis, histoplasmosis, salmonellosis, etc. Fires in garbage dumping areas continue for days. Fires are caused by open burning practice of dry garbage or triggered by heat generated by organic decomposing. Objectionable odour is caused by decomposing organic matter in uncollected garbage. Handling of garbage directly infects the workers with many diseases caused by roundworm, etc. Burning and decomposing garbage causes air pollution. Burning PVC produces toxic pollutants. Leachates from garbage dumps cause water pollution. Uncollected garbage is aesthetically objectionable. It discourages tourists, which is an economic loss. Generating huge quantity of refuse can be considered wastage of resource.

Source Classification and Composition of Wastes

Table 19 shows the different classes of MSW/USW, their origin and characteristics.

Per capita generation of solid wastes in developed countries is very high (USA 2.4 kg/d, Japan 0.94 kg/d) and very low in developing countries (India 0.5 kg/day, Pakistan 0.6 kg/d, Sri Lanka 0.7 kg/d).

The average composition of USW/MSW in India is given in Table 20.

Table 19. Municipal Solid Waste Classification and Characteristics

Sl.No	Waste	Source	Characteristics
1.	Refuse	(a) Domestic (b) Institutional (c) Market/commercial	• Biodegradables (food, vegetables, veg oils etc.) • Non-biodegradables (polythene bags, plastics, packings etc.) • Combustibles (textiles, rubbers, papers etc.) • Non-combustibles (metals, glasses etc.) • Combustibles (papers, polythenes etc.) • Non-combustibles (metals, glasses etc.) • Mainly biodegradables and combustibles.
2.	Burning ash	Solid fuel burning	Generally inert
3.	Construction waste	Construction/ demolition/ modification	Generally inert
4.	Industrial waste	Industries	Hazardous and non-hazardous
5.	Sewer sludge	Sewer cleaning	Biodegradable and organic
6.	Road	Road sweeping	Polythene, waste paper, leaves, dusts etc.
7.	Clinical wastes	Hospitals and clinics	Hazardous and toxic
8.	Agro-waste	Crop yield	Organic, combustible and biodegradable
9.	Animal waste	Animal sheds	Biodegradable
10.	Offal	Butchering, abattoir	Biodegradable

(*Source:* Odisha State Pollution Control Board)

Table 20. Average Composition of MSW in India

Description	Percentage by Weight
Vegetables and leaves	40.15
Grass	3.80
Paper	0.80
Plastic	0.62
Glass and ceramics	0.44
Metal	0.64
Stones and ashes	41.81
Miscellaneous	11.73

(*Source:* Central Pollution Control Board publication)

Management Practice of Municipal Solid Waste in India

The present management practice of urban solid waste in India is most unsatisfactory. Both the municipal staff and the citizens are responsible for the bad state of affairs. The following facts are often encountered in cities and towns.

(a) Householders do not always carry their garbage to the nearest municipal bin. Very often the garbage is thrown in the streets or drains. (b) General public, vendors, etc., throw litter here and there in the market and other public places. (c) Municipal sweepers sweep the road every day but the sweepings are not totally collected for final disposal. They are left as heaps in street corners. (d) Municipal bins are often overflowing will garbage, which is not collected regularly. (e) Stray animals (cows, pigs and dogs) freely roam on the roads and are often found feeding on the garbage. (f) Ragpickers pick up recyclable materials (metals, polythene bags etc.) from the garbage with great risk of health hazard. (g) There is no segregation of wastes at any stage. (h) The collected garbage is not scientifically treated or disposed. (i) Garbage is carried in open trucks or dumpers and haphazardly thrown in low lying or open areas in the outskirts. No consideration is given to geological, physiographical and groundwater conditions in choosing the disposal sites. The reasons for these are attributable to the following managerial and other failures: (i) Lack of awareness amongst the general public, (ii) Lack of public pressure, (iii) Indifference and ignorance of municipal authorities, (iv) Lack of infrastructure and financial resources of the municipalities, (v) Indiscipline and lack of skill of municipal workers, (vi) indifference of employees.

Options of Improved Management

5.1.2 Collection and Storage

Ideally each house should have separate household bins for: (i) Biodegradables (food residue), (ii) Incinerables (plastics, waste paper, etc.) and, (iii) Recyclable and others (metal articles, newspapers, glass, etc.).

The segregated wastes should be taken to similarly separate community bins for each block of houses and the municipal authority should collect the wastes from the community bins for processing and/or transportation to disposal sites. Such collection and storage system exists in most developed industrialized countries where the level of education is high. It may not be very practical in the Indian conditions. However, this system is feasible in many industrial townships and housing colonies after proper awareness generation programmes. In general Indian conditions, recyclable materials can be collected at the storage stage. Since regular and scientific incineration is not in practice in India, incinerables need not be separated. But waste can be segregated (after picking up of recyclable materials) into biodegradable and non-biodegradable. NGOs can play a very important role in the door-to-door collection and segregation. Their role in awareness generation is also very important. Selection and design of the community bins is important.

Following aspects should be considered for selecting the type of bins: (i) Hygiene (exclusion of insects, rodents and odour). It may be possible to achieve with adequate cover and/or spraying of insecticides/special microbial inoculums. (ii) Capacity (adequate volume so that the garbage does not spill). (iii) Weather resistance (impermeable). (iv) Convenience of use by the user and the collector. A colour code can be followed where separate bins are used for separate categories of waste. (v) Aesthetical acceptability. Quick removal of garbage is an important aspect of USW management. A breakdown in this system could create many acute environmental nuisances. For this a proper collection programme and routing of transport vehicles should be planned. Transportation implies conveyance from the point of collection to the point of final disposal, either directly or through a transfer system. The transport vehicle may range from a small wheelbarrow to a cycle rickshaw to a large truck or a dumper depending upon the requirements. The factors that may be considered are the following: (i) Transport - Layout and condition of road, (ii) Method of collection and storage, (iii) Frequency of collection, (iv) Method of loading and unloading, (v) Hygienic and aesthetic requirement (transport vehicles should be covered) (ii) Disposal Methods - The present practice of unscientifically dumping MSW/USW in open or low lying spaces and burning them openly is highly undesirable and should be discontinued. Various disposal methods available are discussed briefly.

5.1.3 Biomethanation

Biomethanation has the same principle as gobar (cow dung) gas plant. Segregated biodegradable waste having high organic content can, in principle, be anaerobically digested like cow dung to recover combustible methane gas and the remaining slurry acts as organic manure. Small anaerobic digesters based on animal dung and human faeces have been very successful. Large operations using other degradable materials have many operational difficulties and are not always cost-effective.

5.1.4 Incineration

Incineration of dry combustible wastes and plastics, etc., is a very common method of disposal in many developed countries. This is the best way of destroying the increasing amount of non-biodegradable polymeric materials like polythene and plastics. This method is again not very viable and cost-effective in Indian conditions at this stage. However, highly infectious hospital wastes are recommended for incineration. Small incinerators are manufactured in India for this purpose.

5.1.5 Pelletization

Pelletization can be an option for wastes of high calorific value like waste paper, grass, dry leaves, etc. The inorganic components of waste are first removed and the components of high calorific value are pulverized and palletized to cubical or cylindrical blocks. These blocks can be used as fuel of good calorific value comparable to that of E-F grade coal. The proportion of combustibles of high calorific value in Indian USW is less which makes pelletization a less attractive option. This, however, has good prospects for agro-wastes.

5.1.6 Composting

Composting of biodegradable component of the MSW is an attractive option. Biodegradation can be done both anaerobically and aerobically. Composting has the following advantages. Technology is simple and does not require much skill. Plant nutrients (N, P and K) are retained. Thus, resource is recovered.

Anaerobic composting is the common practice followed in farming. Anaerobic bacteria do the degradation of biodegradable matters. It is done manually. Degradable organic matter is put in pits with layers of cow dung as source of bacteria and covered with soil. Organic matters are converted to compost manure in about 9 months to 1 year. The operation of the process is simple but the long time taken does not make it an attractive option for disposal of USW. Besides, the compost is not free from pathogens.

Aerobic composting is the process where the bacterial action takes place in the presence of oxygen. The process is a very viable option because of the following: decomposition/degradation is rapid, normally completed within 4-6 weeks.

During the process, temperature increases killing harmful pathogens, weed seeds, insect eggs. The end product is safe to handle.

Some favourable conditions should be maintained for best results. These are: Moisture content should be between 20% to 40%. Excess moisture stimulates anaerobic bacteria. Temperature should not rise above 70° C. Periodic turning of the waste controls the temperature and allows access of air. A carbon/nitrogen ratio of 30 is best suited for the microorganisms. The product has the ratio of < 20. Control of wind and flies is important.

Mechanization can be introduced into the process to accelerate it and the mechanical composting is done in two ways, viz., windrow process and close cell process. The Excel Industries Ltd. Mumbai, has developed a controlled aerobic composting process with the following strategies: (i) Waste sanitation at the points of first collection (bins from where the garbage will be lifted), and (ii) Controlled aerobic composting and mechanical screening of digested compost.

Many plants based on the above principles (Excel's technology) have been established in several cities in India. This technology is ideally suited for large towns where the quantity of garbage collected is high. With low garbage input, it is not cost-effective.

An alternative method of low cost aerobic composting, which is practical and suitable for small towns, has been developed by Ms Almitra H. Patel and submitted to the Supreme Court of India vide the Writ Petition (Civil) No. 888/96 (Almitra H. Patel vs Union of India). This low-cost method, for convenience termed is "bio-treatment", has recently been adopted in some towns. The process, however, does not produce germ-free compost to the extent as in the aforesaid process (Excel technologies). This compost can be compared with the normal farm compost prepared in compost pits considering its hygiene level.

Vermi-composting

Earthworms (verms) are utilized to produce organic manure (compost), to grow mushrooms, vegetables, flowers and crops profitably and as a feed to fish, poultry, pigs and of man. Earthworms (verms) technology is called vermi-technology which involves five components: (i) Vermiculture that is culturing of earthworms mass scale, (ii) Vermicomposting for converting municipal organic waste, agricultural organic waste, canteen waste into manure, using suitable species of earthworms, (iii) Utilization of products like vermi-protein and vermi-fertilizer, for producing vermi-feed as protein source for fish and poultry, and for growing edible mushrooms (Dash and Dash, 1989; Dash and Dash, 1990), using vermi-wash for plant nursery, washing seeds etc. (iv) inoculation of earthworms in the field for waste land reclamation (Senapati *et al.*, 1999; Lavelle *et al.*, 1999; Dash *et al.*, 2010), and (v) to increase crop productivity (Dash *et al.*, 2010).

All technologies centred on utilization of earthworms are called vermi-technology. Vermi-technology is based on biological conversion of organic wastes, especially cellulosic waste materials. About 3000 million tons of organic wastes per year are produced in India. Besides, huge amount of animal excreta and night soil is produced in rural India. Appropriate disposal of these wastes involves application of high cost technology. Vermi-technology involves not only earthworms but also the biochemical activities of soil organisms found in earthworm gut and in organic wastes. The current global interest on this technology has helped to solve some pollution problems and simultaneously helped to recover resources in form of manures and animal protein. The science of vermi-composting took shape during the 20th century. The first vermi-composting plant was started in Holland landing, Ontario, Canada (Appelhof 1980, 1981). Since then the technology has become very popular all over the world with several local modifications (Dash, 2012).

The technology in India using native species was first standardized at Sambalpur University and later applied to field conditions (Dash, 2012). Using certain species of earthworms as the composting agent has been developed as a low cost method of garbage treatment. Extensive works on vermi-composting have been done in the Sambalpur University, Odisha (Dash, 2012) and some other places (Ismail, 2005; Kale, 2005). This method has been found very suitable for treating kitchen wastes at domestic level, in hostels and hotels.

5.1.7 Sanitary Land Filling (SLF)

The wastes are spread in thin layers, compacted to the maximum and covered with soil every day. The environmental problems of rotting garbage in open disposal on land are not encountered in sanitary landfills. On the contrary, sanitary land filling helps in reclamation of otherwise unsuitable land for fruitful use. The selection of site for landfill should be very carefully done, only after careful Environmental Impact Assessment. The following points should generally be considered:

(i)Site should be sufficiently away from the municipal area but not too far to make the transportation very costly, (ii) Internal and approach road to the site should be available, (iii) Area of the landfill site should be sufficiently large to last for a long period (10-20 years), (iv) Water source should be sufficiently away. Two basic land filling operation methods are generally practised. They are: (i) Pit or trench method, and (ii) Area method. In an ideal management practice, the recyclables are separated at source, biodegradable matters segregated and aerobically composted. Of the remaining, the combustible matters are incinerated or palletized (plastics and polythenes not to be palletized). The inert residues are finally land filled.

5.1.8 Regulatory Measures

In exercise of the powers conferred by Sections 3, 6, and 25 of the E.P. Act, 1986 (29 of 1986), The central government made. 'The Municipal Solid Wastes (Management and Handling) Rules, 2000. These rules shall apply to every municipal authority responsible for collection, segregation, storage, transportation, processing and disposal of municipal solid wastes. These rules define the different aspects of the management of these wastes, assign responsibility of municipal authority, state government and the union territory administration, responsibility of CPCB and SPCB, management aspects, annual reports, accident reporting, four schedules and four prescribed forms.

5.2 BIOMEDICAL WASTE MANAGEMENT (BMW)

Biomedical wastes (wastes generated from hospitals, nursing homes, clinics, dispensaries, blood banks, veterinary institutions and animal houses) constitute a very small proportion of the municipal solid waste. Their management (collection, storage, transportation and disposal) is very important because of their highly hazardous nature. Keeping this in mind the Ministry of Environment and Forests has notified the Biomedical Waste (Management & Handling) Rules, 1998 under the Environment Protection Act, 1986. These Rules are applicable to all persons who generate, collect, receive, store, transport, treat, dispose or handle biomedical waste in any form. Biomedical waste means any waste which is generated during the diagnosis, treatment or immunization of human beings or animals or in research activities pertaining thereto or in the production or testing of biological, and including categories mentioned in Schedule-I. Biological means any preparation made from organisms or microorganisms or product of metabolism and biochemical reactions intended for use in the diagnosis, immunization or the treatment of human beings or animals or in research activities pertaining thereto.

The Rules categorize biomedical wastes into 10 categories (Schedule I) for management purpose (Table 21).

Table 21. Biomedical Waste Categories (Cat.)

Cat. 1	**Human Anatomical Waste** (Human tissues, organs and body parts).
Cat. 2	**Animal Waste** (Animal tissues, organs, body parts, carcasses, bleeding parts, body fluid, blood and experimental animals used in research, waste generated by veterinary hospital colleges, discharges from hospitals and animal houses).
Cat. 3	**Microbiology and Biotechnology Waste** (Wastes from laboratory cultures, stocks or specimens of microorganisms, live or attenuated vaccines, human and animal cell culture used in research and infectious agents from research and industrial laboratories, wastes from production of biological, toxins, dishes and devices used for transfer of cultures).
Cat. 4	**Waste Sharps** (Needles, syringes, scalpels, blades, glass, etc. that may cause puncture and cuts. This includes both used and unused sharps).
Cat. 5	**Discarded Medicines and Cytotoxic Drugs** (Wastes comprising outdated, contaminated and discarded medicines).
Cat. 6	**Soiled Waste** (Items contaminated with blood and body fluids including cotton, dressings, soiled plaster casts, linens, bedding and other materials contaminated with blood).
Cat. 7	**Solid Waste** (Wastes generated from disposable items other than the waste sharps such as tubing, catheters, intravenous sets, etc).
Cat. 8	**Liquid Waste** (Wastes generated from laboratory and washing, cleaning, housekeeping and disinfecting activities).
Cat. 9	**Incineration Ash.** (Ash from the incineration of biomedical waste).
Cat. 10	**Chemical Waste** (Chemicals used in production of biological, in disinfection, as insecticide, etc).

The storage, treatment and disposal options for management of biomedical waste are given in Table 22.

The rules also prescribe the standards for incinerators, autoclaving, microwaving and deep burial. Time schedules have been prescribed for the installation of treatment and disposal facilities for hospitals of different sizes. According to the Rules, by 31st December of 2002, all hospitals (including smallest ones) and institutions generating BMW will have complete facilities.

Table 22. Storage, Treatment and Disposal Options of BMW

Waste Category No.	Treatment and Disposal	Type & Colour of Container
1	Incineration/deep burial	Plastic bag (Yellow)
2	Incineration/deep burial	Plastic bag (Yellow)
3	Local autoclaving/micro-waving/incineration	Plastic bag (Yellow) Disinfected container/ plastic bag (Red)
4	Disinfection (Chemical treatment)/autoclaving/ microwaving and mutilation/shredding	Plastic bag/Puncture proof container (Blue/ White translucent).
5	Incineration/destruction and drugs disposal in landfills	Plastic bag (black)
6	Incineration/autoclaving/microwaving	Plastic bag (Yellow) Disinfected container/ Plastic bag (Red)
7	Disinfection (chemical treatment)/autoclaving/ microwaving and mutilation/shredding	Disinfected container/Plastic bag (Red), Plastic bag/puncture proof container (Blue/White translucent)
8	Disinfection by chemical treatment and discharge into drains	No container, only direct discharge into drain
9	Disposal in municipal landfill	Plastic bag (Black)
10	Chemical treatment and discharge into drains for liquids or secured landfill for solids	

Segregation, Packing, Transportation and Storage of Biomedical Waste (BMW). The essential prescriptions are: (a) BMW shall be segregated at source and kept in containers or bags as prescribed along with the colour code. (b) The containers/bags must also have different warning signs prescribed for biotoxic and cytotoxic hazard symbols. (c) If the BMW is required to be transported from its source to disposal facilities outside the premises, the transport vehicle must have warning symbols mentioned above and carry all information in the prescribed form. (d) Transportation must have authorization of the designated authority. (e) Rules framed under the Motor Vehicle Act, 1988 must be followed.

Functions and Responsibilities: The functions and responsibilities of management of the BMW, under the rules, of the different persons/organizations involved are detailed below:

State/union territory governments have established an authority under their control and supervision with such number of members as specified for granting authorization and implementation of the rules. Many states have designated the State Pollution Control Boards as the authority for the purpose.

Besides, they have constituted an Advisory Committee to advise the government and the prescribed authority on matters relating to the implementation of rules. There is an appellate authority to hear any appeal from a person aggrieved with the orders of the authority empowered to grant authorization.

Generator of the Bio-Medical Waste (BMW) and Occupier of Related Facilities:

(a) It is the duty of every occupier of an institution generating BMW to take all steps to ensure that the waste is handled without any adverse effect to human health and environment.
(b) The BMW will be treated and disposed of in the prescribed manner. All the treatment and disposal facilities shall be installed/established within the prescribed time period (different dates for different categories of institutions, the latest date being 31.12.2002).
(c) Every occupier and operator of an institution generating, collecting, receiving, storing, transporting, treating, disposing BMW in any manner (except those providing treatment/service facilities to less than 1000 patients per month) submit an application with the necessary fees to the prescribed authority (Form I) for grant of authorization.
(d) Maintain records related to all aspects of handling BMW.
(e) The occupier/operator can appeal to the appellate authority of aggrieved with any order of the authority granting authorization within 30 days of receipt of the order. (This period can be extended in exceptional cases.)
(f) When an accident occurs in any institution/facility/site handling BMW, the occupier/operator must report the accident (Form III) to the prescribed authority immediately.

Prescribed Authority: The prescribed authority can grant/renew authorization for a period upto 3 years, including one year of trial or refuse (after grant of hearing) the same within ninety days after receipt of the complete application with prescribed fees.

(a) It can make necessary inquiry, as deemed fit, to ensure proper handling of the BMW.
(b) It can also suspend and cancel the authorization after giving reasonable opportunity of being heard.

Appellate Authority: It will hear appeal under the Water Act, and Air Act from any occupier/operator and dispose of appropriately as per the provisions of law.

5.3 MANAGEMENT OF HAZARDOUS WASTE

Any waste, when because of its quantity physical, chemical or infectious characteristics causes significant hazards to human health and environmental quality upon being disposed, treated, stored or transported improperly can be called hazardous waste (generic definition). This can be solid, liquid or gas; the management practices of each type are different from those of the other two. Conventionally, only solid wastes are considered hazardous wastes for management practices. Even radioactive solid wastes are excluded. This chapter only confines to non-radioactive hazardous solid wastes.

The United Nations Environment Program *(UNEP)* describes hazardous wastes as *"Wastes, other than radioactive wastes, which by reasons of their chemical reactivity or toxicity, explosive, corrosive or other characteristics causing danger or likely to cause danger to health or environment, whether alone or when coming into contact with other wastes, are legally defined as hazardous in the State in which they are generated or in which they are disposed or through which they are transported"*. Thus, the United Nations Environment Program (UNEP) leaves to the individual countries to evolve their own definitions of hazardous waste. The Waste Management Council in

India has adopted the following definition of HSW in their meeting in 1990 at Nagpur. "*Any solid waste, other than radioactive wastes, which by reasons of physical and/or chemical or reactive or toxic, explosive, corrosive or other characteristics causing danger or likely to cause danger to health or environment, whether alone or when coming into contact with other waste or environment*". This is a comprehensive but complicated definition.

An acceptable definition is difficult due to the difficulty in identifying suitable parameters for definition. However, a legal definition is essential for regulatory purposes. It establishes the scope for any control program. The main considerations in defining or identifying hazardous wastes are: (a) characteristics of wastes, (b) treatment and disposal options, (c) social, political and economic considerations of the country.

The approaches are listing, fixing minimum threshold concentration above which the waste may be considered hazardous, listing processes of which the waste generated can be considered "hazardous", listing non-hazardous wastes, the rest being automatically "hazardous" (Exclusion).

The Hazardous Waste (Handling and Management) Rules, 1989 lists 18 categories of wastes with threshold concentrations of the hazardous component as hazardous wastes. The latest amendment to the Rules made in 2008 defines HSW on the basis of the characteristics of wastes such as their physical, chemical, reactive, toxic, flammable, explosive or corrosive characteristics, which causes danger or is likely to cause danger to health or environment, whether alone or when in contact with other wastes or substances. These wastes are listed in Schedule-I of these Rules and it includes the processes generating hazardous wastes. Thirty-six names of processes and wastes are listed. Schedule-II of these Rules provides concentration limits in terms of 5 classes (Classes A, B, C, D, E). Class-E is further divided into E1—Flammable; E2—Explosive; E—3-Corrosive; E—4-Toxic; E—5-Carcinogenicity, Mutagenecity, and Endocrinic disruptivity.

The high volume and low effect wastes such as fly ash, phosphogypsum, red mud, slags from pyrometallurgical operations, mine tailings and ore beneficiation rejects are excluded from the category of hazardous wastes. CPCB will issue separate guidelines on the management of these wastes.

Characteristics of Hazardous Waste. The following are some of the important characteristics, which can be attributed to hazardous characteristics.

- Flammability - Flammable wastes with flash point 65.5°C or below.
- Explosive - Wastes which may explode under the effect of flame, heat or photochemical conditions and any other material included in Indian Explosive Act.

- *Ignitability* — Spontaneous ignitability at or below 60°C.
- *Reactivity* — Unstable and violent change without detonation, reacts violently with water, generates toxic gases (HCN, H_2S etc.) when exposed to favourable pH conditions, oxidizing, etc.
- *Corrosivity* — Destroys substances or living tissues on contact (ex. pH < 2 and > 2 corrodes steel at a rate > 6.35 mm/y at 55°C - wastes which may be corrosive by chemical action will cause severe damage coming in contact with living tissue.
- *Toxicity (Acute and Chronic)* — Releases toxic materials (irritant, carcinogenic, mutagenic, teratogenic, etc.) on leaching or in ambient condition. The list includes selected volatile and semi-volatile organics, pesticides,

herbicides and heavy metals. Wastes containing or contaminated with established toxic and or eco-toxic constituents.

- *Infectious* — Carries infective pathogens (Medical waste)
- *Ecotoxic* — Causes immediate or delayed risks for one or more sector environment.

Health and physical hazards being the most important of all the hazards, the criteria for identifying hazardous wastes should be clearly understood (Table 23).

Table 23. Criteria for Identifying Physical and Health Hazards

Sl. No	Criterion	Hazard Range	Waste Hazard
1.	Carcinogen	Proven or potential carcinogen, mutagen or teratogenic	Acute
2.	Corrosive (bio)	Destroys or irreversibly changes living tissues	Acute
3.	Highly toxic	LD 50 < 50 mg/kg LD 50 < 200 mg/kg LC 50 < 200 ppm (parts per million) LC 50 < 2 mg/l	Acute
4.	Toxic	LD 50-500 mg/kg LD 50 200-1000 mg/kg LC 50 200 -2000 ppm LC 50 2-20 mg/l	Hazardous
5.	Irritant	Reversible inflammatory on skin or eyes	Hazardous
6.	Sensitizer	Allergic reactions possible in exposed individuals	Hazardous
7.	Target organ effects	Irreversible/Reversible	Acute hazardous
8.	Physical hazard	Explosive, flammable, reactive, ignitable, corrosive, etc.	Hazardous
9.	Infectious	Pathogen carrying	Acute
10.	Ecotoxic	Hazard for environment	Hazardous

Major Issues of Management of Hazardous Solid Waste (HSW)

The major issues of hazardous waste management are briefly summarized below: (a) Formulation of internationally acceptable definition and classification keeping the requirements of the Basel Convention. Although the UNEP permits each country to evolve its own definition of hazardous waste, the Basel Convention aims at controlling trans-boundary movement of such wastes. For this, it is desirable to have an internationally acceptable definition. India is a signatory of the Basel convention. (b) Promotion of minimization of waste generation through low-waste or no-waste technologies of production, recycling and reuse (*in situ* and *ex situ*). A combination of technological, legislative, economic and informational measures is required for this. (c) Measurement and monitoring HSWs and their fate from generation to final disposal (cradle-to-grave principle). (d) Formulation of guidelines for the segregation, collection, transport and storage. This is to prevent pilferage and leakage for the safety of the operators and the public. (e) Development of safe treatment and disposal methods. (f) Identification of the site of disposal. This should be done very carefully through proper Environmental Impact Assessment (EIA) and other methods. (g) Investigation of abandoned and live disposal sites. A disposal site, whether live or abandoned, needs to be continuously investigated to see if any failure has developed over a period of time endangering the environment (e.g., leachates contaminating the groundwater). Sometimes very old abandoned sites are forgotten. (h) Remediation measures in case of failure of preventive measures. This is often very difficult and expensive. For example, cleaning of contaminated groundwater is very difficult. (i) Information collection and dissemination (training). (j) Awareness generation. (k) Research and Development. A good amount of R&D input is necessary for development of low-waste/no-waste technologies and safe treatment/disposal methods. This is a continuous process. In the Indian scenario, there are many constraints of safe management of HSWs. These include lack of public awareness of the importance of the issues, dearth of knowledge about sources and hazards, poor pollution control and disposal, existence of large number of small scale and tiny industries lacking in financial resources and expertise, lack of combined treatment and disposal facilities, slow and cumbersome judicial procedure, etc.

Basic Management Concept: The basic concepts of management of hazardous wastes are waste avoidance, waste treatment, collection, transportation and storage, disposal. The hazardous solid waste management concept is shown in Figure 63.

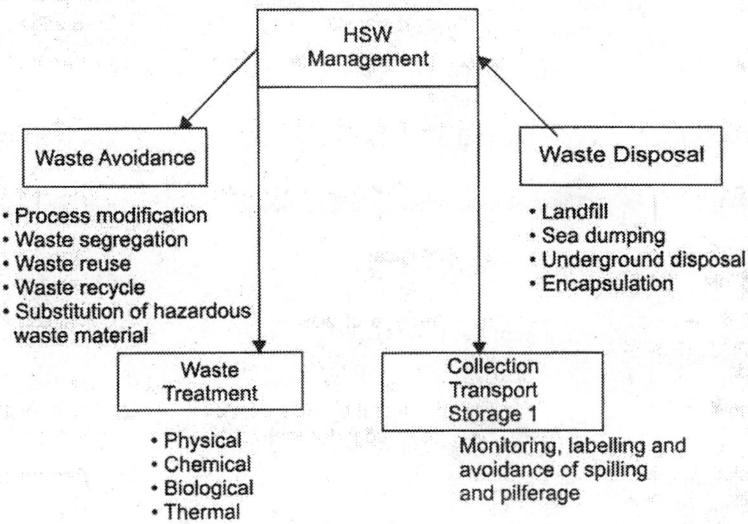

Figure 63. HSW management

Waste Avoidance. Waste avoidance can be done in many ways on case by case basis.

(i) **Process modification:** Industrial process can be altered in such a way that the raw material used is optimized while waste generation is reduced.

(ii) **Waste segregation.** If hazardous and non-hazardous wastes are generated together, segregation reduces the quantity of the hazardous waste making its treatment and disposal processes easy and simple.

(iii) **Waste reuse.** In some cases waste materials can be used with very little processing as a raw material for some other industry. For example, the rejected potliness of aluminium smelters in cement kilns and bagasse of sugar industries for paper manufacturing.

(iv) **Waste recycle.** Waste can be treated and reused in the process. For example, recycling of torn papers of the paper machines in pulp and paper industry.

(v) **Substitution of hazardous waste material.** In some cases substitution of some chemicals in the process can avoid hazardous waste generation. For example, zinc chloride can be used with slight modification in the zinc electroplating process thereby eliminating the cyanide problem.

Waste Treatment. Sometimes the hazardous waste is required to be treated before disposal to change its physical and/or chemical properties for detoxication and easier disposal. The treatment methods can be divided into 4 groups: (i) physical, (ii) chemical, (iii) biological, (iv) solidification.

Table 24 summarizes the different process technologies for hazardous waste (solid, liquid and sludge) treatment and disposal.

Table 24. Summary of Hazardous Waste Treatment and Disposal Technologies

Type of wastes	Treatment	Disposal
Cyanide waste	Detoxification. Biological	Sludge for Landfill
Heavy metal bearing waste	Sludge conditioning and dewatering metal recovery	Landfill
Non-halogenated hydrocarbon including solvents	Thermal treat after solvent recovery	Ash for Landfill
Halogenated hydrocarbon including solvents	Thermal treat after solvent recovery	Ash for Landfill
Wastes from paint, pigment, glue, varnish and printing inks	Thermal / Biological	Ash for Landfill
Waste from dyes and dye intermediate containing inorganic chemical compounds	Vary from the type of waste	Landfill
Waste oil and oil emulsion	Physio-chemical and biological for oil separation and sludge for thermal treat	Ash for Landfill
Tarry waste from refining and tar residues from distillation or pyrolytic treatment	Thermal	Ash for Landfill
Sludge from waste water treatment including incineration ash	Sludge conditioning and dewatering	Landfill
Phenols	Detoxification	Sludge for Landfill
Asbestos		Landfill
Wastes from pesticides and herbicides manufacturing and residues from formulation units	Biological or thermal treat and solidification	Landfill
Acid / Alkaline / Slurry / Slurry Wastes	Physio-chemical treatment and sludge for conditioning and dewatering	Sludge for Landfill
Off-specification and discarded products	Physio-chemical, Biological or Thermal	Ash and Sludge
Discarded containers and liners of hazardous and toxic chemicals and wastes	Liners for Thermal	Containers for Landfill

Thermal Method
- Incineration (heating to very high temperature in the presence of air) - very commonly used.
- Pyrolysis (heating to high temperature in the absence of air) - Its significance in hazardous waste is less. It is important in the recycling of plastics.

The thermal method of treatment is a very common method of treatment for hazardous solid wastes and sludges and therefore, deserves a discussion in greater detail. The thermal process is basically of two types: incineration and pyrolysis.

Incineration is the most important method of treatment of organic and highly toxic hazardous wastes including hospital wastes. The high temperature (usually 1200°C) mineralizes all kinds of organic matters. The mineralized products are slag salts, P205 and gases CO_2 , H_2O, HCl, HF, SO_2, NO_x, etc., depending upon the nature of the waste incinerated. The waste gas may also contain traces of toxic substances like dioxin. Large incinerators have provision for scrubbing to control air pollution. Wastes, which are generally incinerated, are: (i) Slurries, sludges and pasty wastes (oil slurries, dye sludges, distillation residues, tank bottoms, etc.), (ii) Liquids (organic solvent mixtures, transformer oil containing PCB, cutting oil, etc.), (iii) Solids (tarry wastes, pesticides, expired drugs, cosmetics, absorbents, etc., (iv) Waste delivered barrels (barrels containing dyes, drugs, pesticides, etc.), (v) Infectious hospital wastes (bandages, gauges, plastic bottles, body tissues, etc.) A typical large incinerator consists of a combustion chamber, after-burner chamber, pre-cooler, scrubber, exhaust fan and stack. There are many types of incinerators and the choice of the incinerator depends upon the waste type. The solid residue (ash) left after incineration may contain heavy metals. It should be properly disposed usually in secured landfill. Waste heat from very large incinerators is used for power generation in many developed countries.

Incineration is not commonly practised in India. However, there is scope for the use of rotary kilns of cement plants for incineration of certain types of hazardous wastes.

Collection, Transport and Storage of HSW. Sufficient care should be taken to prevent spillage and pilferage of hazardous waste during its collection, transportation and storage. A logbook should be maintained for this. Proper labelling should be done on the containers and transport vehicles. Accidents cause spillage. Therefore, all possible care should be taken to prevent accidents during collection, transportation and storage. If any accident actually occurs, it should be recorded and the competent authority intimated without delay so that remediation measures can be taken up.

Disposal. The options available are landfill, sea dumping, underground disposal, encapsulation. Sea dumping is generally to be avoided because of possible adverse effects on marine life, fishing and navigation. Many national and international laws also control it. International laws prohibit dumping of many hazardous substances like halogenated organics, organo-silicon compounds, mercury, lead and cadmium salts, etc. In spite of international regulations, clandestine sea dumping is taking place.

Hazardous wastes can be disposed of in deep underground mines, which meet specific geological and technical criteria. Salt mines are often used because the hazardous waste has much less chance of interacting with the geological formations there. The very existence of salt in those mines proves that the underground site is not affected by groundwater for millions of years. Disposal in underground mines has much less scope and favour.

Encapsulation followed by deep burial is an option when the waste is very highly hazardous and generated in small quantities. This is a common practice of disposal of nuclear wastes. These are confined in concrete capsules and buried or dumped into sea. There are the however, evidences that the capsules dumped into the seas in the South Pacific Ocean in the 50s and 60s have started leaking, causing radioactive contamination.

Secured landfill, therefore, is the only practical and available option for disposal of hazardous wastes. Liquid wastes are not disposed in landfills. Sludges should be de-watered to the maximum extent before putting in landfills. The disposal site should be selected, designed and managed so that no harmful substance reaches the hydrosphere and the biosphere in unacceptable quantities. Sufficient care should be taken to protect the groundwater sources and ensure mechanical stability of the waste material. It is also desirable that for a cluster of HSW generating industries, particularly for small scale industries, common disposal sites should be identified.

The key factors for site selection are type and quantity of waste, active life of disposal site, traffic condition and geological and geographical condition of the site. Environmental Impact Assessment is required to be done before the final decision.

Secured Landfill Design. A good secured landfill (SLF) should be designed in such a way that there are several barriers which work independently from each other. Ideally the barriers are:

1. Degradation or fixation of pollutants (treatment) prior to disposal.
2. Suitable location of the landfill site should be selected by the aforesaid process so as to prevent migration of pollutants from the waste body to groundwater source or any other sensitive areas like drinking water source.
3. Leachate collection and treatment system.
4. Bottom liner system.
5. Cover liner system.
6. Proper operation and maintenance of the secured landfill.
7. Post-closure activity including notification of site and repairing of barriers.

The Central Pollution Control Board (CPCB) has prepared a standard design of secured landfill, which is shown in Figures 62-64 (source - Dr. D.K. Behera - SPCB, Bhubaneswar). The essential features of the design are: (i) Double impervious liners, (ii) Leachate Collection and Removal System (LCRS), (iii) Leachate Detection System (LDS), and (iv) Closure and final cover.

5.4 HAZARDOUS WASTES (MANAGEMENT AND HANDLING) RULES, 1989 (AMENDED 2000, 2003, & 2008)-(UNDER E.P. ACT, 1986)

Bhopal and other catastrophic accidents gave rise to a new classification of industry – having potential of causing major accidents and 434 such chemicals are listed in Schedule-I under sections 6 & 25 of EP Act, Manufacture, Storage and Impact of Hazardous Chemical Rules,

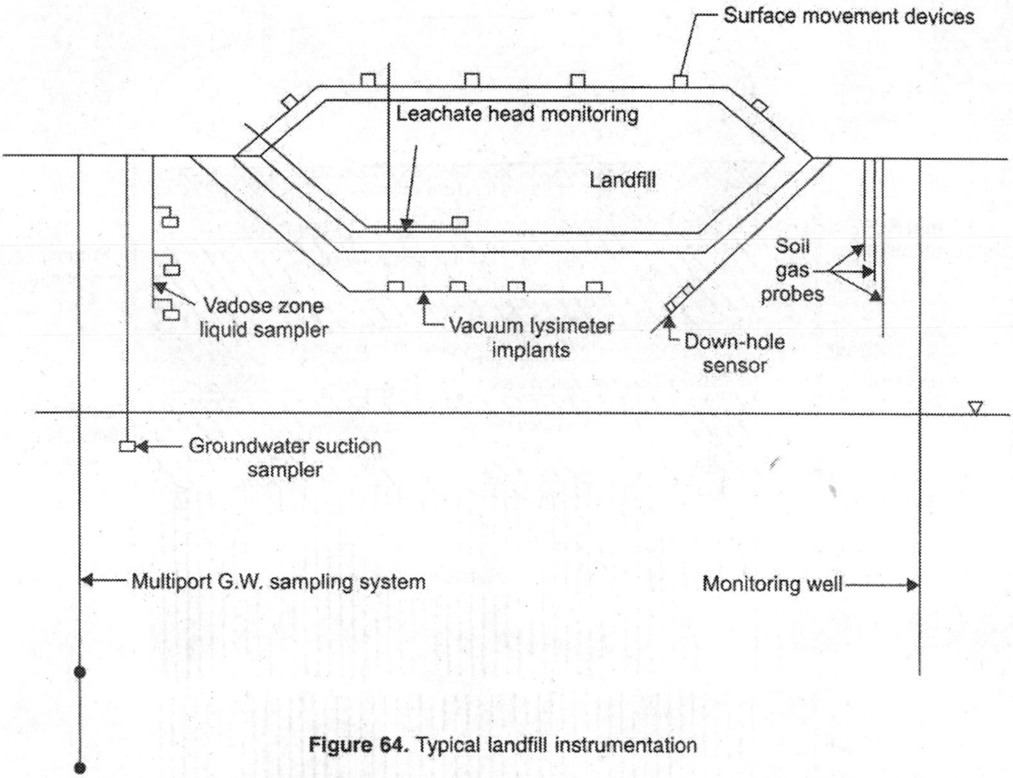

Figure 64. Typical landfill instrumentation

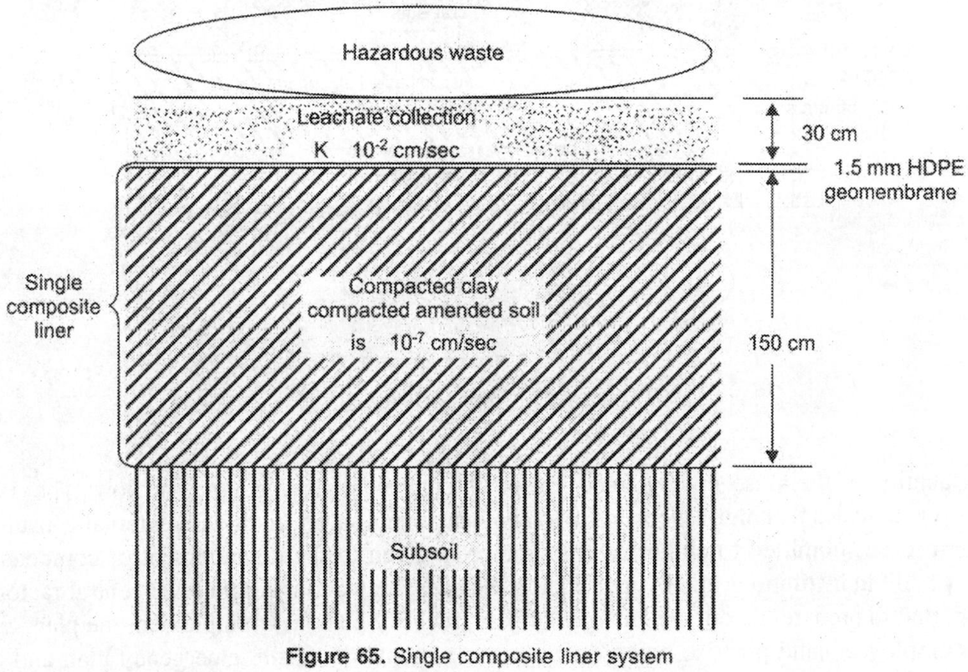

Figure 65. Single composite liner system

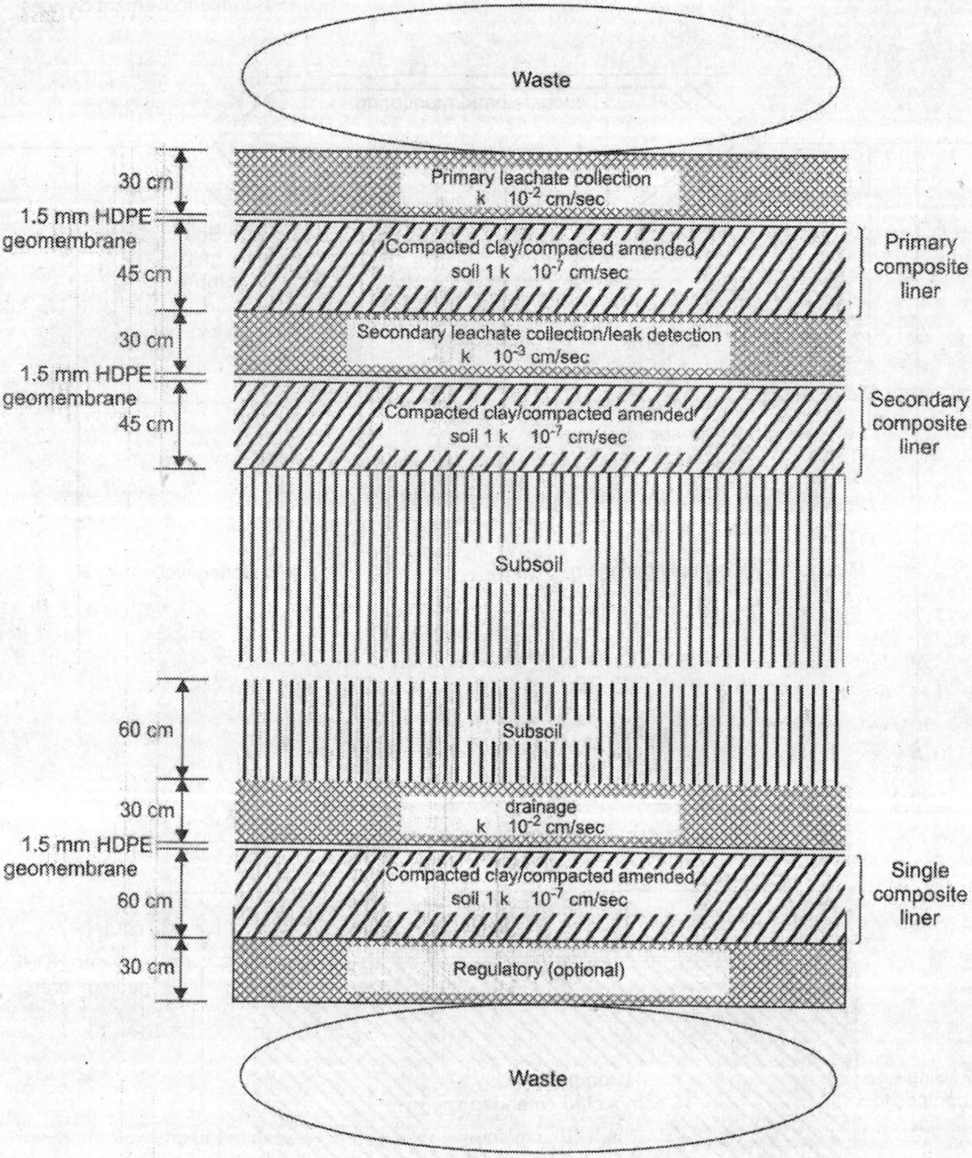

Figure 66. Cover system

1989. Quantity of their use covers three levels of control: high, medium and low. The 1994 amendment stipulates that high level control to conduct annual safety audit with external consultant and report to be submitted to authority. Importance is given to the development of competency for safety audit in institutions and by individuals. Besides, high and medium level central factories are supported to prepare the on-site emergency plan, identify persons to implement the plan, train all their employees, and practise mock drill every six months. Off-site emergency plan and on-site emergency plan formats were prescribed. Violation of provisions is punishable under Section 15 of EP Act.

Hazardous substances, when present in effluents and emissions of a process, are controlled through the Water and the Air Acts respectively. When hazardous substances are present as or with other solid wastes, the above Acts are not very effective. The Ministry of Environment and Forests have, therefore, framed and notified the Hazardous Wastes (Management and Handling) Rules, 1989 under the Environment Protection Act, 1986.

The Rules have again been amended in 2008 Hazardous Material (Management, Handling and Transboundary Movement Rules, 2007)

Applicability. The original Rules (1989) of Hazardous Wastes (Management and Handling) and the amended Rules-2008 of Hazardous Material (Management, Handling and Transboundary movement) include 36 categories, which apply to hazardous wastes/substances generated from specific processes (Schedule I) and those belonging to 5 classes (A-E) based on their concentration limits (Schedule II). The following are the important provisions of the Rules. The amended Rules (2008) include seven chapters containing 26 clauses, 7 schedules and 15 prescribed forms. There are guidelines and regulations for the features. Schedule III Part A gives the list of hazardous wastes applicable for import with prior informed consent; part B includes the list of hazardous wastes applicable for import and export not requiring prior informed consent, and part C gives the list of hazardous characteristics. Schedule IV gives list of HW requiring registration for recycling/reprocessing; Schedule V gives specifications of used oil suitable for reprocessing/recycling and specifications of fuel derived from waste oil; schedule VI deals with HW prohibited for import and export and schedule VII provides the list of authorities and their corresponding duties.

Clause 25 stipulates liability of occupier, transporter, operators of a facility and importer. The occupier and the operator of the facility shall be liable to pay financial penalties as levied for any violation of the provisions under these rules by the SPCB with the prior approval of CPCB. There is provision of appeal under clause 26 and the appellate authority will be the Environment Secretary of the state if the order passed by the SPCB or the Environment Secretary of Government of India if the order is passed by the CPCB.

Authorization by the Pollution Control Board. Any occupier generating HSW and having facilities for collection, reception, treatment, transport, storage and disposal is required to obtain authorization from the respective State Pollution Control Board or Pollution Control Committee for UT areas filing application in the requisite form with the necessary fees.

The Member-Secretary of the regulating agency can grant authorization in the respective form for a period of 5 years at a time after satisfying himself of the appropriate facilities and the technical capacity of the occupier. Authorization can be refused, revoked and suspended only after giving an opportunity to the occupier to be heard. Decision on authorization to be taken within 90 days of the receipt of application.

Renewal of authorization can be granted only if annual returns are regularly submitted and steps are taken for the reduction of waste generation, their recycling and reuse, wherever feasible, and fulfilment of all conditions of authorization, and remittance of processing and analysis fees to the regulating /designated agencies. The occupier/operator has a right to appeal. The state government/ the central government (for Union Territories) have the appellate power.

Packing, Labelling and Transport. The occupier/operator of facility is to ensure safe packing, storage and transport of HW. The packaging shall be properly labelled to be clearly identified. Labels should be strong to withstand physical and climatic conditions. The Central Motor Vehicle Rules and Guidelines should be followed for transport.

Detailed methods of packaging, format for labelling with colour codes, documents to be exchanged between the occupier/operator and the transporter are prescribed under the Rules.

Reporting of Accident. The occupier/operator of any hazardous waste facility is required to immediately report to the Pollution Control Board and all others concerned in the prescribed form, all accidents whether the same occur at the site or during transport.

Disposal Site. The occupier/operator of facility shall be responsible for identifying sites for establishing hazardous wastes disposal facility.

The state government, operator of a facility or any association of occupiers shall identify sites for common hazardous wastes disposal facility in the state. The state government, occupier or any association shall first identify possible sites for disposal facility after preliminary impact assessment. Final selection of the site shall be done after full Environmental Impact Assessment (EIA), public notice inviting objections, suggestions and conduction of public hearing as per the procedures laid down for EIA (to be done by the state government).

Finally, the state government shall acquire or inform such occupier or any such association to acquire the site before notifying the same.

The state government shall undertake to compile and publish periodically an inventory of such disposal sites in the State.

Design and Setting Up of Disposal Facility. The occupier, any association or operator of facility, as the case may be, shall design and set up disposal facility as per the guidelines issued by the central government or the state government. The State Pollution Control Board, which shall monitor its setting up and operation, must approve the design and layout of the facility. Operation and closure of the landfill site shall be done by the occupier/operator of the facility as per the design approved by the State Pollution Control Board.

Management of hazardous waste requires technical skill and proper characterization for disposal so that it does not have long term environmental impact. The options are to be carefully selected considering the composition of waste. The compatible waste should only be sent for landfill. Enforcement of the legislation is highly essential. However, waste management tools such as waste avoidance, waste minimization and waste utilization should be given priority.

5.5 MANAGEMENT OF HAZARDOUS CHEMICALS

A large number of chemicals with hazardous properties are handled in industries and outside. Thus, chemical hazards, minor or major and short-term or long-term are common nowadays. The Bhopal Gas Tragedy in India and the Chernobyl Nuclear Plant Accident in the erstwhile Soviet Union are some of the major technological disasters. It has, therefore, become necessary to evolve management principles and practices for safe handling of hazardous chemicals and tackling technological disasters when they occur.

5.5.1 Hazardous Substances Classification

Hazardous chemicals are classified and labelled as per the United Nations Classification and Definition of Dangerous Goods. A dangerous or hazardous substance may be flammable, explosive, toxic, corrosive, combustible, reactive with air or water, oxidizing, chemically unstable (undergoes decomposition, polymerization, etc.) or radioactive by itself or because of certain substances (e.g., chemicals, heavy metals, pathogenic organisms) present with it. The book deals with only "hazardous" chemicals and excludes radioactive substances. The management practices of both types are entirely different.

United Nations Classification. Hazardous substances are classified under different categories on the basis of their hazardous properties solely for transportation purpose. Each category is further divided into many divisions as shown in Table 25.

- More than 2311 types of chemicals/dangerous goods, commonly transported, are listed in the above categorization.

Table 25. UN Classification of Hazardous Substances

Sl. No.	Category	Division	Description/Definition
1	Explosives	1.1	Substances or articles with mass explosion hazard
		1.2	Substances or articles with projection hazard but not explosion hazard
		1.3	Substances or articles predominantly with fire hazard, along with minor blast hazard and/or minor projection hazard, but not mass explosion hazard
		1.4	Substances or articles which are very insensitive explosives and present insignificant hazard
		1.5	Very insensitive substances which have a mass explosion hazard
2	Gases	2.1	Flammable gases
		2.2	Non-flammable gases
		2.3	Poisonous (toxic) gases
3	Flammable Liquids	3.1	Flash point below – 18°C (0°F)
		3.2	Flash point between – 18°C and 23°C
		3.3	Flash point between 23°C and 61°C
4	Flammable Solids	4.1	Flammable solids
		4.2	Substances liable to spontaneous combustion
		4.3	Substances which, on contact with water, emit flammable gases
5	Oxidizers and	5.1	Oxidizing substances
	Organic Peroxides	5.2	Organic peroxides
6	Poisonous and	6.1	Poisonous (toxic) substances
	Itiologic Materials	6.2	Itiologic (infectious) substances
7	Radioactive Substances	-	Radioactive substances
8	Corrosives	-	Corrosive substances
9	Miscellaneous	-	Miscellaneous dangerous substances

- Each entry in the list is assigned with a UN number to facilitate national and international transportation. A risk classification symbol (alphabet) is assigned to every hazardous substance.
- The alphabets are C, O, E, R, F and T standing for corrosive, oxidizing, explosive, reactive, flammable and toxic respectively.

5.5.2 Properties of Hazardous Chemicals

Flammable Gases and Liquids

These can easily form ignitable mixtures of air and vapour at ambient temperatures. Such mixtures can catch fire by sparks from electrical equipment, static electricity developed during drum filling or other activities, or by naked fire. The flash point determines the flammability character of a liquid. Common flammable gases used in industries and domestic purposes are LPG (Liquid Petroleum Gas), CNG (Compressed Natural Gas) and gaseous hydrocarbons like acetylene. Carbon monoxide (both flammable and toxic) is a common gas generated in many industrial processes. Hydrocarbon solvents, alcohols, ketones, motor spirits and paints are some common examples of flammable liquids. When an accident occurs involving these flammable gases or liquids, apart from various types of fire, serious explosion is also a possibility. Some explosions like the Vapour Cloud Explosion (VCE) and the Boiling Liquid Expanding Vapour Explosion (BLEVE) can be catastrophic. The general precautions to be followed against such hazards are as follows. Clear warning signals against smoking and use of naked flame should be displayed in areas of handling and storage of such substances. Electrical wires and switches should be absent in closed storerooms of flammable substances.

Combustible Substances

These chemicals are likely to continue to burn, if ignited, e.g., nitrocellulose and nitrobenzene. General precautions against hazards of combustion are same as above. Besides, these substances should not be stored in very large quantities.

Corrosive Substances

These substances seriously damage a wide range of materials including metals. They even eat away/destroy/completely burn human skin upon coming in contact.

Some of these substances are sulphuric acid, hydrogen chloride (hydrochloric acid), nitric acid, phenol (carbolic acid), caustic soda, and ammonia liquor. Protective clothing with special protection for eyes should be provided to workers handling such substances.

Toxic Substances

These substances have harmful effects on the human physiology when taken by ingestion (entry through mouth by contaminated food or drink), inhalation (entry through nose in the form of fumes or vapours which can easily pass into the blood stream via the lungs) or absorption through skin by physical contact. Care should be taken to avoid spillage of such substances during storage and handling. Personal protective equipment should also be provided to workers handling such substances.

Oxidizing Substances

These chemicals generate their own oxygen to assist and maintain combustion, e.g., sodium chlorate, potassium nitrate, and ammonium nitrate. Almost all peroxides are oxidizing substances. The normal precautions during storage and handling of such substances are: (i) These should not be stored in close proximity of combustible substances; (ii) Firewalls should be provided if these substances are stored with incompatible materials in the same building.

Reactive Substances

These substances often react with air and/or water vapour producing corrosive, toxic or other harmful substances. When reacting with water, liquids are formed which tend to flow in the storage place causing nuisance. These substances sometimes even react with the container material. The normal safety precaution is to store them in closed containers made of inert materials.

Explosive Substances

Explosion can easily occur with such substances by various means like contact with fire, heating, physical impact and reaction with other substances. Explosion releases a large amount of energy in a very short time. It is associated with sound, heat, shock waves and light. These substances should be handled very carefully. They should be stored in strong walled buildings and away from human habitation and activity.

Appreciation of Hazards

It is essential that the place where a hazardous chemical is stored, handled or transported should have some display indicating the presence, as well as, the nature of hazard of the substance to serve as a warning to the public. This is done through *"Hazard Diamonds"* and *"User Hazard Warnings"* which are coloured pictorial displays (Figures 65-66). But the persons storing and handling hazardous substances are required to know much more about the substance than what the above displays reveal, particularly the safety information. Such information can only be given through a "Material Safety Data Sheet (MSDS)" or "Product Data Sheet (PDS)". The owner or supplier of any hazardous substance is required to provide the MSDS to the workers. This is prescribed under the Factories Act, 1948 (Amended 1987) and Rules framed there under. Figure 65 Hazardous Warning Symbols (CPCB Publication-Hazard Diamonds).

Storage of Hazardous Substances

The important aspects of safe storage of hazardous substances are the location of the site, building design and layout, and the management of the warehouse. Storage of regulatory quantities of the substances requires statutory clearance from the competent authority (factory inspectorate for storage inside factory premises and State Pollution Control Board for isolated storage).

Location of the Site

The ideal location of the store/warehouse should have the following indicative requirements: (i) Away from densely populated areas, and away from drinking water sources (which may get contaminated by accidental release of chemicals); (ii) Away from floodplains and low-lying areas

Classification	Hazard warning sign	Classification	Hazard warning sign
Explosive substance **Class 1**	 (Orange)	Flammable gas **Class 2.1**	 (Red)
Non-flammable compressed gas **Class 2.2**	 (Green)	Toxic gas **Class 2.3**	 (White)
Flammable liquid **Class 3**	 (Red)	Flammable Solid **Class 4.1**	 (Red/White)
Spontaneously combustible substance **Class 4.2**	 (Red/White)	A substance which on contact with water emits flammable gas **Class 4.3**	 (Blue)

Figure 67(a). Hazard diamonds (from CPCB publications)

Classification	Hazard warning sign	Classification	Hazard warning sign
Oxidizing substance **Class 5.1**	 (Yellow)	Organic peroxide **Class 5.2**	 (Yellow)
Toxic sbustance **Class 6.1**	 (White)	Corrosive substance **Class 8**	 (Black/White)
Harmful substance **Class 6.1**	 (White)	Other dangerous substance **Class 9**	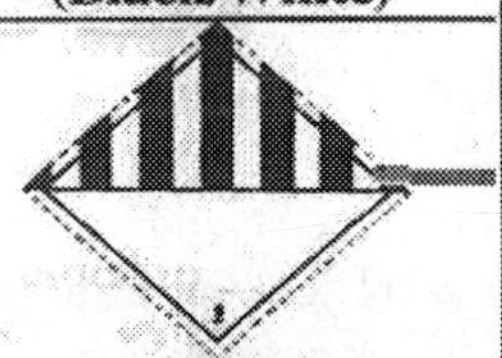 (White)

Classification and indication of general nature of risk	Symbol Black symbol on orange background	Classification indication of general nature of risk	Symbol Black symbol on orange background
Very toxic		Explosive	
Toxic		Oxidizing	
Harmful		Exteremely flammable and Highly flammable	
Corrosive		Irritant	

Figure 67(b)

(floodwater may seep into the storage area and cause water pollution); (iii) Away from external sources of hazard; (iv) Easy access to transport and emergency services.

Site Layout. The following are some of the important safety requirements of site layout. In a large warehouse, incompatible materials should be stored sufficiently separated, preferably in separate buildings. Sufficient space should be provided for safe movement and transport of materials and movement of fire-fighting vehicles. There should be clear access from two sides. Adequate protection should be provided to the buildings, as well as the total site by way of boundary walls, secure fencing, etc. This is to prevent burglary and sabotage. The number of access gates to the site should be decided on the basis of security requirements and emergency considerations. The number of gates ideally should be only one from the point of security but more access is necessary for better evacuation and movement of fire-fighting vehicles. The required number of gates should, therefore, be provided considering all these factors. Good drainage in the area should be provided to prevent waterlogging. Switches should be absent in closed store rooms containing flammable substances.

Design of Building. The following are some of the considerations to be made in the proper design of warehouse buildings. Construction material should be non-flammable and the frame of the building should be reinforced concrete or steel. Warehouse should be substantially closed with good locking arrangement. Walls must be robust and floor impermeable to liquids. Self-closing, properly designed fire door is desirable. Arrangements should be made for good ventilation. Roof and wall vents give good ventilation. Emergency exits other than those afforded by the main door should be provided considering all types of emergencies. These exits should be clearly marked. The main consideration is that nobody should be found trapped in case of emergency. Good drainage system should be provided in stores housing toxic chemicals to prevent uncontrolled release of contaminated fire-fighting water and spilled product. Interceptor pits may be required. Roofing must be capable of keeping out rain water. It should also allow fumes and heat to be vented out in case of a fire. Lightening arrester is essential.

Electrical installations should be strategically planned.

There should be arrangements available for immediately stopping any spillage or leaks and quick cleaning operations. First aid arrangements should be available all the time. Strict control of persons entering into the warehouse is necessary. Workers should be provided with entry permits.

Warehouse Management. A good and organized management practice ensures safety. Some useful management practices are: (i) Good housekeeping is essential, (ii) Inventories of highly hazardous substances should preferably be small, (iii) Packing should be secure and have stable labels with easily understandable internationally acceptable signs, (iv) Working procedure should take "first in-first out" principle as a basis to minimize risk of deterioration of goods, packages or labels, (v) All personnel working in the warehouse should be given the following instructions in writing:

- Safe and correct operations of equipment and storage materials.
- Material safety data sheet of all stored and transported materials.
- Hygiene and safety instructions.
- Emergency instructions and procedures.

(vi) Good record keeping helps to know precisely the quantities of each item available at any point of time. (vii) Sensors for small fires and leaks should be located at strategic places (viii) Risk analysis should be done on the basis of which on-site and off-site emergency plans can be prepared (described in detail later in this chapter) (ix) Training all personnel, by means mock rehearsals, and others (x) All amenities for good hygiene and personal protective clothing and equipment should be provided to all working personnel.

Transport of Hazardous Chemicals

At present there are (2009) about 33 million registered vehicles in India plying on 3.05 million kilometers of road network. Thus, there are about 11 vehicles per km of road, which is one of the lowest in the world. In the last 50 years the number of vehicles on the road have increased 80 times whereas the road length has increased only 5 times. The increased road congestion, poor maintenance of roads and vehicles, and lax enforcement of road safety rules are responsible for high rate of road accidents in India. There are about 11 accidents per thousand vehicles in India. This is indeed very high in comparison to developed countries.

Causes of Transport Emergency

The major causes of escape of hazardous chemicals during transportation are: (i) Defective valves, (ii) Missing gasket, (iii) Overfilling/under filling of tanker, (iv) Overexposure to temperature/pressure variation, (v) Collision with other vehicles/objects, (vi) Bad roads, (vii) Vehicle's mechanical failure, (viii) Speed violation, (ix) Driver's negligence/ignorance, (x) Public negligence/ignorance, (xi) Defective design of tank cars.

The HAZCHEM code is the Emergency Active Code. It tells about all the actions to be taken in case of accidental fire or spillage. A reference HAZCHEM code is presented in Table 24.

Apart from the display of the Emergency Information Panel on the body of the vehicle, the driver should also carry safety instructions with him. This document is called the *Transport Emergency Card (TREM Card)*. This is very useful to the local police, fire brigade and hospitals after a transport emergency. The TREM Cards have the following format.

Fire Hazard

As seen in the table, fire is the cause of second largest number of accidental deaths in India, next only to road accidents. It happens in homes, offices, public places and industrial premises. Fire is also a major cause of accidents in industries. Hence, it is useful for any industrial manager to learn the basic principles of cause and prevention of fire, as well as, the methods of fire-fighting.

Fire is the result of certain combustion processes. Combustion is the reaction between a combustible material (fuel) and air (oxygen). Mere contact between the fuel and oxygen will not cause fire. A minimum temperature (ignition temperature/flash point) is necessary for the start of fire. Hence, fuel, oxygen and heat may be considered the three components of fire. Controlling fire requires control of these components. With greater understanding of the chemistry of fire, another component may be added. In the analysis of the detailed chemical mechanism of fire, the original fuel molecules combine with oxygen molecules in a series of very fast successive reaction steps involving intermediate transient species, called the free radicals. Such type of reactions are known as chain reactions. It is also possible to control fire by controlling chain

Table 26. Accidental Deaths by Natural and Unnatural Causes in India in 1997
(Nityananda, 2000 - quoted by Behera, 2008)

Sl.No.	Cause	No. of Deaths
A	**Natural Causes (Flood, Cyclone etc.)**	50,247
B	**Unnatural Causes**	
1.	Air crash	16
2.	Collapse of structure	2,126
3.	Drowning	21,821
4.	Electrocution	4,583
5.	Explosion of bombs, boilers, gases, etc.	933
6.	Falls 6,172	
7.	Factory and machine accidents	669
8.	Fire 25,166	
9.	Firearms	1,496
10.	Sudden deaths (abortions, epileptic fits, etc.)	11,041
11.	Killed by animals	771
12.	Mines or quarry disaster	614
13.	Poisoning (food, liquor, toxic gases, snake bite, etc.)	21,552
14.	Stampede	19
15.	Suffocation	584
16.	Traffic accidents	
	(i) Road accidents	74,204
	(ii) Rail road accidents	1,501
	(iii) Other railway accidents	12,769
17.	Other causes	14,665
18.	Causes not known	14,293
	Total	2,33,903

- *Source:* National Crime Records Bureau, Report on Accidental Deaths and Suicides in India, 1997. Extracted from a paper published in Industrial Safety Chronicle, June 2000 by T. Nityananda.
- Maximum road accidents resulting in deaths are caused by goods transport vehicles (27.5%) followed by passenger buses (16.8%).
- When a transport vehicle carrying hazardous chemical meets with a road accident, the impact can be serious due to the escape of the hazardous substance. This can be considered a "Transport Emergency" and included in the police district's emergency plan.

reactions through the free radicals. Thus, chain reaction is also a necessary component of fire. The four components, viz., fuel, oxygen, heat and chain reactions can be represented by a "Fire Pyramid" (Figure 69).

Chemical Hazards

Chemical accidents in industrial premises include fire, explosion, gas leaks, spills of hazardous substances, accidents during transportation of hazardous chemicals, and exposure to ionizing radiations. The impact of such accidents can be localized (confined to the immediate workplace)

Table 27. Hazchem Code

Emergency Action Code Scale for Fire or Spillage

1. JETS
2. FOG
3. FOAM
4. DRY AGENT

Code	Action	
PV	FULL	
R		
S	BA	
SV	BA for FIRE only	DILUTE
T	BA	
T	BA for FIRE only	
W V	FULL	
X	BA	
Y V	BA for FIRE only	CONTAIN
Z	BA	
Z	BA for FIRE only	
E	CONSIDER EVACUATION	

Notes for Guidance :

- FOG : In the absence of equipment a fine spray may be used
- DRY AGENT: Water must not be allowed to come into contact with the substances at risk.
- V: Can be violently or even explosively reactive
- BA: Breathing apparatus plus protective gloves.
- DILUTE: May be washed to drain with large quantities of water.
- CONTAIN : Prevent, by any means available, the spillage from entering drains or water course.

SUBSTANCES	HAZCHEM CODE
(1) PETROL	3 YE
(2) METHYL ALCOHOL	2 PE
(3) L.P.G.	2 WE
(4) AMMONIA LIQUEFIED	2 PE
(5) SULPHUR	2 Z
(6) KEROSENE	

or widespread. Some of the impacts, particularly health related ones, may be long term and even extend to the next generation. Technological hazards of greater magnitude and impact can be termed "disaster", e.g., Bhopal tragedy. Chemical hazards are becoming increasingly common with progressive industrialization. Clear management principles and practices for handling such emergencies arising out of chemical hazards are necessary.

Basic Principles of Handling Technological Hazards

The basic principles of handling all technological hazards, including chemical ones, are: avoidance, prevention and mitigation. Avoidance means to avoid the occurrence potential of the hazard. This can be done by various ways, i.e., using of safer chemicals, having small inventories, operation at lower temperatures and pressures, etc. These options are, of course, subject to availability of technology and economic viability. Avoidance also requires proper location and layout of a factory and also the control of all nearby developments after the establishment. Prevention means

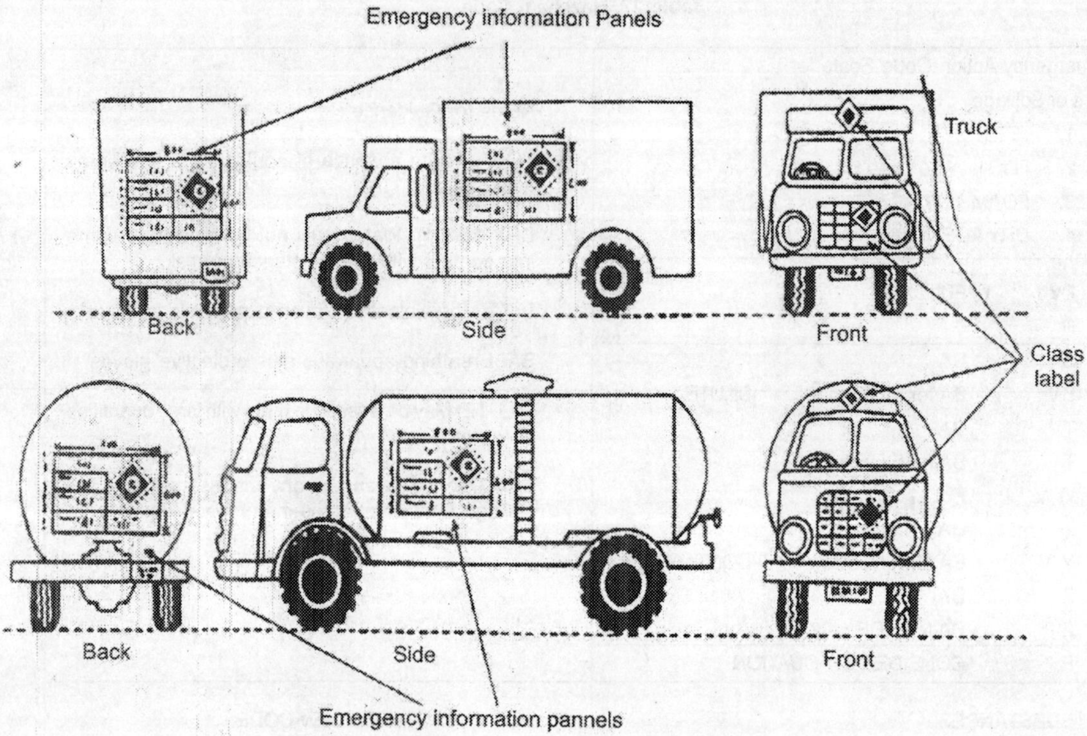

Figure 68. Emergency information panel (EIP)

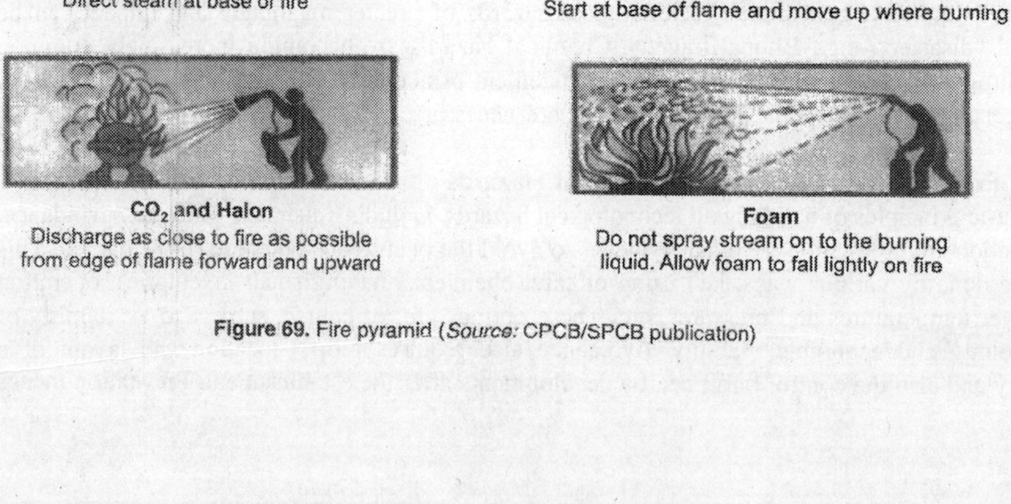

Figure 69. Fire pyramid (*Source:* CPCB/SPCB publication)

reduction of probability of accidents (hazards) in a given situation. This requires steps for preventing failures, improving detection (leaks, etc.), laying down shut-down procedures and methods, having proper relief site layout, smooth operation and maintenance. The objective of mitigation is to reduce impact when an accident occurs. Emergency action plans, both on-site and off-site, are prepared and rehearsed to achieve this objective.

Practical Methods of Prevention and Control of Technological Hazards

Appropriately designing all safe installations, including equipment and machinery, is the main aspect of preventing technological hazards. These include: (i) **Location of Various Installations.** At the macro level planning, different hazardous installations (industries, stores, etc.) should be adequately separated. Similarly, other activities around each of them should be controlled. These are necessary to reduce the impact of industrial accidents. (ii) **Site Layout.** Site layout of each installation should be carefully planned with particular care taken to avoid any cascading effect in case of an accident in any particular unit. (iii) **Hazard Analysis**. Hazard potential of each unit/site/process is required to be analyzed scientifically with the help of experts and accordingly provisions made. (iv) **Use of Checklists.** Checklists prepared by professionals often provide readymade initial step of designing installations. (v) **Use of Recognized Standards.** Adherence to various recognized standards for performance of plants/machineries and processes, quality of materials, emissions, etc., prepared by professional bodies go a long way in designing substantially safe installations.

Risk Assessment in Connection with Hazardous Substances and Natural Events

"Risk" is the likelihood of a specified undesirable event (hazard) with specific consequences. It is a measure of the expected losses due to a hazardous event of a particular magnitude occurring in a given area over a specific time period. It is a combination of the probability of the occurrence of the event and its consequences. All human activities have risks of hazard, low or high. The level of risk is a function of the nature of hazard, vulnerability of the elements affected, and economic value of the elements. A *"high risk"* activity has a high probability and high consequences of hazard. In public perception, industrial activity, particularly in chemical industries, is a high-risk one (Table 25). The relationship between the risk, hazard and vulnerability is: Disaster Risk = Hazard + Vulnerability.

A proper risk management reduces the probability and/or consequences of the hazard. As for example, air travel is normally expected to be risky because of the inherent probability of air crash and its disastrous consequences. A sequence of safety measures using computers has drastically reduced the probability of air crash although consequences remain as high as before. This has made air travel not riskier than other modes of travel.

An analysis of the past chemical hazards in Indian industries reveals that those incidents have resulted from one or more of the following causes: (i) Design/construction failure, (ii) Operating error, (iii) Equipment failure (including due to operation error), (iv) Inadequate maintenance, (v) Insufficient supervision and training, (vi) Natural phenomenon, (vii) External interference, (viii) Most of these incidents result in fire or other accidents and sometimes in explosion and toxic release.

Table 28. The Risk & Disasters

Y ↑ Consequences		
	Earthquake Lightening accident air crash	Industrial accident Accident during auto racing
	Accident while walking on footpath Accident during physical exercise	Normal road accident Kitchen fire Accident on 2-wheeler

Probability of occurrence → X

Risk Analysis (Hazard Analysis) is the estimate of the likelihood of the hazard based on engineering evaluation and mathematical techniques. This is used to predict the probability and frequency of occurrence of the hazard and its consequences.

Risk Assessment is the process by which the results of risk analysis are used in the decision making process. Answers to some vital questions are provided by risk assessment. Some of them are: Does the industrial plant have appropriate design and layout to localize any minor event without a serious chance of it spreading to other parts of the plant? Is it appropriately located so as not to have unacceptable risk of spreading into the neighborhood community (houses, schools, hospitals, bus terminals etc.)? Is its location appropriate in relation to other industrial plants around so that any incident occurring in one plant does not spread to others in a "domino effect"? Do all the emergency plans take full account of the entire spectrum of all possible accidents and their potential effects (worst case scenario)? Risk assessment essentially consists of identifying the potential hazards, estimating their likelihood (frequency or probability) and their consequences.

Risk Analysis and Control Techniques

There are various methods of risk analysis and control techniques – both qualitative and quantitative. Some of them are listed below.

- **Checklists.** In this method all aspects that require special attention learnt from earlier experiences are listed. These lists are an effective means of making sure that points that have gone wrong earlier and resulted in unsafe conditions are not missed.
- **Hazard Indexing.** It is perhaps the most widely used method use to identify fire, explosion and toxic release hazards in the design of an existing or proposed plant. Various types of indices have been developed (e.g. DOW and MOND indices). These indices take into account the properties, quantity and the manner of use of the concerned material. Risks are ranked in a way to indicate actions to be taken.
- Frequency of accidents per year and number of deaths due to accidents are plotted and the unacceptable and acceptable regions are studied along with the Alarp Region (F-n

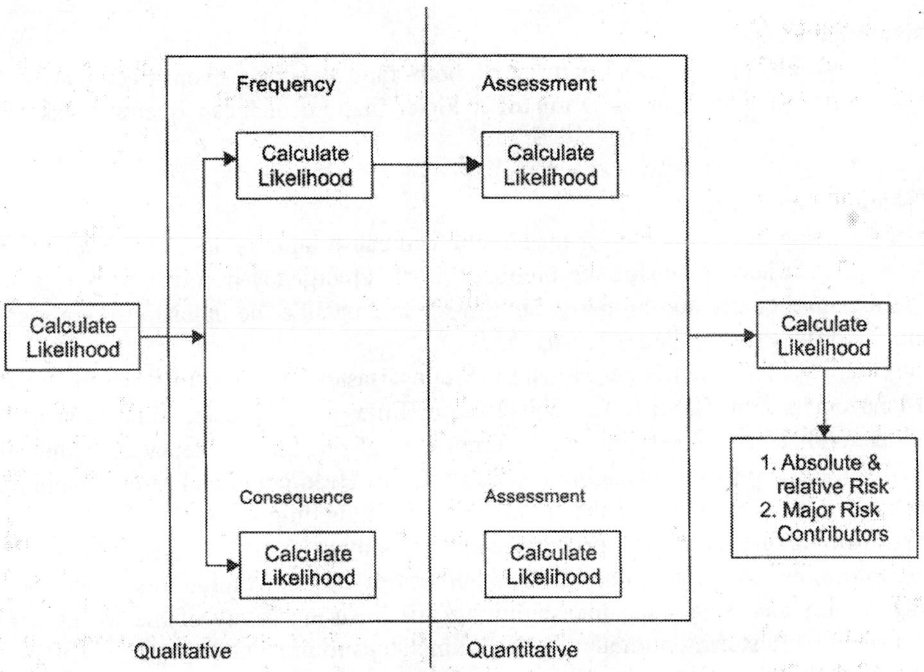

Figure. 70. The Process of risk assessment

curve for Societal Risk) and then efforts for reduction of risk to a level that is as low as reasonably practicable are made.

HAZOP (Hazard and Operability) Studies

This method is basically a qualitative method but can be developed to a semi-quantitative one by incorporating some quantification. HAZOP study is carried out by an interdisciplinary team which systematically reviews the process to find out the ways by which a complex system can deviate from its planned method of operation, identify the consequences of such deviations and recommend actions necessary to prevent hazards resulting from them.

Fault-Tree Analysis (FTA)

This is a quantitative procedure for hazard analysis with a *top-down* approach. It requires the construction of a logic diagram (fault tree) which traces from an undesirable event (say, explosion) all causes down to the roots that can ultimately lead to the event.

Event-Tree Analysis (ETA)

It is a similar logic diagram like the FTA but works from *bottom-up*. It begins with a particular initial event (say, power failure) and brings out all possible effects of that initial event stressing how a single failure (event) can have many effects.

Cause-Consequence Diagram

It is a technique which incorporates features of both fault-tree and event-tree analyses. It presents the sequence of events in the form of a logic diagram and can quantify risks of a system.

Emergency Management Plan (EMP)

An emergency occurring in any factory or installation can cause injuries, loss of life, damage to property or disruption inside or outside the premises. If the emergency becomes uncontrollable, it can cause serious loss of life and property, both inside and outside the industrial premises and in the neighborhood. It is then called a *"disaster"*.

Emergency Management Plan is necessary to meet a disaster situation. It is also referred to as Disaster Management Plan (DMP). The objectives of Emergency/Disaster Management Plan should include the following: (i) Controlling the occurrence, localizing the emergency and eliminating the hazard, (ii) Welfare of persons managing the disaster, (iii) Head count and rescue operations, (iv) Rescuing people, (v) Treatment of the injured, (vi) Safeguarding others by steps including evacuation, (vii) Minimizing damage to property and environment, (viii) Informing and assisting relatives, (ix) Informing and collaborating with authorities, (x) Informing the news media, (xi) Preserving records and organizing investigation, (xii) Ensuring safety of the works before personnel re-enter (xiii) Restoring normalcy, (xiii) Taking steps to prevent recurrence. This list is only indicative and not exhaustive, (xiv) Emergency Management Plan is made for both on-site and off-site of the factory premises.

Preparation of the on-site Emergency Plan is the responsibility of the occupier of the factory/ facility. An Emergency Coordinating Officer (ECO) should be designated to co-ordinate activities during emergency.

Off-site Emergency Management Plan and On-site Emergency Management Plan

The following are the important features of an on-site and off-site Emergency Management Plan.

Formulation of Plan and Emergency Services. The following should be taken into consideration for the formulation of the plan: (i) Worst event scenario, (ii) Route of the worst event, (iii) Time scale and size of lesser events (very often a large event is preceded by lesser events, (iv) Consequences of events, (v) Procedure of raising alarms, communications, etc., (vi) Appointment of key personnel (Emergency Officer, etc.), (vii) Creation of Emergency Control Centre, (viii) Action on-site, (ix) Action-off-site.

(i) **Planning Shut-down Procedures:** Depending upon the nature, size and gravity of emergency, total or partial shut-down of the factory may become necessary. Clear guidelines and procedures should be laid down for the purpose.

(ii) **Rehearsing Emergency Procedures:** Regular rehearsal of procedures makes the organization fit for quick and efficient response to emergency situations.

(iii) **Plan Appraisal and Updating:** Emergency plans should be periodically appraised and updated.

Components of Off-site Emergency Planning

The following should be looked into while preparing the emergency plan:

Organization, communication, availability of emergency equipment and medicines, availability of specialized knowledge, voluntary organizations whose help can be sought, chemical information (in case of release of toxic substance, meteorological information (this gives information about area of maximum fallout of the released toxic gas), emergency measures, public information, assessment at the end (for future guidance).

The Emergency Coordination Officer of the factory has much greater role and responsibility when the impact of accident inside the factory premises spills over to the neighbourhood. The off-site emergency plan should clearly define the role and responsibilities of the ECO.

Roles of Different Organizations. In case of a serious technological disaster, various organizations, other than the factory management, have important roles to play to control and mitigate the impact. Some of them are: Police, fire services, medical authorities, technical expert sources, regulatory authorities (factory inspectorate, pollution control board etc.), Local authorities and district administration, voluntary organizations, nearby industries, media.

CHAPTER 6

Energy Management: Global Climate Change

The year 2007 was a landmark year in the history of environmental movements in the world. The Nobel Committee has recognized that global warming is a matter of serious concern for mankind. We have to act urgently to save the planet for our existence and continuance by awarding the prestigious prize to Mr. Al Gore for championing the cause and to UNO's Intergovernmental Panel for Climate Change (IPCC) for providing conclusive scientific evidence that anthropogenic activities are interfering in nature's functioning and aiding significantly in causing global warming, climate flip flop, sea level rise, etc. Dr. R.K. Pachauri, being the Chairman of IPCC was honoured with the prize along with Mr. Gore. The message for 2008 World Environment Day was 'CO_2, Kick the habit for Low Carbon Economy.' The message for 2009 was 'Your Planet needs you: Unite to combat Climate Change'. The message for 2010 was 'Many Species, One Planet, and One Earth'. The year 2010 was declared by the UNO as 'the International Year of Biodiversity' and the message for the decade, 2011-2020 is 'Biodiversity Conservation'. The year 2011 has been declared by the UNO as 'the International Year of Forests'. All these messages show the importance of climate change, and forest and biodiversity conservation for the mankind.

In 1987, unusually high waves in the Indian Ocean inundated about a quarter of the urban area in the capital island of Male. The sea water flooded farms and washed away reclaimed lands in Maldives. Mr. Maumoon Abdul Gayoom, President of the Maldives, citing scientific evidence of sea level rise as glaciers melt and warmer water expands, made a serious appeal before the United Nations General Assembly in October, 1987 to save the Maldives. He echoed the problems of small islands, river deltas, coastal areas, big cities like Kolkata, London, New York and other cities.

An estimate shows that more than 630 million people will search for safer ground if sea level goes on rising. This will involve massive economic disruption and huge migration of people making climate change a real economy and security threat.

The warming of the planet also provides more energy to fuel climate disturbance causing stronger storms, cyclones, hurricanes, etc.

Climate change is popularly understood to mean the effect of global warming.

6.1 CLIMATE CHANGE: HISTORY AND FACTORS

It is believed that the current warming up of the globe started a few thousand years ago while most of the ice was still present in poles, Greenland and Himalaya-like high mountains.

But now it is estimated that about half of the ice sheets and glaciers covering Canada, Iceland and Europe are also melting. Ice in the Arctic, the Antarctic, Greenland and even Himalayas is melting and all the glaciers are shrinking. Climate flip-flop is now very common. During the last few hundred years of human activities, particularly, industrialization and urbanization, ecosystem fragmentation have caused serious damage to the planet culminating in climate flip-flop that every nation is now concerned.

In 1824, French Genius Joseph Fourier discovered why our planet's climate is so warm - tens of degrees warmer than a simple calculation of its energy balance would suggest. He observed that the sun brings heat and the earth radiates heat back into space but the numbers did not balance. He called it l'effet de serre – the Greenhouse Effect. Physicist John Tyndall on June 10, 1859, six months before the publication of Origin of Species by Charles Darwin demonstrated by a series of experiments at the Royal Institution in London that some gases absorb radiant heat and keep the earth warmer. Tyndall actually put Fourier's ideas to laboratory test. He commented that 'The atmosphere admits the entrance of solar heat, but checks its exit; and the result is a tendency to accumulate heat at the surface of the planet'. In 1897, Svante Arrhenius, who was awarded Nobel Prize in chemistry in 2003 calculated how much global warming a doubling of CO_2 in the atmosphere would cause. He predicted a 4-6°C rise (2-4°C – that IPCC scientists find). Arrhenius, being Swedish was not troubled by his finding rather he was happy. The cycle of day and night is due to the earth's movement. The day length and seasons are due to its tilt and position. Axis of rotation tilts at 23.44 degrees from the vertical. Hence, during the northern summer (southern winter), the northern hemisphere is tilted towards the sun and the southern hemisphere away from the sun. This accounts for temperature difference in summer and winter. In northern winter (southern summer) the position is reversed. In summer solar day is longer. The earth rotates on its axis once every 24 hours as it orbits the sun. Days and nights are unequal except spring and autumn equinoxes because of the earth's tilt. In 1950s Charles Keeling and his associates started to measure CO_2 in Antarctica and in Mauna Loa in Hawaii far away from any sources. By 1960, Keeling proved that CO_2 concentration was indeed on the rise. Now we know the Keeling Curve. In 1988, the Intergovernmental Panel of Climate Change was founded by United Nations Organization to analyze the issue.

In 1992 at Rio-Earth Summit the historic treaty was signed,' the Framework Convention on Climate Change. Its goal 'Stabilization of GHG concentrations in the atmosphere at a level that would prevent dangerous anthropogenic interference with the climate system. Milankovitch, a Mathematician, in his study in 1936 opined that three basic variations in the Earth's movement affect global climate. These variations are: (i) variations in the earth's orbit around the sun follow one lakh year cycle, (ii) the tilt of the earth's axis takes 41,000 years to complete a cycle, (iii) a 23,000 year cycle is created by a top-like wobble of the earth's axis. These cycles together affect the planet's climate. As per these cycles, earth scientists, meteorologists and physical scientists tell us that the planet should not have been in a period of so much warming. But this is not happening.

In the 5th century rightly calculated by Bhaskaracharya for the first time in the world that the earth takes 365.25875684 days to orbit the sun. Around March 21 (vernal equinox) and around September 22 (autumn equinox), earth's axis passes through upright position and none of the hemisphere is inclined towards the sun. On these days day's and nights are of equal duration. Solastices are the longest and shortest days in the year. June 21-summer solstice (longest day), December 21 winter solstice (shortest day) in northern hemisphere and the opposite in southern hemisphere. These earth processes are happening but the earth's atmospheric temperature is rising causing global warming. Scientific evidences indicate that the anthropogenic activities are aiding to the global warming.

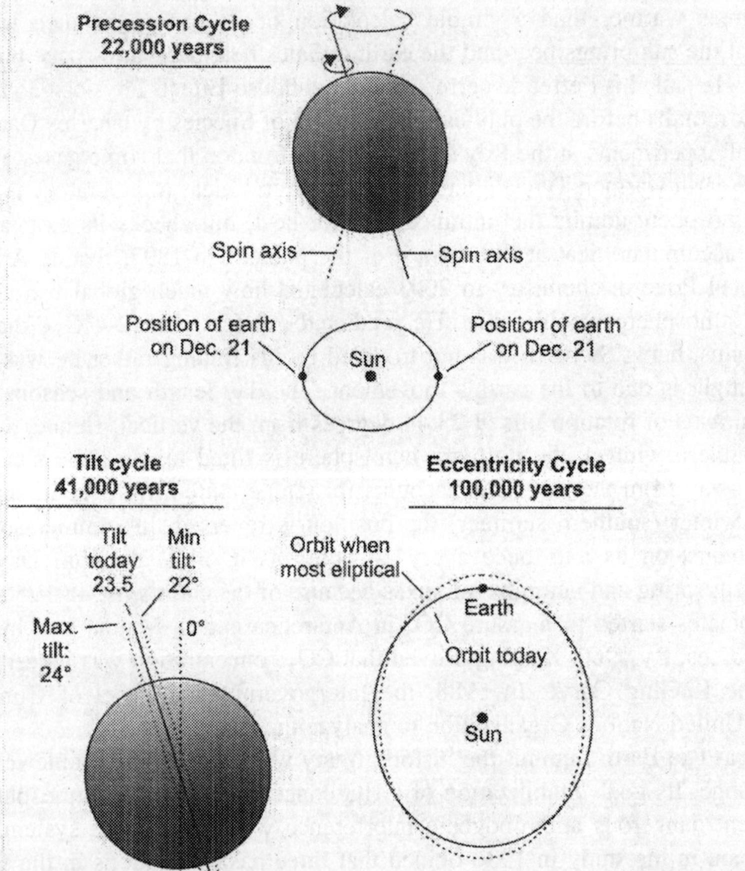

Figure 71. Milankovitch cycles (*Source*: Kunzig and Broecker, 2008)

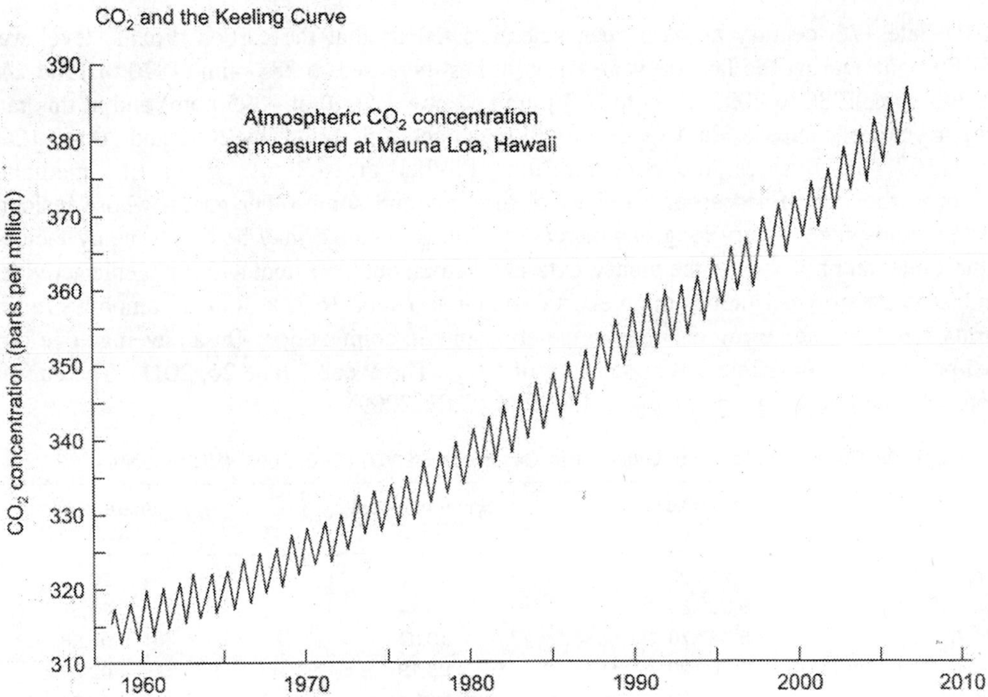

Figure 72. Keeling curve (*Source*: Kunzig and Broecker, 2008)

6.2 GREENHOUSE GASES (GHG)

The following gases are called greenhouse gases, produced largely by human activities:

1. Carbon dioxide (CO_2): Source (i) Automobiles (ii) Industrials (iii) Anthropogenic: Increased from 280 ppm to about 400 pp. Absorbs heat at three bands (nm): 2.3-3.1, 4.1-4.5, 13-18μ, Residence time (RT) : > 30 years to centuries, Global Warming Potential (GWP) = 1.
2. Methane (CH_4): Source (i) Organic matter decay under anaerobic conditions (ii) Agriculture fields. Increased from1 ppm to > 2 ppm. Absorbs heat at two bands (nm): 3.2 & 7.6μ. Residence time 14 years, GWP = 25.
3. Nitrous Oxides (NOx): Source (i) Automobiles, (ii) Industries: Increasing. Absorbs heat at band (nm): 7.66μ RT:114 Yrs, GWP-298.
4. HFCs/ Perflurocarbons (PFCs)/SF6 : Source (i) Refrigerants (ii) Foam (iii) Fire extinguishers, (iv) Aerosol products (v) Some mineral based industries- Increasing. Absorbs heat at bands (nm): 7-12μ RT: 1.4 to 270 years, PFC-10,000-50,000 Yrs, GWP = 124-14,800-22800.
5. Water Vapor: Source (i) Evaporation, (ii) Transpiration: Evaporation increasing. Absorbs heat at bands (nm): 1 to 8μ, Residence time ~ 9 days.

(*Source:* Forster, P. et al., 2007. 4th Assessment Report of IPCC, CUP, Cambridge)

Taking the late 17th century as base year, scientists tell us that the carbon dioxide level was around 280 ppm. During the last100 years or so, it has increased to 383 ppm (1870 to 1986-240 ppm to 340 ppm, 1986 to 2005 - 340 to 383 ppm and now (2010) at ~395 ppm) and at this rate (2 ppm per year) of increase, the CO_2 level will reach about 550 ppm by 2050 and 700 to 1200 ppm by 2100 AD. Besides, the concentration of other green house gases like methane, chlorofluorocarbons, perflurocarbons, oxides of nitrogen and some other gases, whose resident time in the atmosphere is very long has increased. Climate change may be due to many factors, i.e., natural internal processes in the planet, external factors, but persistent anthropogenic activities from industry, use of fossil fuel as main energy source, transport (650 million automobiles run in the world), land use, etc., bring changes in the atmospheric composition. On an average one litre of diesel/petrol on burning releases about 3 kg of CO_2 ('The Week', June 26, 2011). The current emissions of green house gas is given in Table 28 (CSE, 2009).

Table 28. Current Emissions of Greenhouse Gases (2005/2007) (CSE, 2009) (Million tonnes)

Country	Total emission 38,725.9 (2005)	Share of global GHG (%)	Share of World Population (%)
1. China	7,219.20	19.12	20.19
2. USA	6,963.80	18.14	04.59
3. EU(27)	5,047.70	13.37	07.58
4. Russian Federation	1,960.00	05.19	02.22
5. India	1,852.90	04.91	16.94
6. Japan	1,342.70	03.56	01.98
7. Brazil	1,014.10	02.69	02.89
8. Germany	977.4	02.59	01.28
9. Canada	731.6	01.94	0.50
10. U.K.	639.8	01.69	0.93
11. Mexico	629.9	01.67	01.60
12. Indonesia	594.4	01.57	03.41
13. South Korea	422.8	01.12	0.73

Recent data shows that the top ten CO_2 producers (percent wise) are ('The Week', June, 2011) are (i) China-22.3 (ii) USA-19.91 (iii) Russia-5.5 (iv) India-5.24 (v) Japan-4.28 (vi) Germany-2.69 (vii) Canada-1.90 (viii) U.K.-1.84 (ix) South Korea-1.72 (x) Iran-1.69.

The recent estimate of carbon emission per year from 2006-2009 amounts to 36.3 gigatonnes (Meinhausen et al., 2009) and 49 gigatonnes from 2009-2011 per year by UNEP, 2011. Indian emission of Greenhouse gas has increased to more than 2000 million tonnes per year.

6.3 HISTORICAL BURDEN OF GREENHOUSE GAS EMISSIONS (1980-2005)(CSE, 2009)

Country	Million tons
1. USA	134,600.9
2. Former USSR	76,465.6

Contd.

Contd.

3. China	68,459.9
4. Japan	26,994.8
5. Germany	24,164.7
6. India	18,206.7
7. U.K.	15,025.2
8. Canada	13,054.1
9. Italy	10,692.5
10. France	10,171.4

6.3.1 Key Factors

Excessive consumerism is a factor for global warming.

Patterns of consumption food habits and recycling processes have influenced growth in energy demand and GHG emissions. The specific GHG emissions from food production and processing are much lower in India than in developed countries, as seen in Table 28. (Based on TERI analysis from various data sources).

Besides, the average American has an ecological footprint of nine global hectares (carbon footprint of 20.1).The average European ecological footprint is half that of the USA– about 4.5 global hectares. Indian ecological footprint is estimated at 1.9 (carbon footprint is about 1.2). The ecological footprint of a Malawi, Haiti, Bangladeshi, and Nepali is hardly 0.5 global ha - not enough to provide basic food, sanitation, shelter, etc. Hence, ecosystems are collapsing and need immediate attention for conservation. In view of this the UNO message for the World Environment Day is significant.

(*Source:* Global Footprint Network & TOI, 25th November, 2009)

Table 29. Pattern of Food Consumption and Greenhouse Gas Production (Release of carbon dioxide in tons per million kcal of food energy) (based on TERI Publication_

	For Food Production	For Food Processing	Total
India	0.07	0.03	0.1
China	0.07	0.03	0.1
U.K.	0.20	1.50	1.7
Germany	0.30	1.50	1.8
The Netherlands	0.60	1.30	1.9
Australia	0.20	1.8	2.0
U.S.A.	0.20	2.0	2.2

6.3.2 Industrialization

Another key factors are industrialization, and transport, which release huge quantity of gaseous pollutants containing greenhouse gases, which trap heat. The pollutants also cause marine pollution causing damage to biodiversity, especially planktons, which act as a sink for GHG.

Table 30. Natural Sinks are Decreasing (billion tons of carbon, 1 ton C = 3.67 ton CO_2

Global carbon budget-sinks	Mean				Per cent decrease per year
	1959-'06,	1970-'99,	'90-99,	'00-06	
Land	1.9	2.0	2.7	2.8	1.87
Ocean	1.9	2.0	2.2	2.2	1.25
Atmosphere	2.9	3.1	3.2	4.1	1.89
Total	5.7	7.1	8.1	9.1	

Source: Centre for Science Education, New Delhi, 2009

6.3.3 Deforestation is the Key to Global Warming

This is to be prevented and new forests are to be developed. The total forest area in the world is about 4 billion ha, fifty-two per cent of forests are in low latitudes (O-25 degree N&S – Tropical Zone). High latitude forest (Boreal: 50-75 degree N&S) account for 30%, mid latitudes Temperate zones account for 18% of forests of the globe. Besides, there are additional 1.7 billion ha of open woodland, scrub, shrub, etc., lands and about 69 million ha of plantations (31 million ha in tropics & 37.6 million ha in mid-latitude mainly in China) exist. (FAO, 1995)

Saving the rainforests will be an essential first step. Deforestation is one of the largest contributors to climate change. Rainforests provide countless services to humanity, often unnoticed. Fifty percent of the world's biodiversity are found in rainforests. The Amazon forest releases 20 billion tons of moisture every day, helping to water crops around the world. Healthy rainforests absorb about 10% of man's carbon emissions every year. Deforestation releases more CO_2 than all the transport. Fifteen million hectares of tropical forests are lost every year - larger than the size of England. About 50% of best selling products in supermarkets of developed countries contain palm oil, linked to rainforest clearance in southeast Asia.

Brazilian farmers make $3000/ha by clearing forests and growing soybeans for export.

Subsistence agriculture in Africa clears forests. Rainforests may disappear in the next 50 years. How you shop determines the future of rainforests. More than 40 million dollars may be needed over the next five years to tackle the problem. Source: The Prince's Rainforests Project. (The Prince of Wales - Prince Charles - Rainforests: The Burning Issue, 2009).

6.4 EFFECTS ON GLACIERS RECEDING

The data on retreat of glaciers in the Himalayan region is given below (ISRO - India Today, 2007).

Glacier melting in the Himalayas is projected to increase flooding, rock avalanches and affect water resources in the next 20-30 years. This will be followed by decreased river water flow as the glaciers recede causing problems for agriculture, other aspects of human use. It may bring colossal environmental problems for the people in India (Table 31).

The year 2005 was the warmest on record and the ten warmest years have all occurred after 1980. Warming of Earth's Oceans have resulted in more powerful tropical storms, supercyclones, hurricanes, tsunami, etc. Weather related disasters have become common. Scientists (IPCC)

Table 31. Himalayan Glaciers Melting (ISRO-data)

Sl. No.	Glacier	Basin	Glacier Area sq km	Retreat Total	In Metres Rate / Yr.
1	Miyar		87.8	757	16.43
2	Shaune Bange	Satluj	8.8	923	26.4
3	Bilare Bange	Satluj	2.8	90	2.6
4	Parbati		48.44	6569	214
5	Samudra Tapu		77.67	802	21
6	Chipa	Dhauliganga	5.0	1050	26.92
7	Meola	-do -	14.0	1350	34.62
8	Jhulang	-do -	3.3	400	10.53
9	Gangotri	143	535	28.1	
10	Dokariana Bamak	-do -	5.8	585	16.7
11	Meru Bamak	-do -	4.7	395	17.2

have predicted that average air temperature would rise by 1.4 to > 4.8°C and sea levels by 0.3 and > 2.9 meter in 21st century.

6.4.1 Effect on Biodiversity

Changes in the range and distribution of biodiversity, loss of biodiversity and trees blooming earlier, change in productivity have been predicted and happening. They may affect agriculture and decrease cereal productivity in tropical latitudes. Fish production is affected.

Rivers and lakes in colder regions are freezing much later than earlier, and melting much earlier than before and the thawing of permafrost is happening. Africa appears to be at the greatest risk from the projected effects of global warming even though their emissions have been very small compared to developed countries.

Migratory animal species are more vulnerable to climate change as they use several sites, habitats and diverse resources during migration for their survival. Animal migration is a function of seasonal changes in climate. In winter, the feeding grounds in northern latitudes freeze, making the aquatic plants and fish unavailable to many animals. These animals migrate south in order to survive. The migratory pattern and habitat will be affected with climate changes in north and south.

Small sea fish krill forms the base of food chain for many animals. It is known that krill are not tolerant to warmer water and with even a marginal temperature rise in ocean water, krill may perish causing disaster to the population of other animals, like big fish, penguins, albatrosses, seals whales and affect the oceanic food chain.

6.5 CLIMATE CONTROL POLICIES: (KYOTO PROTOCOL 1997)

In 1997, the global community met at Kyoto in Japan to work out a mechanism for controlling GHG emissions. Policy decisions taken during this conference have been termed Kyoto Protocol. According to the mandate of this Protocol, all countries are grouped into two categories. Those consuming energy above the global average mostly advanced countries like the USA, Russia, Japan, Europe, Australia and East European countries are called Annex-1 countries (Developed) and the rest are called Non-Annex-1 countries (Developing). According to Kyoto Protocol, Annex-1 countries have to bring down their GHG emissions to less by 5.2% average from the base level of 1990, keeping in mind their economic development, population growth, etc.

If for some reason they are not in a position to bring down the consumption level to below 1990 level, they are allowed to go and reduce the GHG emission in the developing countries where the efficiency of energy consumption is also lower and there is a need to consume more energy for ensuring their development.

Any reduction made in the specific CO_2 emissions can be considered as being reduced in the respective country. Alternatively, any organization or industry in the Non-Annex-1 country reducing the GHG emissions can trade those emissions with the Annex-1 countries.

This financial instrument of selling GHG emission is called carbon trade under Clean Development Mechanism. Kyoto Protocol for carbon trading will operate between 2008–2012.

The International Protocol which regulates GHG emissions – Carbon Trading – essentially means exchanging points earned by the reduction of GHG for money. This has emerged as a huge opportunity for developing countries where GHG emissions are much below the fixed quota. Developing economies are not expected to meet emission targets. Companies in developing countries can earn carbon credits by investing in clean technology. The principle is based on the fact that climate change is a global problem that requires a global solution.

Global cooperation on technology transfer is important and developing countries will need access to climate-friendly technology. Global Environment Facility (GEF) has a critical role to play in the co-development and transfer of technology and it can be made through several different channels.

Technology transfer must be accompanied by capacity building. Though UNFCCC has made substantial progress in evolving the mechanism for inter-state sale of carbon emission credits, there are still some gray areas, which are being resolved from time to time. Carbon trading is in full swing in many developing countries like Brazil, Mexico, China and India despite the fact that the USA did not ratify the Kyoto Protocol. They wanted that large economies like China, India, Brazil, etc. should take some steps to control carbon emission. However, they have agreed for Bali Road Map of December, 2007. Carbon trading is moving across all the countries in a very rapid way. A market of around 9 billion tons prevailed in 2006-2007 and expected to grow up to 300 billion tons (1000 billion dollars) by 2012.

The organizations can reduce energy consumption or release of any of the six gases by adopting cleaner options (Clean Development Mechanism) and claim reduction in GHG emission.

The Kyoto Protocol further stipulates that the time period allowed for GHG emission reduction commences from January 2000 and ends up by 2012. The accounting for Annex-1 countries begins from 2008 and ends with 2012 (first crediting period). To reduce the GWP (global warming potential) from the green house gases, industries can undertake any of the following CDM projects: Increase in methane gas (biogas) consumption, increasing the use of biomass in place of fossil fuel for energy generation, fuel switching from coal to biomass (biomass gasification), switching over to hydroelectric power, energy efficiency projects, fuel switching from coal to gas, improving energy efficiency at the user end, improved agriculture practices and increasing carbon sink potential.

At present the prices of certified emission reduction (CER) range between 15-26 URO per ton of CO_2. Prices vary depending on the type of GHG emissions. Renewable and methane captures are at the top of the list and energy efficiency at the lower end. As the accounting period approaches (2012) the prices may increase further. Size of the project is determined based on the total emissions saleable over accrediting period.

IPCC scientists have forecast three models of CO_2 increase in atmosphere in the near future:

1. CO_2 equivalent in atmosphere, < 445-490 ppm - Average temperature rise 2-2.4°C. Sea level rise 0.4-1.4 meter.
2. CO_2 equivalent in atmosphere, ~590-710 ppm - Average temperature rise 3.2 - 4.0°C. Sea level rise 0.6-2.4 meter.
3. CO_2 equivalent in atmosphere, ~855 - 1200 ppm - Average temperature rise 4.9 - 6.4°C. Sea level rise 1.0 - 3.7 meter. The target of IPCC is to persuade the world nations to control their emissions to pre-1990 level by, say, 2015 so that model 1 will operate. Arresting climate change will require transforming the global economy from a high carbon to low carbon energy base. High carbon base includes coal and petroleum. Low carbon base is corn oil, jatropha oil, biomass gasification. No carbon base is solar, wind, hydroelectricity, hydrogen and nuclear.

Bali Road Map (2007)

UNO organized the conference in 2007 at Bali. The slogan was 'No Time Left- Act Now'. There were 10,000 participants, 187 govt. representatives and the conference was held from December 3-14, 2007 and the conference adopted Bali Road Map: a new negotiating process was to be concluded in 2009 & expected to lead post-2012 to international agreements.

Salient Features:

1. Launching Adoption Fund (AF).
2. Reducing GHG emissions.
3. Technology Transfer is made simple.
4. USA and Australia agreed for post-2012 agreement and they argued for some commitment from developing countries, especially from China, Brazil and India for reduction of GHG.
5. The Message: The World cannot afford to wait.

Countries are to address the question, a shared vision of long-term cooperative action, carbon emission reduction, taking into account social and economic conditions and other relevant factors.

Countries must negotiate the question of 'enhanced action on technology' but countries shirk from clarifying what they wish to do to mitigate climate change.

Recent Developments in International Negotiations

Poznan, Poland - Climate Change Conference (December 1-12, 2008): UNFCC-14th Conference of Parties (COP) to solve the problem of erosion of trust between developed and developing countries on implementation of Bali Road Map was held at Poznan. Over 3000 delegates from 186 countries participated in the conference. Developing countries will need huge amount of money every year till 2015 to adapt to climate change effects according to the Human Development Report of UNDP, 2007. At present the availability of the fund is meager and developed countries are not contributing as expected. GEF has been handling money till now over climate change, but least developed countries (LDC) found the process too cumbersome. Besides, UNFCCC has found that CDM process cannot properly account for energy efficiency projects in the building sector.

There was a policy shift in the USA after Mr. Barack Obama became President and Mrs. Hillary Rodham Clinton was appointed as Secretary of State with regard to Climate Change. I quote some portions of the address of the Secretary of State Mrs. Clinton delivered at 17 Major Economies, forum on Energy, Climate on 17th April, 2009. 'It is an environmental issue, a health issue, an economic issue, an energy issue and a security issue. It is a threat that is global in scope, but also local and national in impact.' Desertification and rising sea level generate increased competition for food, water and resources. But we have also increasingly seen the dangers that these transpose to the stability of societies and governments. We see how this can breed conflict, unrest and forced migration. She stresses on four points. These are:

1. Climate change is a clear and present danger to our world and demands immediate attention, the science is conclusive. 2. The US is determined to make up for lost time, both at home and abroad and the USA is committed to address this issue and to act. 3. The countries should pull together and work towards a successful outcome of the UN climate negotiations later in the year at Copenhagen 4. We all must cooperate and new policy and new technologies are needed to resolve this crisis. The international business on CDM will be huge; their priority area being to make homes and buildings more energy efficient. On one hand it is very encouraging but there is an element of business interest which makes developing countries worried. They fear that the developed countries may vouch for imposing restrictions on carbon emissions. The press clip in Times of India dated 23rd May, 2009, justifies their fear. The first draft for negotiations on the climate change policy beyond 2012 released on 19th May, 2009 include two options for developing economies like India to deviate their emissions from the current baseline by 15-30% by 2020 or reduce by 25% from 2000 level by 2050. This provision violates the UNFCCC's original text and also the spirit of Kyoto protocol.

India has advocated for CDM policy reform. Developed countries advocate that carbon capture and sequestration (CCS) from coal fired power plants should be included among CDM projects. Many developing countries have reservation on carbon capture mechanisms, especially underground capping. Many western countries are not interested in following Kyoto protocol and desire a new protocol beyond 2012.

However, some good progress has been made in India on this matter. CO_2 produced in >80 power plants in India can be collected and pumped underground to store for indefinite period. This is known as Carbon Sequester and Storage Technology (CSST) and is being attempted in industrially advanced countries.

For underground storage suitable geological formations such as porous and leak proof rocks are required (underground abandoned coal mines may be suitable). A major part of Indian off-shore region has soft sedimentary rocks which are considered ideal for carbon sequestration and storage (CSS). India annually burns 300 million tonnes of coal in power plants and generates equal amounts of CO_2 from this source. If CSS technology materializes, India's off-shore sediments will be a fertile field for future carbon sequestration. In recent years there have been many international conferences on CSS technology in New Delhi attended by delegates from world over to discuss this possibility. Thus, India's huge off-shore region not only offers promise of large oil and gas reserves, it has enough space for underground storage of CO_2 sequestered from thermal power plants. Research funding in this field and policy intervention will be required.

Every nation wants enhanced economic development, even it shows concern for global warming and emissions. The first draft for negotiations on the climate change policy beyond 2012 released on 19th May, 2009 at Bonn, Germany include, two options for developing economies like India, to deviate their emissions from the current baseline by 15-30% by 2020 or reduce by 25% from 2000 level by 2050.This has generated lot of heat in the negotiations and at Copenhagen in December 2009. This provision deviates from UNFCCC's original text and also the spirit of Kyoto protocol.

The 20 nation Major Economic Forum (MEF) met in London on 19th & 20th October, 2009. (Chairman - Mr. Ed Miliband, Minister, British Energy and Climate Change, Co-Chairman - Mr. Todd Stern of USA, Head of Climate Change Policy). Note: Developing countries (DC) rejected the suggestion of International monitoring of GHG and mandatory GHG reductions for DC, although the co-chairman, Mr.Todd Stern of the USA argued in favour and stated that by 2030, China and developing countries will contribute 97% of GHG emissions of the world. However, they agreed on three points. Rich nations to take on internationally - binding commitments on reducing GHG (Kyoto, Bali protocols) and developing countries to take domestic action to cut the GHG emissions. UNO has to play a more active role in the governance of flow of finances to help developing countries counter climate change. Countries agreed to scale up public finances significantly for GHG reduction.

India's Voluntary Policy Shift

Considering about 8% GDP growth rate per annum in 2002-2009, the estimate of GHG from all sources in 2000 in India was about 1485 million tons , per capita emissions about 1.1 ton. This was about 3% of total global emissions. An assessment of the current and projected trends indicate that green house gas emissions grew @ 4% per annum during 1990 & 2000 and are projected to grow further due to developmental needs. The absolute level will not be less than 5% of global emissions in 2020. (Sharma et al., 2006 - Current Science). In India, the estimate is >3000 million tons of GHG emission by 2020. India has announced 25% cut in emission level by 2020 taking 2005 as the base year before the Copenhagen meet. It means that the dependence on energy from coal to renewable will receive priority.

Prime Minister's council on climate change has approved eight missions under India's National Action Plan on climate change.

(i) Achieving energy efficiency; 'Perform, Achieve and Trade' (PAT) mechanism.
(ii) Promoting renewable energy.
(iii) Promoting sustainable development, especially through clean technology development & transfer.
(iv) Promoting afforestation, and enhanced forestation (from 20.6% to 33% of land cover) to increase sink factor.
(v) Promoting sustainable agriculture. The National Solar Mission has approved enhancement of solar energy generation. On 21st October, 2009 India and China had signed a MoU for collaborating on climate change issues at mutual and international level.

India has installed a base of 20,000 MW of renewable energy and the plan is to increase it to 70,000 MW by 2020–2030. This is part of the programme of energy security for the country. The PM's office has announced that by 2015, India will save about 5% of annual energy consumption and nearly 100 million tons of CO_2 emissions per year.

India, in collaboration with Iceland, hopes to soon start exploring the possibility of geothermal energy in Ladakh, Chhattisgarh, and many other areas (Energy Minister, Government of India, 2011-Times of India). India launched a 83 kg small observation satellite (IMS-I) in April, 2008 On 18th October, 2008 Mr. G. Madhavan Nair announced further actions to be taken: India plans to launch two climate satellites (one 50 kg micro satellite for climate study and the second satellite (remote sensing) will monitor GHG (CO_2 & CH_4) emission in polar orbit. The satellite will contain 2 optical instruments: (i) a multispectral camera, (ii) a hyper-spectral camera to operate in visible and near infrared regions. These actions indicate India's concern and positive voluntary actions.

The policy centres around gradually switch over to renewable source of energy. The dependence on coal was 80% and the plan is to gradually reduce the dependence on coal 55 to 40% by 2030 and simultaneously taking vigorous steps to depend on solar, biomass gasification, nuclear etc. (Figure 73) (Source: Govt. of India Publication)

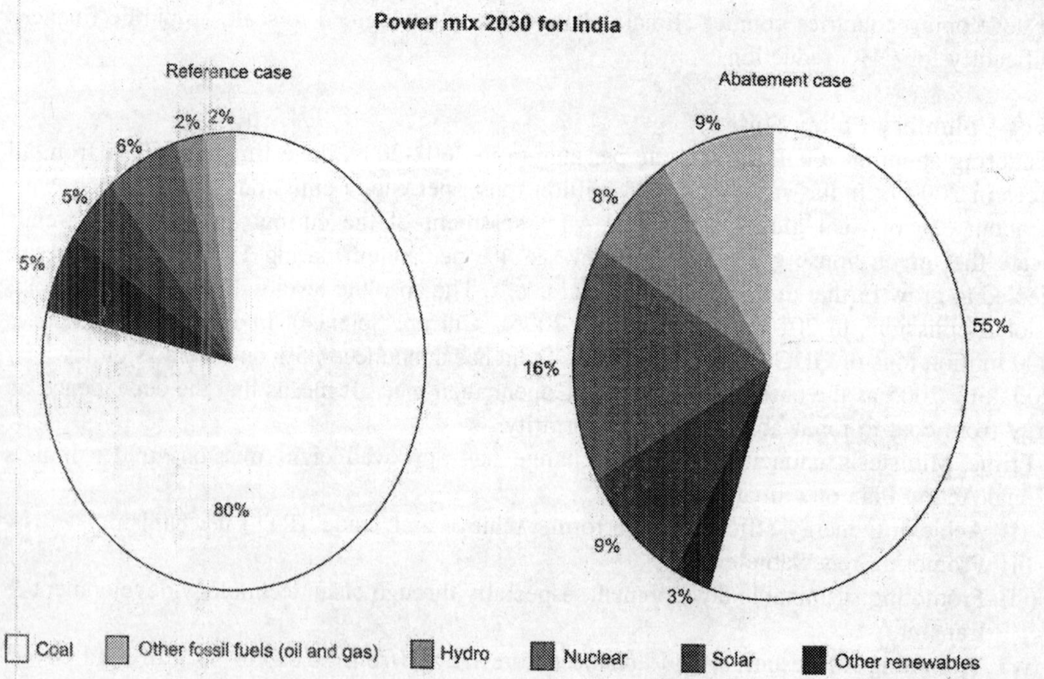

Figure 73.

Copenhagen: December 7-18, 2009

The Copenhagen Conference was attended by 193 countries and 120 Heads of States. The deliberations resulted in developing the following: (i) No specific emission targets set for the developed countries (ii) Consensus was to keep temperature rise to below two degrees celsius by 2050, but no strong commitment was made. Emphasis was on mobilization of financial resources for supporting reforestation efforts of developing countries and scaled-up funding for poor countries, including long term cooperative action (fast-tracked fund) of $30 billion during 2010-2012. The USA will take initiative to mobilize $100 billion by 2020.

Summary of Copenhagen Conference—Proceedings:

(i) Most of Annex-1 countries wanted a new deal replacing Kyoto Protocol (5.2% cut of 1990 level). Non-Annex countries insisted upon retaining Kyoto and action in 2008-2012. Kyoto Protocol survives-discussions to continue

(ii) Consensus (120 out of 193 countries) agreed to allow upto 450 ppm CO_2 & 2°C rise in temp. by 2050.

(iii) Outcome was voluntary emission cuts by BASIC countries and retention of Kyoto. (A political agreement was signed - neither supported by the UNO nor a legal document)

(iv) International monitoring was not accepted.

(v) Consultations yield a political accord and not a legally binding treaty.

(vi) UNO-UNFCCC meeting in Mexico in 2010 did not introduce punitive measures for violation of International agreements.

Johansberg 2012 and Rio de Janeiro (Rio + 20), 2012 and Doha 2012 Conferences adoped green economy concept. This concept has been discussed in chapter 2 of this book.

Energy Security and Climate Change: Indian Situation

There is increased need of energy in agriculture, industrial and service sectors as population continues to grow and to meet the developmental needs. Modern way and standard of living demand huge energy from unsustainable consumerism, transport facilities and increased construction work and other aspects of human use. In 1947 India had very low electricity generating capacity. At present India has the capacity to generate >1,70,000 MW (>115 times growth) with about 80% load factor. In spite of this increase, India is not able to meet the demand of energy from the farm, industry and service sectors. Hence, the situation has become critical. In the 10th and 11th plans, additional 27,283 MW & 78,700 MW could be achieved. It has been estimated that by 2020, the energy production capacity will reach 2,20,000 MW. However, per capita energy consumption in India is only about 700 units per year compared to about 2600 units at international level in industrially developed countries.

Table 32 gives the per capita income and energy use in the world.

India has huge reserves of thermal grade coal and therefore states such as Odisha, Jharkhand, Chhatisgarh and some other with abundant coal reserves attract investors to set up thermal power plants if fresh water is available. Coal, therefore, occupies important position in power sector. As two major rivers such as Mahanadi and Brahmani flow in Odisha, and the coal mining areas of Angul-Talcher and Ib valley are situated near the rivers Brahmani and Mahanadi respectively, many thermal power plants have been established and many are in the pipeline in these areas and

Table 32. Per Capita Income & Energy Use in the World

GDP/Capita ↓	KW/Capita →	<1	<2	<4	<5	<6	<7	<8	<9	<10	< 12
< $5000		India	Brazil, China			Russia					
10000			Argent-ina	World Average				South Arabia			
20000					Spain						
25000						France					Canada
30000						UK					
40000						Japan					USA

likely to be set up there. There is huge pressure on the rivers for fresh water. There is huge pressure on land for making the provision of ash ponds.

Pollution Load

Thermal power plants are not environment friendly as these plants generate huge amount of greenhouse gases and pollutants such as SO_2, NOx, Cox, SPM, fly and bottom ash, metallic dust, etc. About 120 -150 million tons of fly ash is generated annually in India (Jain, 2010).

One estimate (Paribesh Samachar, 2010) shows that the pollution load from 1 MW of Indian coal based thermal power generation amounts to:

~19 tons of CO_2 per day
>136 kg of SO_2 per day
>7 tons of fly ash per day
>60 kg of particulate matter per day

Green House Gas Emissions

Carbon dioxide is the dominant green house gas and it is not yet considered a pollutant in most countries of the world. Three categories of coal based thermal power plants (TPPs), depending upon the type of fuel used operates in most of the states in India. These categories are:

Category-I, fuel is only coal; either pulverized or sized, Category-II, fuel may be low grade coal, washery rejects, and char. These TPPs use Atmospheric Fluidized Bed Combustion (AFBC) or Circulating Fluidized Bed Combustion (CFBC) boilers and these plants are usually small (usual capacity < 50 MW), Category-III, TPPs which use waste heat of some other processes to generate steam and the plants are usually of low capacity. About 70% of our energy source (~170000 MW) is fossil fuels, especially coal and lignite (Times of India news). The distribution is approximately as follows:

- 119000 MW - Coal based,
- 18700 MW - Gas based
- 1330 MW - Diesel based.

- Ash utilization is only 30%–40% in brick making, road construction, forest soil fertilization cement making, and in agriculture, etc. (Jain, 2010). Hence, it is a huge problem.

The industrial pollution load in India on the basis of the data given above.

(i) Particulate Matter - 60 kg/day/MW × 1,19,000 MW thermal power = 7140 T/day __ 2.61 million Ton/year

(ii) SO_2 - 136 kg/day/MW × 1,19000 = 16184 Ton/day 5.91 million ton/year

(iii) CO_2 - 0.79 ton/day/MW × 1,19000 MW = 94010 ton/day 34.31 million ton /year

Ash - 4-7 Ton/day/MW × 119000 MW = 4, 76,000 to 8, 33,000 ton/day = about 174 million ton - about 304 million ton/year. > 80 mega thermal power plants operate in India and some are coming up.

The Sink Potential

The total forest area in the world is 4 billion ha. Fifty-two per cent of forests are in low latitudes (O-25° N&S – tropical zone). High latitude forest (Boreal: 50-75° N & S) account for 30%. Mid latitudes - temperate zones account for 18% of forests of the globe. Besides, there are additional 1.7 billion ha of open woodland, scrub, shrub, etc. lands and about 69 million ha of plantations (31 million ha in tropics and 37.6 million ha in mid latitude mainly in China) exist. (FAO, 2005, 2006).

Forest and tree cover of the country was 78.37 million ha in 2007 (FSI, 2009), which was 23.84% of the geographical area and this includes 2.82% tree cover. Table 33 gives the forest and tree cover of the country in 2007 (FSI, 2009).

Table 33. Forest and Tree Cover in India

Class	Area (million ha)		% of Geographical Area (G.A.)
Forest Cover VDF (very dense)	8.35	2.54	Note: 55.51 million ha <1000 m, 11.67 m.ha.
MDF (medium dense)	31.90	9.71	<1000 to 3000 m
and			1.91 m. ha < 3000 m
Open Forest	28.84	8.77	altitude.
Total Forest Cover	69.09	21.02	
Tree Cover (Tree patches < 1ha With canopy density >10%)	09.28	02.82	
Total Forest & Tree Cover	78.37	23.84	
Non-forest: Scrub	04.15	01.26	
Non-forest	255.49	77.72	
Total G.A.	328.73	100	

GHG Removal

Forest Survey of India Report, 2009 states that over the last two decades, the national forestry legislation and policies have transformed India's forests into a significant net sink of GHG. The carbon stocks stored in the country's forests and tree cover have been estimated as 6,622 million tons in 2005 with an annual increase of 38 million tons (equivalent to 138 million tonnes of CO_2) since 1995 (carbon stock was 6,245 million tones). It has been estimated that the CO_2 removal by India's forests and tree cover was enough to neutralize about 9.31% of India's total emissions (CO_2 equivalent) at 2000 level. In 2000 India's level of emissions was estimated as ~1485, million tonnes (Sharma et al., 2006; Shukla, 2006). Out of it 9.31% of amounts to ~138.25 million tonnes. Thus, it appears that 78.37 million ha of forest with 12% tropical evergreen category, 34% tropical moist deciduous, 30% tropical dry deciduous, 5% tropical thorn, 6% subtropical pine, and 11% Himalayan temperate category and tree cover could neutralize 138.25 million tonnes of GHG per year amounting on the average to 1 ha of forest and tree cover neutralizing 1.764 tons of GHG per year (equivalent to about 0.5 tons of carbon per ha per year) (FSI Report, 2009, Kishwan et al., 2009, Melkenia, 2009). This is a gross estimate and the site specific estimates would be different.

Carbon in Forest Biomass and Soil

This average value appears to be an underestimate as it does not differentiate the rate of primary productivity on an altitudinal gradient, type of forests, the succession stage of the forest and the ground vegetation. However, this shows the importance of forests and tree cover and the urgent need to increase forest and tree cover in India.

The grasslands, scrub lands, crops also neutralize GHGs and this has not been estimated separately. The other GHG sinks are soil, water bodies and planktons in the water bodies including bays and oceans. Kishwan et al. (2009) have also estimated component-wise carbon in India's forest biomass and soil in 1995 and 2005 (Table 5). The total estimate for 2005 was 3755.811 million tons of carbon in soil amounting to 55.4723 tons per ha.

The total estimate amount of carbon in forest biomass was 2865.739 million tons amounting to 0.3310 ton of carbon per ha of biomass and 42.32 tons of carbon per ha of biomass. The tropical dry deciduous, moist deciduous, littoral and swamp forests contribute significantly to India's SOC pool. This situation can be improved if efforts for forest conservation are effective.

Odisha—A Case Study

Odisha has a total geographic area of about 1,55,707 km^2 (4.74% of the country) and of this 31.38% of area is under forest cover. The distribution of forest cover is given below.

30 districts: 12 districts with > 33% forest cover 05 districts with >20% & < 33% FC 13 districts with < 20% FC (6 districts < 10%FC)

The recorded forest area of the state is 58,136 km^2 (37.33% of the geographic area) but the forest cover in the state based on October-December, 2006 satellite data interpretation is 48,855 km^2 (48,855 ha (31.38% of the geographic area).

In terms of forest canopy density classes, Odisha has 7,073 km^2 very dense forest, 21,394 km^2 moderately dense forest, and 20,388 km^2 open forest (FSI, 2009)). Out of 30 districts, only 12 districts of Odisha have forest cover exceeding the national target of 33% forest cover for each district. Another 4 districts have forest cover exceeding 23.8% but less than 33% and 13 districts have forest cover less than 20%. Some districts such as Bhadrak, Jagatsinghpur and Puri have forest cover of less than 5% and districts such as Baleswar, Kendrapara and Jajpur have forest cover less than 10% of the geographical area of the district.

The industries have been concentrated in districts such as Angul, Dhenkanal, Sundargarh, Jharsuguda, Sambalpur, Balasore, Jagatsinghpur, Jajpur, and Cuttack. The GHG sink potential of Jagatsinghpur, Jajpur, Jharsuguda, Baleswar, Bhadrak, Cuttack, Puri, is low. These are important districts from industrial development point of view. Further concentration of thermal power plants in Angul, Dhenkanal, Jharsuguda are to be avoided.

Regulatory Measures

Carbon dioxide, a green house gas is not considered a pollutant in India and in most of the countries. It should be considered as a pollutant if the emission concentration is very high than its natural range of occurrence in the atmosphere. Environmental Protection Agency (EPA) in the USA has declared carbon dioxide as a pollutant and has brought it under environmental regulatory provisions (Raha and Mishra, 2009). They have also cited a legal case, which has been filed at the New South Wales, Australia Land and Environment Court at curbing carbon dioxide pollution from coal fired thermal power plants. If the court declares CO_2 as a pollutant, the case will be a very positive step controlling climate change. In India, thermal power from coal based plants is the most important energy source. More than 80 mega thermal power plants operate in India and it is the right time to debate whether carbon dioxide should be considered a pollutant in India.

Scientific studies show that the level of CO_2 in the atmosphere should not be less than 150 ppm for plants to continue the process of photosynthesis. However, plants usually grow better and produce better flowers and fruits at higher level of CO_2 (Happer, 2011). The present level of CO_2 in the atmosphere is conducive for good photosynthetic activity. Evolutionary history says that most of the green plants evolved at CO_2 levels of several thousand ppm, not less than 10 times higher than the current level in the atmosphere.

About 57 million years ago in the Eocene period of Cenozoic era, the volcanic activity generated huge amount of oxides of carbon and other gases as the geologists and evolutionary biologists tell us. The level of CO_2 was perhaps not less than 5000 ppm in the atmosphere. All forms of animals and many flowering plants and ancestors of modern man had already evolved in the planet by that time as scientists tell us (Table 34). Was the high concentration of CO_2 detrimental to living organisms at that time? It may be that the organisms were adapted to high temperature and the biodiversity was not as rich as it is now. But the fact remains that the adaptive potential of biodiversity, especially human beings is phenomenal.

Human beings and most of the animals will survive and perform their functions without having much CO_2 in the air but with higher concentration of CO_2 in the atmosphere, physiological functioning, especially respiratory gas exchange would be very difficult. In other words, there may not be a lower limit but there is an upper limit that man and most of the vertebrate animals can tolerate.

NASA has conducted extensive studies on human tolerance for CO_2 for astronauts and NASA recommend an upper limit of 5000 ppm of CO_2 for space missions for one thousand days, assuming total pressure of one atmosphere. USA Navy recommend an upper limit of 8000 ppm for cruises of ninety days in the submarines (Happer, 2011). Green plants, however, will do their functions better in increasing CO_2 level in the air up to a very high concentration with other environmental conditions remaining the same as at present. For us, the important issue is the productivity of crops and other plants providing food to us under increased CO_2 concentrations.

Table 34. The Ages of Life on Earth (based on Reader's Digest publications)

Age	Events	Life
Precambrian		
4.6 billion years ago	The Earth is formed	No Life
4.5 billion years ago	The Moon is formed	No Life
3.8 billion years ago		Single celled organism
3.3 billion years ago		Cyanobacteria or Blue Green Algae
2.1 billion years ago		Single celled organism with a nucleus ,
720 million years ago		Multicelluar Animals
Paleozoic		
Cambrian - 550-505 million years ago		Trilobites & other marine animals with hard cell
Ordovician - 505-483 million years ago		Fishes without jaws & corals
Silurian - 438-408 million years ago		Land plants & jawed fishes
Devonian - 408-360 million years ago		Land animals, insects & amphibians
Carboniferous - 360-286 million years ago		Reptiles
Permian - 286-245 million years ago		Reptles diversity
Mesozoic		
Triaseric (245-208 million)-Juraseric (208-144 million)		Reptiles Evol. Peak. Evolution of Birds & Mammals
Cretaceous (144-65 million)		
Cenozoic		
Tertiary period (65-1.8 million years ago)		Birds diversity
Paleocene (65-57 million years ago)		Flowering plants, mammals & primates appear
Eocene (57-34 million years ago)		Ancesor of modern man)
Oligocene (34-23 million years ago)		Other mammals
Miocene (25-5 million years ago)		Homo erectus
Pliocene (5-1.8 million years ago) to 50000 years		Homoneanderthalensis, H. cromagnon, H. sapiens
Holocene Quaternary Perid (12,000 years ago to present)		Modern man (H. sapiens sapiens) (wise man)

As it appears, higher concentration of CO_2 upto a certain level will increase productivity if the temperature regime, availability of nutrients and water do not create stress. But increasing CO_2 level in the atmosphere is increasing the level of atmospheric temperature. Figure 72 shows a generalized graph showing the relationship of the intensity of sunlight, air temperature and rate of photosynthesis in C_3 and C_4 plants (Dash and Dash, 2009). In high air temperature, the rate of photosynthesis goes down, especially in C_3 plants (most of the plants and crops) (Figure 74).

IPCC shows serious concern on rise of temperature in the atmosphere and in the ocean. Besides, the rise of temperature is thought to be the cause of glacier melting, migration of biodiversity northward, loss of productivity, flooding of coastal ecosystems and human settlements.

Increasing CO_2 Level in the Air

Before industrialization in Europe, the average CO_2 concentration in the atmosphere was around 280 ppm and during the last 200 years, the concentration has increased to about 393 ppm (113

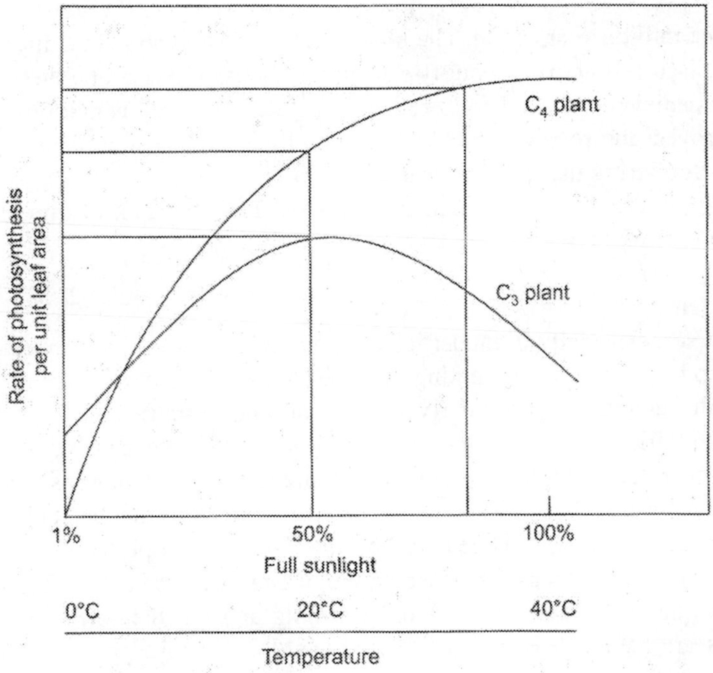

Figure 74. Relationship between intensity of sunlight, temperature and rate of photosynthesis in C_3 and C_4 plants. Rate of photosynthesis for unit leaf area in different sunlight and temperature conditions (Dash and Dash, 2009).

ppm increase). The current rate of burning of fossil fuels, the rate of increase in CO_2 concentration has been estimated to about 2 ppm per year. At this rate of increase, it would take 300 years for CO_2 to reach a concentration of 1000 ppm in the atmosphere. The IPCC report (2008) shows that during there 150-200 years post industrial period the average temperature of the atmosphere has increased to about 0.8 degree Celsius. They also predict that with the current rate of increase in CO_2 and other green house gas emissions, the temperature will increase by 2-4 degree celsius, or more, which will be detrimental to many aspects of our crop productivity, prevalence of disease, housing security, etc. especially in tropical countries. Air temperature rise may enhance crop productivity in temperate climate but glacier melting and appearance of vector-borne diseases will increase. In general temperature rise will reduce crop productivity in tropical and subtropical countries. In view of this they advocate to change to alternate energy sources urgently so that CO_2 and other green house gas emissions are reduced.

Many scientists are of the opinion that since the Paleozoic era (~ 550 million years before), it was assumed that the ocean currents involving the fluid flow pattern and salt belt, the continental drift, massive volcanic eruptions in initial periods, the planet's orbital parameters (Milankovitch cycles), variations in sun's output of all types of radiations, and some other causes were the reasons for temperature increase making the planet conducive for life. Besides, the atmospheric gases played, an important role in the heat balance of the planet.

In recent times scientists have found a strong corelation between CO_2 concentrations and the planet's temperature by studying ice-core records of the cycles of glacial and interglacial periods during the last million years or so. The planet's climate is always changing and there may be many reasons as discussed above. About twelve to ten thousand years ago there was warming of the planet called medieval warming followed by the "little ice age" which brought famine as the crops were destroyed due to severe cold. Since the little ice age, the planet is warming up slowly and steadily. But during the last 200 years, the level of greenhouse gases, particularly CO_2 level has increased and increasing due to human activities. Therefore, lot of importance is being given to adopt 'green technologies'.

International Scenario

Many private enterprises, especially in industrially developed countries, have invested heavily on green technologies and their role in promoting climate change programmes cannot be ruled out. However, most of the countries, particularly the developing countries such as India, China, Brazil, Mexico, South Africa, Argentina, etc. depend upon coal for their energy.

The leaders of green technologies are the industrialized western countries, (West European countries, USA, Canada) Australia and Japan and hence the world environmental politics involving clean development technologies (CDM) centered on the international protocols.

Considering the scientific facts as discussed above, it can safely be concluded that CO_2 level in the atmosphere is one of the factors of global warming and not the sole factor. The serious environmental issues are habitat loss, damage to regional/local landscapes, increasing pollution load, particularly hazardous chemicals and wastes, mining activities, unplanned industrialization and massive transport system. Although carbon dioxide level of 393 ppm or much higher level does not create hindrance in the functioning of the living world, it absorbs and retains heat and increases the temperature of the atmosphere. The temperature rise creates problems for the living and non-living world and biological and physical processes. In view of this all efforts are to be made to prevent further fast rise of atmospheric temperature. Inclusion of carbon footprint of industries in EIA document will be a progressive and proactive concept and will be in the national interest.

Biomass forms important component of energy source for rural India and few hundred million people depend upon biomass as energy source. India produces 300 million tons of sugarcane annually and Bagasse can be used to produce butanol on a large scale. Biomass energy for rural India project is an US $8.62 million project supported by Global Environment Facility (GEF) through UNDP, India-Canada Environment Facility, Government of India and Government of Karnataka. This project will provide socio-economic and environmental benefits. (Dash, 2012). Energy from biomass gasification sources should be vigorously promoted.

Algae can be used as efficient GHG sequesters. Algae require non-agriculral land, fresh water pond sources and shallow marine areas (brackish water, saline break water, saline shallow coastal areas, etc.) for their mass cultivation. Algae are better GHG sequesters than land plants. About 1 million ha of wasteland is available for algal cultivation. Besides the brackish water lake like Chilika can be utilized for microalgae (seaweed) cultivation. Shallow coastal region in east coast can also be used for algal culture and to sequester GHG. Algae can be used for carbohydrate and protein source as cattle feed and for agar-agar preparation. Seaweed (algae) grown in seacoast ponds enriched with thermal power plant flue gas may produce net primary production of 20 g per sq. meter per day ,which amounts to 73 tons NPP per year per ha (amounts to about

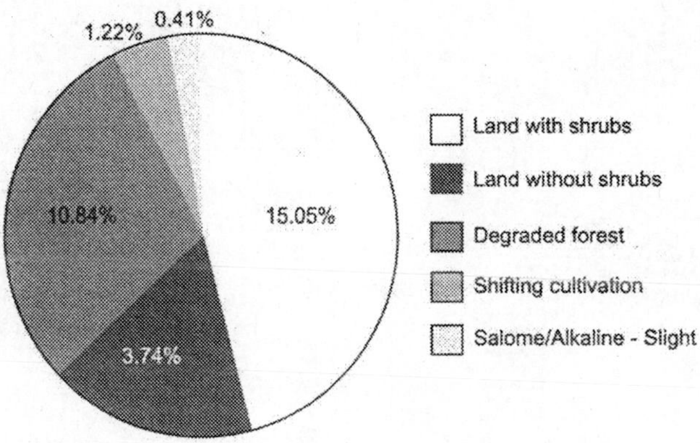

Figure 75. Types of wasteland in India with potential for plantation and for Algal culture (from Satya Dash, 2012)

438 tonnes CO_2 per ha per year).These efforts will help to neutralize GHG emissions to some extent. Fresh water algae and soil algae can also sequester GHG. Research in this discipline will be profitable for the country ((Times of India news, 2010).

References

A Guide to Manufacture, Storage and Import of Hazardous Chemicals Rules, 1989, published by Ministry of Environment and Forest, Govt. of India, 1992.

A Report of the Intergovernmental Panel on Climate Change, 2007 (4 volumes), UNEP, Switzerland.

Asian Development Bank, 1991. *Guidelines for Social Analysis of Developmental Projects*, Manila, The Philippines.

Barrett, B.F.D. and Therivel, R., 1991. Environmental Policy and Impact Assessment in Japan, Chapman, and Hall, Routledge, New York, p. 149.

Behra, A. and Dash, M.C. 1999. Environment status of Sambalpur-Burla-Hirakud Complex, Orissa Pollution Control Board, Bhubaneswar, 112 Pages.

Behera, D.K., 2008. 'Management of Hazardous Wastes', in: M.C. Dash's and K.C. Acharya (ed.), *Environmental Management and Sustainable Development in Industries*, Interscience Institute of Management and Technology, Bhubaneswar.

Bezborah, Pranjal and Dutta, Mitali Chelleng, 2004. Corporate Values and Ethics, *Vanijya*, 14:73-86.

Bisset, R., 1983. 'A Critical Survey of Methods for Environmental Impact Assessment, An Annotated Reader' in: T.O'Riordan and R.K.Turner, (Eds), *Environmental Planning and Management*, Pergamon Press, Oxford, England, 168-186.

Buhenne-Guilmin, F. and Glowka L., 1994. 'An Introduction to the CBD' in: Krattiger A.F., McNeely J.A., Lesser, W.H., Miller, K.R., Hill Y. St. and Senanayke, R. *Widening Perspectives on Biodiversity*, IUCN, The World Conservation Union and the International Academy of the Environment.

Bull. A.T., 1994. *Microbial Biodiversity: Issues and Actions*, University of Kent, UK, 7, IUMS Congress.

Burslem, D.F.R.P., Garwood, N.C. and Thomas S.C., 2001. Tropical forest diversity - The Plot Thickens. *Science*, 291, 606–607.

Brundtland, Harlem Gro (ed.), 1987. *Our Common Future: The World Commission on Environment and Development* United Nations, Oxford University Press, U.K.

Bukowitz, W.R. and Williams, Ruth L., 2004. *Knowledge Management Field Book*, Pearson, New Delhi.

Canter, L.W. and Hill, L.G., 1979. *Handbook of variables for Environmental Impact Assessment*, Ann Arbor Science Publishers and Ann Arbor, Michigan.

Canter, L.W., 1986. *Environmental Health Impact Assessment, Pan American Health Impact Assessment*, Pan American Health Organization, Metepec, Mexico, pp. 232-247.

Canter, L.W., 1993. Pragmatic Suggestions for Incorporating Risk Assessment Principles in EIA Studies, *The Environmental Professional*, 15(1), pp. 125-138.

Canter, L.W., 1996. *Environmental Impact Assessment*, International Edition, McGraw-Hill Inc., New York, p. 660.

Census. 2011. Government of India, New Delhi.

Centre for Science and Environment (CSE), New Delhi.2009. *Climate Change: Politics and Facts*, Centre for Science Education, New Delhi.

Central Pollution Control Board, 2000. Guidelines for Developing Greenbelts, New Delhi and other Publications.

Chakraborty, S.K., 1998. *Human Values for Managers*, Wheeler, New Delhi.

Choudhury, S. Nanda, 2010. 'Industrial Health Hazards and Environmental Management Model in Industrial Belts of North Orissa: A Case Study of Balasore', A D.Sc.thesis of Fakir Mohan University, Balasore.

Cloud, P.E.Jr., 1969. Resources, Population and the Quality of Life (Quoted by E.P.Odum, 1971).

Confederation of Indian Industries, Publications.

Crosby, A.W., 1986. *Ecological Imperialism: The Biological Expansion of Europe*. Cambridge University Press, pp. 900-1900.

Cutter, Susan L. (ed.), 1994. *Environmental Risks and Hazards*, Prentice-Hall Inc., New Jersey, USA.

Cunningham, W.P. and Saigo, W., 1990. *Environmental Science*, W.C. Brown, New York.

Darwin, C., 1883. On the Formation of the Mould, *Proceedings of the Geological Society of London*, 2:574-576.

Darwin, C., 1881. The Formation of Vegetable Mould through the Action of Worms with Some Observations on their Habits, John Murray, London.

Das, R.C. and Behera, D.K., 2008. *Environmental Science, Principles and Practice*, Prentice Hall of India, Delhi.

Dash, M.C. 2012. *Charles Darwin's Plough: Tools for Vermi-Technology*, I.K.International Publishers, New Delhi/Bangalore, p. 185.

Dash, M.C., 2010. 'Environment, Energy and Development from Stockholm to Copenhagen and Beyond the Celebrations', *The Bioscan* (Special Issue), 1:1-11.

Dash, M.C., 2010. A Comparison of Industrial Green House Gas Emission (GHG) and Carbon Sink Potential of Forest Vegetation in Orissa, A Fast Thermal Power Growing State in the Context of Climate Change. *The Ecoscan*, 4:147-152.

Dash, M.C., 2010. 'Climate Change: Facts and Politics' (In Oriya language), *Bigyan Diganta*, 6th issue, pp. 3-14, Orissa Science Academy, Bhubaneswar.

Dash, M. C., Saxena, K.G and Giri, Sohan., 2009. 'Vermitechnology for Wasteland Reclamation, Plant Productivity and Composting: A Review in Indian Context', *International Journal of Ecology and Environmental Sciences*, 35(2-3): 163-185.

Dash, M.C., 2009. 'Bioresources as a Tool for Food Security, and Sustainable Development for Rural Livelihood in India in the Context of Industrial Development and Environmental Protection: An Overview', *The Ecoscan* 3(3 & 4), pp. 201-208.

Dash, M.C., 2009. Presidential Address in the 4th National Congress of National Environmentalists Association, Aurangabad, Maharashtra, India.

Dash, M.C. and Dash, Satya Prakash, 2008. Conservation and Sustainable Management of Belowground Biodiversity: A Review on the Functional Role of Soil Fauna in Indian Ecosystems with Particular reference to Earthworms, *International Journal of Ecology and Environmental Sciences*, 34(3):223-243.

Dash, M.C. and Dash, S.P., 2009. *Fundamentals of Ecology*, Tata-McGraw-Hill Publ., New Delhi.

Dash, M.C., 2007. Save the Planet from Global Warming, *Society of Geoscientists & Allied Technologist Bulletin*, 8(2), 43-59.

Dash, M.C. (Ed), 2006. The State of Environment of Orissa, MOEF, New Delhi and SPCB, Bhubaneswar.

Dash, M.C., 2000. Sustainable Development and Environmental Protection in Orissa and Role of Pollution Control Board: An Overview, *Paribesh Samachar*, SPCB,Bhubaneswar, pp. 10-16.

Dash, M.C., Behera, D.K. and Behera, B.K. 2000. Industrial Chemicals Handled in Orissa, SPCB, Bhubaneswar, 192 pages.

Dash, M.C. and P.C.Mishra., 2001. Man and Environment. Macmillan India Publishers.

Dash, M.C.2013. Sustainable Development: The journey from Rio-1992 to Rio-2012 and Beyond. The International Journal of Ecology and Environmental Science, 39(1):1-21.

Dash, Satya Prakash, 2012 .Indian Biotechnology: The Roadmap to the next Decade and Beyond, Government of India, Department of Biotechnology and Association of Biotechnology Led Enterprises, 135 pages.

Dilip Kumar, 2012.Technology Driven Fisheries and Aquaculture for Rural Livelihoods, In: Sustainable Development of Fisheries and Livestock for Food Security (Khillare, Y.K., M.C.Dash, and B.N.Pandey, Ed, Narendra Publishing House, New Delhi. 41-52 pp.

Disaster Management in India - A New Direction, 2007. National Disaster Management Authority (NDMA), Government of India, The Times of India, Delhi.

Disaster Prevention and Mitigation: A Compendium of Current Knowledge, Volume II Preparedness aspects, 1984. UNO, New York.

Down to Earth, New Delhi, 2007-2012 (Articles on Climate Change and Related Issues *Encyclopedia of Life Support Systems*, EOLSS Publishers, Oxford, 2002.

Economic Survey, Government of Orissa, 2005-2006.

Edwards, C.A. and J.R.Lofty., 1972. Biology of Earthworms, Chapman and Hall, London.

Environmental Management System, Central Pollution Control Board, Ministry of Environment & Forests, 2001, pp. 1-27.

Envis Newsletter, 2006. Centre for Environmental Studies, Government of Odisha, Bhubaneswar.

Fatesingh, Himansusekhar, 2010. Energy Generation and Conservation (In Oriya), *The Samaj*, 26th December Issue.

'acts at your Finger Tips, 2002. Reader's Digest Publications, India.

ood and Agriculture Organization (United Nations Organization), 1984. Status of Food and Agriculture, Rome

Food and Agriculture Organization (United Nations Organization), 1985. Year Book of Forest Products, Rome.

Forest Survey of India Report, 2009. Government of India, MoEF, New Delhi.

FAO, 2005. *State of the World's Forests*, FAO, Rome.

FAO, 2006. Global Forest Resources Assessment 2005: Progress Towards Sustainable Forest Management. FAO Forestry Paper 147, FAO, Rome.

Gahan, Padmavati, 2011. *Personal Communication on Corporate Governance.*

Geiger, R. 1941 The Climate near the ground, Cambridge, Massachusetts, Harvard University Press.

Girsberger M.A., 1999. *Biodiversity and the Concept of Farmers' Rights in International Law; Factual Background and Legal Analysis*, pp 283-291, in Th. Cottier, Series on Global Economic Law No. 1.

Gopinath,Vedula, 2011. *Management of Corporate Governance and Accountability*, Ph.D. thesis submitted to Sambalpur University.

Government of India Country Report on Animal Genetic Resources of India. 2005. Department of Animal Husbandry and Dairying, Ministry of Agriculture, Government of India, New Delhi.

Green Cities-Urban Environmental Solutions, 2000. *Global Issues* (Electronic Journal), Public Affairs Office, U.S. Embassy, New Delhi, pp. 1-39.

Hagerty, D.J., Pavoni, J.L. and Heer, J.E. Jr., 1973. Solid Waste Management, Van Nostrand Reinhold, New York, pp. 242-262.

Happer, William, 2011. *The Truth about Greenhouse Gases*, National Wildlife Federation, USA.

http://in.rediff.com/money/2007/jan/16wef.htm

http://www.indiatogether.org/2005/jun/hlt-mdgoals.htm

http://www.funonthenet.in/about_india.ppt.

India Today, New Delhi, 2005-2007. Articles on Global Warming and Related Issues.

Jain, M.K., 2010. *Suitability of Fly Ash as a Mine Void, Fill Material - A Critical Review*, Minenvis, 64, pp. 1-6.

Jain, R.K. et al., 1973. *Environmental Impact Assessment Study for Army Military Programs*, Technical Report, D-13, U.S. Army Construction Engineering Research Laboratory, Champaign, Ill.

Indian Chamber of Commerce, Publications.

Indian Standard Environmental Management Systems - Specification with Guidance for Use, 1997. Bureau of Indian Standards, New Delhi, pp. 1-16.

India's Best B-schools" Business World, 6 September, 2004.

Indira Gandhi Open University, New Delhi. Publications on Science and Environment.

Ismail, Sultan Ahmed, 2005. *The Earthworm Book*, Other India Press, Goa pp. 101.

Kalam, Abdul A.P.J. (ed.), 2010. *Vision Earth-2030*. Safeguarding the Earth, Low Carbon Fut not Low Growth, (by Ajay Mathur) and Imperatives of a Low Carbon Future (R.K. Pach The Economic Times Presentation.

Kale, Radha, D. and Dinesh, M.S., 2005. 'Earthworm Component of Soil Biota', in: *Pr of National Workshop on 'Conservation and Sustainable Management of Bel Biodiversity*, KFRI, Kerala, India.

Kashmanian, R., Keenan, C., Wells, Richard, 2010. Corporate Environmental Leadership: Drivers, Characteristics, and Examples. Wiley Periodicals, Inc. (Online)

Khillare,Y.K.,Dash,M.C. and B.N.Pandey.2012.Sustainable Development of Fisheries and Livestock for Food Security, Narendra Publishing House, New Delhi, 222 pages.

Kishwan, Jagdish, Pandey, Ran Dadhwal, V.K., 2009. *India's Forest and Tree cover: Contribution as a Carbon Sink*, Indian Council of Forestry Research and Education, Dehradoon, pp. 1-12.

Kump, Lee R., 2011. *The Last Great Global Warming, Scientific American*, 57-61.

Kunzig, Robert and Broecker, Wallace, 2008. Fixing Climate, Green Profile, London.

Karmachari, S.B.and Singh, S.K., 1992. Biomass and Net Production of Teak (*Tectona grandis*) in dry tropical region in India. *Forest Ecology and Management*, 55, pp. 233-247

Kishwan, Jagdish, Pandey, R. and Dadhwal, V.K., 2009. *India's Forest and Tree cover: Contribution as a Carbon Sink*, Indian Council of Forestry Research and Education, Dehradun, pp. 1-12.

Lavelle, P., Brussaard, L., Hendrix, P. (ed.), 1999. Earthworm Management in Tropical Agroecosystems, CABI Publishing, U.K., pp. 300.

Lee, N. 1983. Environmental Impact Assessment Review, *Applied Geography*, 3, pp. 5-27.

Lieth, H., 1977. The Gross Primary Productivity Pattern on the Land Vegetation: A First Attempt, *Tropical Ecology*, 18, pp. 109-115.

Lieth, H., 1972. 'The Net Primary Production of the Earth with special emphasis on the Land Areas', in: R.H. Whittaker, (ed), *Perspectives on Primary Productivity of the Earth*. Symposium at the American Institute of Biological Science, Second National Congress, Miami, Florida.

Lieth, H. 1972. 'Modeling the Primary Productivity of the World', *Tropical Ecology*, 13, 125-130.

Lee, N., 1983. 'Environmental Impact Assessment: A Review', in *Applied Geography*, 3, pp. 5-27.

Lee, N., 1988. *An Overview of Methods of Environmental Impact Assessment*, Environmental Impact Assessment Workshop, Seville, Spain.

Lein, J.K., 1988. 'An Expert System Approach to Environmental Impact Assessment', *International Journal of Environmental Studies*, 33, 13-27.

Leopold, L.B. *et al*., 1971. *A Procedure for Evaluating Environmental Impact*, Circular 645, U.S. Geological Survey, Washington, D.C.

Mahadevan, T.N. and Misra, U.C., 1999. Concepts in Disaster Prevention Management and Control for a Typical Industrial Area, Scavenger (Society for Clean Environment), 30 (3 & 4), 1-8.

Mahapatra, J.K. 2011. Personal Communication.

Meinhausen, N., Hare, W., Raper, S.C.B. et al., 2009. Greenhousegas emission targets for limiting global warming 2°C. Nature 458: 1158–1196.

Miller, G. Tyler Jr. 1996. Living in the Environment-Principles Connections and Solutions, 9th edition, Wadsworth Publishing Company, Singapore.

Miller, G. Tyler, Jr. 1996. Living in the Environment, Principles, Connections, and Solutions, Wordsworth Publishing Company, Belmont.

Ministry of Environment and Forests, 2008. Notification, New Delhi, 24th September, 2008.

Mishra, P.C., Mishra, B.K., Tripathy, P.K., Meher, K. and Pradhan, M.K., 2009. Corporate Social Responsibility: A Case Study on Quality of Life of People around Bargarh Cement Works of Orissa *India, Current Research Journal of Social Sciences*, Maxwell Scientific Organization, 3: pp. 93-110.

Misra, S.K., 2008. Sustainable Mining, Environmental Management and Sustainable Development in Industries', In: (M.C. Dash and K.C. Acaharya (ed), Proceedings Volume, Interscience Institute of Management & Technology, Bhubaneswar.

Mitchel, J.K., Devine, N., Jagger, K. 1999. Contextual Model of Natural Hazard Environmental Risk and Hazard (Susan L. Cutter, Ed)., Prentice Hall of India Ltd.

Melkania, N.P. 2009. 'Carbon Sequestration in Indian Natural and Planted Forests', in Indian Forester, pp. 380-392.

Mohanty, R.P., 2003. 'Towards Knowledge Management - A Case Study,' *Information Technology Management*, Vol.2, No. 3 .

Multi Disciplinary Centre on Safety, Health and Environment, Bhubaneswar- their Publications.

Naik, Chita Ranjan (SPCB), 2011. *Personal Communication.*

Nath, Pradosh N. Mrinalini, 2000. 'Organizational Practices for Generative Human Resources in Non-Corporate Research & Technology Organization", Journal of Intellectual Capital, 01: 2000.

Nature's Mighty Powers, Extreme Weather, 2008. Reader's Digest Publications, India.

Nayak, C.R. and Dash, M.C., 2000. Environment status of Angul-Talcher Area, SPCB, Bubaneswar, 139 pages.

Simon, Andrew, 2008. The Final Countdown: 100 Months to Save Our Planet, Guardian-G2, dated August, 2008.

Neelamegham, S. 'India Inc in the New Era of Globalization', *Journal of Marketing & Communication*, Vol. 1, Issue I, pp. 28-33.

Odum, E.P. 1971.Fundamentals of Ecology, Saunders, Philadelphia.

Orissa Resettlement and Rehabilitation Policy 2006. Government of Orissa,Bhubaneswar.

Orissa Tottering on Tragedy, 2001. *Down to Earth*, October, 15, Centre for Science and Environment, New Delhi.

Paribesh Samachar, 2010. 'Biodiversity-Ecosystems Management and the Green Economy', Volume XV and XVI, pp. 1-25, State Pollution Control Board, Odisha, Bhubaneswar.

Pedersen (Ed.), 1993. *Environmental Assessment of Products - A course on Life Cycle Assessment*, 2nd edn., UETP-EEE, Helsinki.

Pollution Control Acts, Rules, and Notifications issued thereunder, 2006. Central Pollution Control Board, 2006.

Pradhan, M.K., 2008. Safety, 'Health and Environmental Management Practices in Bargarh Cement Limited of Orissa in the context of Globalization', Ph.D. thesis of Sambalpur University, Odisha.

Proceedings of the Seminar on Inter-Sectoral Co-operation in Fly Ash Management, 1998. Mahanadi Coalfields Limited & Mining Geological & Metallurgical Institute of India, pp. 109.

Raha, Debashis and Mishra, P.C. 2009. First Ever Legal Action on Carbon Dioxide Pollution and Its Future Consequences. The Ecoscan 3(3&4): 209-210.

Rain Forests: The Burning Issue, 1996. The Prince's Rainforests Project, Forest Stewardship Council, London, pp. 48. The Prince's Rainforests Project. (The Prince of Wales - Prince Charles- Rain Forests: The Burning Issue, 1996).

Reddy, M.V. (ed), 1995. *Soil Organisms and Litter Decomposition in the Tropics*, Oxford & IBH Publishing Co. Pvt. Ltd., New Delhi, pp. 274.

Reddy, M.V. (ed.) 2008. *Wildlife Biodiversity Conservation*, Daya Publishing House, New Delhi, pp. 390.

Robbins, S.P. and Decenzo, David, A., 2001. *Fundamentals of Management*, Pearson Education, Asia, Singapore.

Rout, D.K. and Dash, M.C. 1998. Environment Status of Bhubaneswar. Orissa Pollution Control Board, Bhubaneswar, 87 pages.

Sahu, Sanjat, 2011. Personal Communication on Biodiversity Research Papers.

Schneider Electric, 2010. 'A Watt Saved is a Watt Shared'. *The Week*, September, 2010, pp. 6-7.

Senapati, B.K., Lavelle, P., Giri, S., Pashanasi, B., Alegre, J., Decaens, T., Jimenz, J.J., Albrechrt, A., Blanchart, E., Mahieux, M., Rousseaux, L., Thomas, R., Panigrahi, P.K. and Venkatachalam, M., 1999. In-Soil Earthworm Technologies for Tropical Ecosystems, In: Lavelle, P., Brussaard, L. and Hendrix (ed.), pp. 199-237, *Earthworm Management in Tropical Agroecosystems*, CABI Publishing, U.K.

Sharma, A.1987. Resources and Human Well-being , Presidential address, Indian Science Congress, 74th session,Benaras..

Singh, J.S., and Joshi, M.C., 1979. Primary Production, in *Grassland Ecosystems of the World* (ed.), R.T. Coupland, Cambridge University Press, London, pp. 197-218.

Sinha, Sachin, 2000. Getting Strategically Ethical, *The Journal of the All India Management Association*, 39(7).

Sharma, S., S. Bhattacharya and Garg, A., 2006. Greenhouse Gas Emissions from India: A Perspective, *Current Science*, 90(3), 326-333.

Sharma, Subhash. (2002). Character Competence of the Corporation, Journal of Human Values, Management Centre for Human Values, IIM, Calcutta, 8(2).

Shukla, P.R. 2006. 'India's GHG Emission Scenarios: Aligning Development and Stabilization Paths', *Current Science*, 90(3), pp. 384-395.

State Pollution Control Board, Odisha - Officials for personal communication (especially - Mr. Sidhanta Das, Er.Nihar Sahoo, Er. (Dr) A.K. Swar, Mr. B.N. Bhol, Mr. C.R.Naik, Mr. Anupam Behera, Er. Bijoy Behera, Er. R.N. Prusty, Er. Simachal Dash, Mr. B. Patjoshi, Dr. S.S. Pati)

Sustainable Development: Learning and Perspectives from India, 2002. Centre for Environmental Education, UNDP, and Government of India, Ministry of Environment and Forests, New Delhi, pp. 1-71.

Swain, S. and Behera, N. 1998. 'Biomass and Net production of *Tectona grandis* (Teak) in a Regenerating Teak Forest'. *Ecology, Environment and Conservation*, 4 (2 & 3), pp. 1-7.

SPAN, 2005-2008. USIS, Kolkata (Articles on Global Warming, Climate Change, Energy Scenario)

Singh, Gurdeep, 2009. 'Environmental Assessment of Fly Ash from some Thermal Power Stations for Reclamation of Mined Out Areas', in: *Proceedings of Indo-Italian Conference on Emerging Trends in Waste Management Technologies*, Organized by MIT College of Engineering and Maharashtra Institute of Technology, Pune, pp. 38-45.

Sohrab, 1998. ISO 14001 Environmental Management Supreme Standards. A Mainstay of Sustainable Development, Asia Pacific Tech. Monitor, *Environmental Management* Vol. 15(5), Sept-Oct 1998, pp 9-17.

Society of Geoscientists and Allied Technologists, 2009. *Vision Document on Mineral Development-2020 for Odisha*, SGAT for Department of Steel and Mines, Government of Orissa, Bhubaneswar.

Sahoo, Nihar, 2008. *Environmental Impact Assessment*, in: M.C. Dash and K.C. Acharya (ed), Environmental Management and Sustainable Development in Industries', Interscience Institute of Management and Technology, Bhubaneswar.

Sahoo, Nihar 2011. Storage of Hazardous Materials, A Technical Guide, United Nation Environment Programmer.

Swar, A.K. 2008. Pollution Control Measures in Mineral Based Industries and Role of SPCB, in: M.C. Dash and K.C. Acharya(ed), *Environmental Management and Sustainable Development in Industries*', Interscience Institute of Management and Technology, Bhubaneswar.

Tata Energy Research Institute, New Delhi, Publication on Energy and Climate Change.

The Air (Prevention and Control of Pollution) Act, 1981, 2007, Current Publications, Mumbai.

The Environment (Protection) Act, 1986, 2006. Professional Book Publishers, New Delhi,

The Knowledge Society-Government of India, New Delhi (2002).

The Water (Prevention and Control of Pollution) Act, 1974, 2007, Universal Law Publishing Co. Pvt. Ltd., New Delhi.

The Week, 2011. June Issue, Mid-Year Special, Kottayam, Kerala.

Taking on Climate Change Move, Government of India, New Delhi, February 6, 2010.

Tripathy, P.K., Behera, D.K. and Behera, B.K. 1999. Status Report on Management of Chemicals in Orissa, State Pollution Control Board, Bhubaneswar.

UNEP 2011. *Towards Green Economy*.

Unger, S.H. 1994. *Controlling Technology: Ethics and the Responsible Engineer*, John Wiley, New York.

Urry, John. 2011. *Climate Change and Society*, Syndetic Solutions, LLC.

Vermiculture Biotechnology for Waste Management, 1999. Central Pollution Control Board, New Delhi, pp. 18.

World Bank, 1982. *The Environment, Public Health, and Human Ecology: Consideration for Economic Development*, Washington, D.C.

World Health Organization (WHO), 1987. *Health and Safety Component of Environmental Impact Assessment*, Copenhagen.

Index